50% OFF FSOT Test Prep C

Dear Customer,

We consider it an honor and a privilege that you chose our FSOT Study Guide. As a way of showing our appreciation and to help us better serve you, we have partnered with Mometrix Test Preparation to offer you **50% off their online FSOT Prep Course.** Many Foreign Service Officer Test courses are needlessly expensive and don't deliver enough value. With their course, you get access to the best FSOT prep material, and you only pay half price.

Mometrix has structured their online course to perfectly complement your printed study guide. The FSOT Test Prep Course contains **in-depth lessons** that cover all the most important topics, over **1,700+ practice questions** to ensure you feel prepared, more than **900 flashcards** for studying on the go, and over **150 instructional videos**.

Online FSOT Prep Course

Topics Covered:

- Writing
- Unites States Government
- United States History, Society, Customs, and Culture
- World History and Geography
- Economics
- Mathematics and Statistics
- Management Principles, Psychology, and Human Behavior
- Communications
- Computers and Internet
- And More!

Course Features:

- FSOT Study Guide
  - Get access to content from the best reviewed study guide available.
- Track Your Progress
  - Their customized course allows you to check off content you have studied or feel confident with.
- 4 Full-Length Practice Tests
  - With 1,700+ practice questions and lesson reviews, you can test yourself again and again to build confidence.
- FSOT Flashcards
  - Their course includes a flashcard mode consisting of over 900 content cards to help you study.

To receive this discount, visit them at www.mometrix.com/university/fsot/or simply scan this QR code with your smartphone. At the checkout page, enter the discount code: **FSOTAPEX50**

If you have any questions or concerns, please contact them at universityhelp@mometrix.com.

SCAN HERE

APEX test prep

in partnership with

Mometrix
TEST PREPARATION

FREE

Free Study Tips Videos/DVD

In addition to this guide, we have created a FREE set of videos with helpful study tips. **These FREE videos provide you with top-notch tips to conquer your exam and reach your goals.**

Our simple request is that you give us feedback about the book in exchange for these strategy-packed videos. We would love to hear what you thought about the book, whether positive, negative, or neutral. It is our #1 goal to provide you with quality products and customer service.

To receive your **FREE Study Tips Videos**, scan the QR code or email freevideos@apexprep.com. Please put "FREE Videos" in the subject line and include the following in the email:

a. The title of the book

b. Your rating of the book on a scale of 1-5, with 5 being the highest score

c. Any thoughts or feedback about the book

Thank you!

FSOT Study Guide 2024-2025

6 Practice Exams and Prep for the Foreign Service Officer Test
[2nd Edition]

J. M. Lefort

Table of Contents

Welcome

Dear Customer,

Congratulations on taking the next step in your educational journey, and thank you for choosing APEX to help you prepare! We are delighted to be by your side, equipping you with the knowledge and skills needed to make this move forward. Your APEX study guide contains helpful tips and quality study material that will contribute to your success. This study guide has been tailored to assist you in passing your chosen exam, but it also includes strategies to conquer any test with ease. Whether your goal is personal growth or acing that big exam to move up in your career, our goal is to leave you with the confidence and ability to reach the top!

We love to hear success stories, so please let us know how you do on your exam. Since we are continually making improvements to our products, we welcome feedback of any sort. Your achievements as well as criticisms can be emailed to info@apexprep.com.

Sincerely,
APEX Team

FREE Videos/DVD OFFER

Achieving a high score on your exam depends on both understanding the content and applying your knowledge. **Because your success is our primary goal, we offer FREE Study Tips Videos, which provide top-notch test taking strategies to help optimize your testing experience.**

Our simple request is that you email us feedback about our book in exchange for the strategy-packed videos.

To receive your **FREE Study Tips Videos**, scan the QR code or email freevideos@apexprep.com. Please put "FREE Videos" in the subject line and include the following in the email:

   a. The title of the book
   b. Your rating of the book on a scale of 1-5, with 5 being the highest score
   c. Any thoughts or feedback about the book

Thank you!

SCAN HERE

Test Taking Strategies

1. Reading the Whole Question

A popular assumption in Western culture is the idea that we don't have enough time for anything. We speed while driving to work, we want to read an assignment for class as quickly as possible, or we want the line in the supermarket to dwindle faster. However, speeding through such events robs us from being able to thoroughly appreciate and understand what's happening around us. While taking a timed test, the feeling one might have while reading a question is to find the correct answer as quickly as possible. Although pace is important, don't let it deter you from reading the whole question. Test writers know how to subtly change a test question toward the end in various ways, such as adding a negative or changing focus. If the question has a passage, carefully read the whole passage as well before moving on to the questions. This will help you process the information in the passage rather than worrying about the questions you've just read and where to find them. A thorough understanding of the passage or question is an important way for test takers to be able to succeed on an exam.

2. Examining Every Answer Choice

Let's say we're at the market buying apples. The first apple we see on top of the heap may *look* like the best apple, but if we turn it over we can see bruising on the skin. We must examine several apples before deciding which apple is the best. Finding the correct answer choice is like finding the best apple. Although it's tempting to choose an answer that seems correct at first without reading the others, it's important to read each answer choice thoroughly before making a final decision on the answer. The aim of a test writer might be to get as close as possible to the correct answer, so watch out for subtle words that may indicate an answer is incorrect. Once the correct answer choice is selected, read the question again and the answer in response to make sure all your bases are covered.

3. Eliminating Wrong Answer Choices

Sometimes we become paralyzed when we are confronted with too many choices. Which frozen yogurt flavor is the tastiest? Which pair of shoes look the best with this outfit? What type of car will fill my needs as a consumer? If you are unsure of which answer would be the best to choose, it may help to use process of elimination. We use "filtering" all the time on sites such as eBay® or Craigslist® to eliminate the ads that are not right for us. We can do the same thing on an exam. Process of elimination is crossing out the answer choices we know for sure are wrong and leaving the ones that might be correct. It may help to cover up the incorrect answer choice. Covering incorrect choices is a psychological act that alleviates stress due to the brain being exposed to a smaller amount of information. Choosing between two answer choices is much easier than choosing between all of them, and you have a better chance of selecting the correct answer if you have less to focus on.

4. Sticking to the World of the Question

When we are attempting to answer questions, our minds will often wander away from the question and what it is asking. We begin to see answer choices that are true in the real world instead of true in the world of the question. It may be helpful to think of each test question as its own little world. This world may be different from ours. This world may know as a truth that the chicken came before the egg or may assert that two plus two equals five. Remember that, no matter what hypothetical nonsense may be in the question, assume it to be true. If the question states that the chicken came before the egg, then choose your answer based on that truth. Sticking to the world of the question means placing all of our biases and assumptions aside and relying on the question to guide us to the correct answer. If we are simply looking for answers that are correct based on our own judgment, then we may choose incorrectly. Remember an answer that is true does not necessarily answer the question.

5. Key Words

If you come across a complex test question that you have to read over and over again, try pulling out some key words from the question in order to understand what exactly it is asking. Key words may be words that surround the question, such as *main idea, analogous, parallel, resembles, structured,* or *defines.* The question may be asking for the main idea, or it may be asking you to define something. Deconstructing the sentence may also be helpful in making the question simpler before trying to answer it. This means taking the sentence apart and obtaining meaning in pieces, or separating the question from the foundation of the question. For example, let's look at this question:

> Given the author's description of the content of paleontology in the first paragraph, which of the following is most parallel to what it taught?

The question asks which one of the answers most *parallels* the following information: The *description* of paleontology in the first paragraph. The first step would be to see *how* paleontology is described in the first paragraph. Then, we would find an answer choice that parallels that description. The question seems complex at first, but after we deconstruct it, the answer becomes much more attainable.

6. Subtle Negatives

Negative words in question stems will be words such as *not, but, neither,* or *except.* Test writers often use these words in order to trick unsuspecting test takers into selecting the wrong answer—or, at least, to test their reading comprehension of the question. Many exams will feature the negative words in all caps (*which of the following is NOT an example*), but some questions will add the negative word seamlessly into the sentence. The following is an example of a subtle negative used in a question stem:

> According to the passage, which of the following is *not* considered to be an example of paleontology?

If we rush through the exam, we might skip that tiny word, *not,* inside the question, and choose an answer that is opposite of the correct choice. Again, it's important to read the question fully, and double check for any words that may negate the statement in any way.

7. Spotting the Hedges

The word "hedging" refers to language that remains vague or avoids absolute terminology. Absolute terminology consists of words like *always, never, all, every, just, only, none,* and *must.* Hedging refers to words like *seem, tend, might, most, some, sometimes, perhaps, possibly, probability,* and *often.* In some cases, we want to choose answer choices that use hedging and avoid answer choices that use absolute terminology. It's important to pay attention to what subject you are on and adjust your response accordingly.

8. Restating to Understand

Every now and then we come across questions that we don't understand. The language may be too complex, or the question is structured in a way that is meant to confuse the test taker. When you come across a question like this, it may be worth your time to rewrite or restate the question in your own words in order to understand it better. For example, let's look at the following complicated question:

Which of the following words, if substituted for the word *parochial* in the first paragraph, would LEAST change the meaning of the sentence?

Let's restate the question in order to understand it better. We know that they want the word *parochial* replaced. We also know that this new word would "least" or "not" change the meaning of the sentence. Now let's try the sentence again:

Which word could we replace with *parochial,* and it would not change the meaning?

Restating it this way, we see that the question is asking for a synonym. Now, let's restate the question so we can answer it better:

Which word is a synonym for the word *parochial*?

Before we even look at the answer choices, we have a simpler, restated version of a complicated question.

9. Predicting the Answer

After you read the question, try predicting the answer *before* reading the answer choices. By formulating an answer in your mind, you will be less likely to be distracted by any wrong answer choices. Using predictions will also help you feel more confident in the answer choice you select. Once you've chosen your answer, go back and reread the question and answer choices to make sure you have the best fit. If you have no idea what the answer may be for a particular question, forego using this strategy.

10. Avoiding Patterns

One popular myth in grade school relating to standardized testing is that test writers will often put multiple-choice answers in patterns. A runoff example of this kind of thinking is that the most common answer choice is "C," with "B" following close behind. Or, some will advocate certain made-up word patterns that simply do not exist. Test writers do not arrange their correct answer choices in any kind of pattern; their choices are randomized. There may even be times where the correct answer choice will be the same letter for two or three questions in a row, but we have no way of knowing when or if this might happen. Instead of trying to figure out what choice the test writer probably set as being correct, focus on what the *best answer choice* would be out of the answers you are presented with. Use the tips above, general knowledge, and reading comprehension skills in order to best answer the question, rather than looking for patterns that do not exist.

Bonus Content and Audiobook

You can access numerous bonus items online including all 6 practice tests for this study guide and the audiobook. Go to apexprep.com/bonus/fsot or scan the code below.

After you go to the website, you will have to create an account and register as a "new user" and verify your email address before you begin.

If you need any help, please contact us at info@apexprep.com.

Study Prep Plan for the FSOT

 **Breathe**

Reducing stress is key when preparing for your test.

 Build

Create a study plan to help you stay on track.

 **Begin**

Stick with your study plan. You've got this!

1 Week Study Plan

Day 1	Day 2	Day 3	Day 4	Day 5	Day 6	Day 7
Communication	Mathematics and Statistics	World History and Geography	FSOT Practice Tests #1 & #2	FSOT Practice Tests #3 & #4	FSOT Practice Tests #5 & #6	Take Your Exam!

2 Week Study Plan

Day 1	Day 2	Day 3	Day 4	Day 5	Day 6	Day 7
Communication	Computers	Economics	Management	Mathematics and Statistics	United States Government	United States Society and Culture

Day 8	Day 9	Day 10	Day 11	Day 12	Day 13	Day 14
World History and Geography	English Expression	Situational Judgment	FSOT Practice Tests #1 & #2	FSOT Practice Tests #3 & #4	FSOT Practice Tests #5 & #6	Take Your Exam!

30 Day Study Plan

Day 1	Day 2	Day 3	Day 4	Day 5	Day 6	Day 7
Communication	Media Relations	Preparing and Using Email	Consumer Economics	Management	Laissez-faire Management Styles	Mathematics and Statistics

Day 8	Day 9	Day 10	Day 11	Day 12	Day 13	Day 14
Interpreting Categorical and Quantitative Data	Statistical Measures	United States Government	The Federal Government	United States Society and Culture	Early American Foreign Policy	World History and Geography

Day 15	Day 16	Day 17	Day 18	Day 19	Day 20	Day 21
Geography	Foreign Policy and World Geography	English Expression	Conventions of Standard English Spelling and Punctuation	Situational Judgment	FSOT Practice Test #1	Test #1 Answer Explanations

Day 22	Day 23	Day 24	Day 25	Day 26	Day 27	Day 28
FSOT Practice Test #2	Test #2 Answer Explanations	FSOT Practice Test #3	Test #3 Answer Explanations	FSOT Practice Test #4	FSOT Practice Test #5	FSOT Practice Test #6

Day 29	Day 30
Take a break!	Take Your Exam!

Introduction to the FSOT

Function of the Test

The Foreign Service Officer Test (FSOT) is one of the first steps for candidates wishing to join the State Department as a Foreign Service Officer. Successful completion of the test allows the top candidates to proceed to the Foreign Service Officer Assessment (FSOA) and continue down the path to a career in the State Department.

Test Administration

The FSOT is administered online by Pearson Vue. Candidates must submit an application within five weeks before the available testing window, but registration closes three days before the testing window begins. You must provide one valid form of identification, which must be government-issued, have your photo and signature, and not be expired. Do not bring extra materials or personal items into the testing room other than a cell phone (which must not be used during the exam). The official eligibility requirements also state that candidate must be a US citizen, be between 20 and 59 years old, and be available for worldwide assignment by the State Department.

The exam lasts 210 minutes, with the timer beginning when the exam begins. 30 minutes are provided for writing the essay.

Test Format

There are 153 multiple-choice questions on the test, divided into three sections. The **Job Knowledge** section includes a wide array of questions, both specific and general knowledge, about communication, computers, economics, management, mathematics and statistics, the United States government, United States society and culture, and world history and geography. There are 60 Job Knowledge questions. The **English Expression** section includes questions about proper use of the English language in reading, writing, and comprehension. There are 65 English Expression questions. Finally, the **Situational Judgment** section presents a series of situations and asks the candidate to choose which of the provided responses would be best and which response would be worst. There are 28 Situational Judgment questions on the test. Additionally, there is an essay, which may ask candidates to draw on any of the other topics or from the candidate's life experiences. The exact nature of the essay is not given ahead of the test.

Some versions of the test may include additional, ungraded questions. These ungraded questions are included by the State Department for research purposes.

Scoring

Candidates should receive an email with their test results for the multiple-choice section of the exam at the email address registered to their account. They may also view their scores online in their Pierson Vue account. It may take up to three days for the scores to appear. The essay is scored later, during the candidate's Qualifications Evaluation Panel, if certain criteria are met; the essay will not be graded if the multiple-choice section of the test has not been completed within the specified time or if the candidate's score did not meet the minimum cut-off.

Communication

Foreign service officers must be skilled at clear and effective communication, whether they are communicating with members of their team, government officials, news media, or citizens. This study guide will cover general communication principles as well as more specific skills.

General Tips for Effective Communication

Effective communication consistently features the following characteristics:

- **Respect:** Respect is an innate human need, and it is critical to show respect for others in all conversations. This may seem obvious when speaking with government officials or authorities, but it is just as important when interacting with coworkers and team members. This is especially important when delivering bad news or discussing unpleasant topics, as proper respect can help soften the blow.
- **Awareness:** When a person shows awareness in communication, they may also be described as "reading the room." This refers to being aware of when a topic or tone may be inappropriate. An effective and aware communicator is also someone who learns from mistakes and can reorient their communication in the moment. Aware speakers will notice the impact of their speech and steer the communication to reinforce or avoid certain topics as necessary. A speaker with a strong awareness of their audience can communicate with ease about any topic.
- **Confidence:** For a speaker to build trust with their audience, they must convey confidence. Speakers should never assume that this will just come naturally. Instead, they can use a few tricks to help maintain confidence. Confident speakers make eye contact with audience members and use a strong yet natural tone of voice with a focus on sounding competent and trustworthy. Minimal reference to speech materials, such as a script or teleprompter, also help a speaker exude confidence.
- **Conciseness:** It can be easy to fall into a trap of thinking that a strong communicator is one who explains everything in as much detail as possible. However, this can easily lead to rambling speech or confused listeners. Instead, a good communicator knows when to be simple and concise. Shorter speeches are often remembered more easily, especially if the focus stays on the key points. A good communicator is someone who can take a complex topic and streamline it into the most important information.
- **Connection:** Good communicators know how to keep their audiences engaged. The use of visual aids or audience participation can keep listeners interested in and focused on the material. Alternatively, sharing a quick, relevant story or using appropriate humor are also ways to keep listeners engaged. These strategies can also serve a secondary purpose of personalizing a speech or dialogue, making listeners feel more at ease with the speaker.

Communicating Within a Team

A foreign service officer might initially overlook the importance of effectively communicating with coworkers and team members. Management officers are often coordinating with many different agencies and staff members, so clear communication is vital to keeping operations moving smoothly.

There are four main styles of communication: passive, passive-aggressive, aggressive, and assertive. **Passive** communication is always indirect and may be emotionally manipulative, focusing on self-blame or apology. In contrast, **aggressive** communication is very direct and expressive, while tending to be self-centered and accusatory of others. **Passive-aggressive** communication sits between these two extremes, typically combining the indirectness of passivity with the self-centeredness of aggression. Passive communication could be useful on occasion, such as when someone is presenting negative news, but usually all three of these communication styles are considered ineffective.

The fourth and preferred communication style is **assertive** communication, which is characterized by self-confidence, appropriate levels of honesty, tactful directness, and empathetic understanding of others. Striking the right balance in all these areas can make assertive communication the most difficult to practice, but it is usually the most effective style.

There are a lot of small tips you can consider to keep things moving efficiently. Use email communications to schedule meetings or communicate logistics in advance. However, some sensitive matters are best discussed at an in-person meeting instead. One-on-one meetings can help individual workers identify problems they're having and address solutions to them, while larger team meetings are better for collecting feedback and sharing news or plans. Having a clear agenda for every meeting helps make each one as productive as possible.

Keep in mind that the most important aspect of keeping motivation high is to make everyone feel like a respected team member. When collecting input from your team, be inclusive and listen to all feedback. Avoid too much technical language when possible and thank team members for their contributions. Regardless of whatever decision is ultimately made on an issue, make it feel like a team decision. Members will be happiest when they all feel connected to the team.

Research Tips

When making presentations or reports, you must conduct research to gather accurate information. Finding the information you need can be challenging. You may need to search news articles, databases, encyclopedias, or internet archives and articles. The most important thing to remember is the difference between primary, secondary, and tertiary sources and what sources are appropriate for research.

Primary sources are direct sources of information and research. If you're looking up population information, then a primary source would be the most recent census results, providing direct information about a population. Primary sources are usually the best possible sources, especially for hard facts like statistics.

Secondary sources provide second-hand information that may involve commentary or analysis. If you're looking up population information, then a secondary source would be another department's review of the most recent census information. Secondary sources are better used to provide supporting arguments for your analysis.

Tertiary sources are sources that simply compile or index information. If you're looking up population information, then an example of a tertiary source would be a database of census reports. Tertiary sources aren't suited for use in presentations or reports themselves, but often can help you identify primary or secondary sources to examine instead.

To find the information you need, you must know how to efficiently use computer databases and search engines. Many databases or search engines allow you to filter results according to certain specifications. For example, when performing a Google search, you can put a phrase inside quotation marks to search for exact matches and exclude partial matches. If you include an asterisk in that phrase, it will act as a blank and allow any word to fit in that spot. There are many other modifiers, and while the exact execution of these modifiers may differ between search engines, the purpose behind them is the same – to allow you to fine-tune your search so you can find exactly what you want.

As you gather research, be sure to cite sources in either footnotes or a source list, depending on how your research is presented. Be aware of how the format (such as a PowerPoint presentation or paper report) affects how and when you should cite sources. In an informal, private conversation between you and a colleague, it's okay to be casual about referencing your sources. However, in a formal report to your superior, you should always cite sources correctly and accurately. If you fail to do so, it may confuse readers or even lead to punishments for committing plagiarism.

In summary, start by casting a wide net when conducting research, using databases, search engines, encyclopedias, and large tertiary sources. Use the tools, filters, and modifiers available to you to narrow your search to the exact information you need. Then seek out primary and secondary sources to use in your reports and presentations, and cite them correctly.

Public Speaking Tips

Public speaking doesn't always come naturally to people. Even experienced public speakers may find themselves occasionally caught off guard or nervous. Focus on the following tips when preparing for an oral presentation.

- **Keep calm:** While this is easier said than done, doing your best to remain calm before and during a speech is the key to success. Some people may prefer to practice their speech over and over so that when they finally present in public, they feel prepared. Others may decide to speak directly to certain individuals in the crowd to help narrow their focus and lessen the pressure. Still others may decide to go with the flow and speak authentically in the moment. Your own approach may be unique to you, but whatever you choose, keeping calm during a speech helps you come across as a strong speaker.
- **Clear direction:** Your speech or presentation should have a clear flow to it – a beginning, middle, and end. One good way to begin is by introducing yourself as well as the topic you are presenting. You can also open a speech with a strong hook to engage listeners and entice them to want to learn more. Stay focused on the topic; an occasional interjection of appropriate humor or a related story can help ease tension and make the presentation more human, but remember to avoid straying too far from the primary focus of the speech. A strong and memorable speech or presentation is concise and clear.
- **Practice:** Public speaking is a skill, and the best way to improve at a skill is to practice. Pretend you're giving a short speech about your preferred topic in the mirror during your morning routine. Set aside time to practice an upcoming presentation in your office before the meeting later that week. Even just a few minutes of practicing one or two lines before going onstage can help relieve anxiety and build public speaking skills.

Mass Media Tips

When you need to disseminate information or news to the public, **mass media** outlets are the best way to do so. Mass media includes not just television or radio stations, but also magazines, social media sites, and online news blogs. Members of the public learn about news through various platforms, often depending on factors such as age, income, or ease of access.

Mass media is a powerful tool for shaping public interests. It can be used to influence what members of the public view as important or unimportant in society. It can even play a role in news suppression, as some media outlets let ulterior motives dictate what stories are covered or ignored. However, there are still many ways to use the influence of mass media to convey news or messages to the public.

The **agenda-setting theory** suggests that the news stories the media chooses to prioritize reporting on will change public perception of that news. A news organization that chooses to primarily report on news about an ongoing war will increase its readers' or viewers' beliefs that other local or social issues are less important than war issues. This basic theory has been expanded into **framing theory**, which asserts that public opinion is shaped not just by what is covered by the news, but also how it is presented. For example, a public protest can be perceived very differently depending on whether the reporting focuses on the reasons for the protest or the damage caused by it. The former paints the protest as the public exercising their rights, while the latter makes it sound more like a destructive riot. Such a powerful strategy should be handled with care, as **cultivation theory** states that regular readers or viewers will begin to believe more and more messages from that media source and even change their own worldview to match. For example, if a news station starts to report on war events with a positive focus on battles that their home country is winning, many of the station's viewers will be influenced to believe that the war is going well for them, even if their country is actually losing the war.

Mass media messages are most effective when they are simple and communicated through an appropriate outlet. For example, if you are running a recycling initiative to get younger people to recycle more often, you would want to focus your efforts on a media campaign that younger people are more likely to see and react positively towards. Many younger people are more accessible online or through social media, so a digital social media campaign will likely be more effective than running ads in the newspapers or on the radio. Keeping the message clear and engaging is also important, so a short series of video clips may be more effective than a longer, text-based post. In general, mass media is most effectively used by considering the target audience and how to best reach them.

Here are a few types of mass media and the advantages of each:

- **Television:** Television is a good way to widely circulate news or information. While the number of households using television services is declining, it is still popular and effective at distributing messages to a wide range of people.

- **Newspapers:** Newspapers are the best way to reach a specific and dedicated local audience. While many people don't read newspapers regularly, they are particularly popular with older people and those with strong local ties. They can be a useful niche platform for certain messages.

- **Radio:** Radio broadcasts can be an effective method of spreading news in certain situations. The most common place someone might be listening to the radio is while driving, and while many traditional stations have a limited local range, satellite radio is capable of consistent broadcasts anywhere.

- **Social media:** Online social media sites are the best way to communicate with a younger adult audience. Popular sites like Facebook, Twitter, or Instagram are capable of quick, concise messaging that can be easily shared around the world. Social media can also allow for more creative messaging due to site limitations – for example, Twitter's character limits or Instagram's focus on photos and videos.

- **News blogs:** Many news organizations now publish most of their news online. With some searching, you can likely find a news site for just about any topic no matter how specific or niche. This allows an organization to easily communicate information to target audiences according to their interests, such as releasing sports news on a dedicated sports news website.

Media Relations

Media relations refers to the relationship between an organization and various media outlets. Working with the media allows an organization to more easily communicate policy decisions or new information to the public. However, the organization has no control over what the media chooses to say about it, so it is important for the organization to maintain positive relations with the journalists or reporters involved, which can lead to more favorable coverage for the organization.

The people involved with media relations in an organization will need to be experts in mass media and its influence. They will need to know who to contact at different media outlets, what types of stories each outlet produces, how the public perceives or will perceive the information, what audiences will be reached through different outlets, and more. It can be a difficult and comprehensive endeavor, and public perceptions can change rapidly. However, it's a critical job in terms of keeping media and public perception of an organization as favorable as possible.

Public Diplomacy

When communicating with foreign states or a foreign public, you are engaging in a form of **diplomacy**. Diplomacy refers to communications with a foreign government or state, usually to discuss mutual interests or foster positive relations. **Public diplomacy** is the same type of communication but with the public citizens of that foreign state.

Instead of fostering positive relations between your home country and a foreign country, public diplomacy focuses on the relations between your home country and the public citizens of the foreign country. The difference is slight, but how a foreign public perceives your home country can have strong effects on governmental diplomatic relations as well. This should always be done as transparently as possible; foreign public citizens will react negatively to false or deceptive information, making the message difficult or impossible to control. Therefore, keeping the information clear and accurate is the best strategy.

Engaging in public diplomacy is often done in a similar manner to that of working with mass media. Cultural exchanges allow the citizens of two different countries and cultures to learn more about each other and come to a deeper understanding of the values they share. Visitor exchange or student exchange programs go even deeper by allowing people to directly learn through visiting or studying in each other's countries. However, language barriers may sometimes cause obstacles in disseminating information, and translators should be careful to choose words that convey the intent of the message without coming across the wrong way. This can be even more problematic when the foreign country has very different cultural customs, so any messages should be carefully considered to avoid cultural blunders.

Diplomatic Goals

When engaging in diplomatic action between two countries, there is almost always a specific goal or compromise in mind. These may be categorized as follows:

- **Militaristic:** A country may wish to empower their military through training exercises or a shared strategy.

- **Economic:** A country may want to open new markets or improve existing ones through trade agreements.

- **Environmental:** A country may seek aid for recovery from a natural disaster or preventative efforts to combat a future one.

- **Humanitarian:** A country may seek an alliance or have refugees because of an ongoing war.

Each country may have one or more goals in mind when approaching diplomacy, and thus diplomacy is best considered as a process of negotiations between two or more countries attempting to reach a compromise on their goals. These negotiations are a balance of persuasion, rewards, and concessions. Diplomats often use persuasive arguments first, and then discuss rewards and concessions between the countries to reach a compromise. Diplomacy, by its very nature, does not include violence as an option. However, warnings of violence may be used to pressure other nations. Pressure can also be applied through the use of propaganda or public events to get support from the foreign public and encourage a country's government to accept a certain concession or outcome.

Practice Quiz

1. Which of these qualities of communication can be described as an innate human need?
    a. Connection
    b. Confidence
    c. Awareness
    d. Respect

2. Which of the following is an aspect of being an aware speaker?
    a. Shifting the tone of a speech to empathize with the audience
    b. Sharing an appropriate joke to keep the audience engaged
    c. Keeping the speech short and sweet
    d. Speaking in a strong tone of voice

3. Which of the following is NOT a sign of a confident speaker?
    a. The speaker is making eye contact with many members of the audience.
    b. The speaker is frequently pausing in the middle of sentences.
    c. The speaker rarely glances at the teleprompter.
    d. The speaker has a strong, enthusiastic tone of voice.

4. Which tone of communication is generally the most preferred?
    a. Passive
    b. Aggressive
    c. Assertive
    d. Passive-aggressive

5. You have a complaint about a fellow team member, who is often belligerent and rude. Which of the following describes the most appropriate time and place to bring it up?
    a. An email to the team member about your complaint
    b. A private meeting with your boss in their office
    c. During the next full team progress meeting
    d. Casually mentioning it to your boss in the break room

See next page for answer explanations.

Answer Explanations

1. D: Respect for other humans, both giving and receiving it, is an innate human need that makes people feel happier. Choice *A*, connection, can also help improve happiness but is not an innate human need in the same way that respect is, so it is incorrect. Choices *B* and *C* are not human needs, so they are incorrect.

2. A: An aware speaker is flexible and can shift the tone of their speech to empathize with the audience at any moment. Choice *B* is a sign of connection with the audience, not awareness, so it is incorrect. Choice *C* is a sign of conciseness, so it is also incorrect. Choice *D* is a sign of confidence, so it is also incorrect.

3. B: A speaker that is constantly pausing in the middle of their sentences will not convey confidence in their speech to the audience. Confident speakers will make eye contact, use a strong tone of voice, and try to memorize their speech without referring to teleprompters or aids, so Choices *A*, *C*, and *D* are all incorrect.

4. C: Assertive communication uses an appropriate level of self-confidence and respect, so it is usually the best choice of tone. Passive communication can be specifically used for handling bad news, but it is not a commonly preferred tone of communication, so Choice *A* is incorrect. Neither aggressive nor passive-aggressive communication are preferred in any situation, so Choices *B* and *D* are incorrect.

5. B: Complaints about hostile team members should be kept private between you and your superior, so a private meeting is the best choice here. A direct email to the employee in question could be misunderstood or lead to a conflict, so Choice *A* is incorrect. Bringing it up during an all-team meeting may derail the meeting and create an open conflict, so Choice *C* is incorrect. Offhandedly mentioning the complaint during a break may trivialize it, so Choice *D* is incorrect.

Computers

It is important for anyone working in today's modern world to be comfortable using computers. Several basic computer operations that people need to know how to use include word processors, databases, spreadsheets, PowerPoint, email, and web browsers.

Word Processing

Knowing how to write text on a computer is an essential skill that everyone needs to know. There are several different programs available, but the most famous is most likely Microsoft Word. Other examples of word-processing software include Google Docs and WPS Office. All word processors are functionally the same.

After opening any word processor, users are greeted by a blank document. This is where all of the writing will occur. Typing anything on the keyboard will make it appear on the document. At the top of the screen is where numerous features are found, and it is important to become familiar with this area. All of these options give users the chance to customize their document.

There is always a menu that has options for saving and printing the document, usually on the top left. On Word, this is labeled as "File." Here, users have the option of opening, printing, sharing, exporting, and saving the document. Users can also start a new, blank document to work on and open a new file.

On most word processors, the home screen, or first tab, is where the user can choose different fonts and styles for their writing. Font is how the words appear on the screen, and there are numerous options available. Next to the font choice is the size of the font. There are several sizes already preselected, but users can also enter a custom value. This is also where users can choose to bold, italicize, or underline their text. Users can also change text color and highlight text.

Every word processor also has options for changing how the document is formatted. This changes how the text is organized. For example, there is a button for changing the alignment of the text, or how it lines up on the document. The button looks like several lines stacked on top of each other.

Any tab labeled "Insert" or similar is where users can add pictures, graphs, tables, videos, and other elements. This is also where headers and footers are inserted. Headers and footers will appear on every page in the document and usually contain information like the page number, name of the document, or date. The "Insert" tab is also where special characters can be added to the text. These are symbols that do not appear on the keyboard, such as math symbols and markers for other languages.

Features under tabs like "Layout" and "Format" change how the document physically appears. Users can change the page margins, which is the space surrounding the document. Orientation is how the document is displayed on the screen. Landscape is a horizontal viewpoint, while portrait is a vertical viewpoint. Most documents start out in the portrait orientation. Paragraph spacing is how much space is in between each line of text. Some writing styles, like APA, require all text to have double spacing in between each line. Other ways of organizing are also found under this tab, such as creating bullet points or numbered lists.

Word processors are automatically installed with features like word count, dictionary, translator, and grammar and spell check. If an error occurs, the program notifies the user. Incorrectly spelled words might have a red underline, or the program could offer its suggestions on how to correct the error. Most of these errors can be fixed by right clicking the screen and choosing an option. Right clicking is also where a few useful shortcuts, like "Cut," "Copy," and "Paste" are located.

Databases

There is more information in the world now than ever. It is important to store these vast amounts of data to organize and analyze them. Unlike spreadsheets, databases can hold enormous amounts of information from a variety of different sources. Databases can be created by coding languages like Python and R, or with a tool like Microsoft Access.

To begin, users can either open an existing set of data or create a new table themselves. As in other Microsoft products, most basic features can be accessed by clicking "File" or "Home." This lists useful options like opening, saving, printing, or creating a new database. To create a database, users will click on "Create" or a similarly named option to open a set of options. From these options, users can customize their database by labeling each row and column to anything that they need. Users can input their data directly onto the created table.

Databases can be organized and filtered to find useful information. For example, if the user wants to sort all columns by alphabetical order, selecting this option will automatically reorder them. Microsoft Access also has a built-in version of SQL (structured query language), which is a tool that filters the information on the database. For example, users can filter results to only show customers who are male and live in Florida. Users will select this option from the different columns and rows listed.

Databases can be customized in a variety of ways. They are fully customizable, and users can modify them to suit their needs. Fields, or categories, can be added or modified to help organize the data and add more information to the database. Macros are a smart way to automate tasks that would normally be very tedious. For example, users can create macros that automatically update a field with new information. Databases can also be combined with existing technology, like a business's accounting or financial software, to create even more detailed pictures about what the data is showing.

Database output includes features like reports, forms, queries, and exports. Reports summarize the information in a database in the specified manner, like with a sales chart or customer report. Forms are used to input data into the database but also display specific information about the data. Queries search for specific information in a database. Data export refers to the ability to take the raw data from the database and extract it somewhere else. Common export formats include CSV and Excel files. This is a great way to create a backup for the data in case the original data is lost. It also makes it easier to share data with other teams or individuals who need a copy of the information.

One of the benefits of using databases is that they minimize data redundancy. Redundancy refers to the same data being stored in multiple locations. This can create problems when the information is not properly formatted or is transferred to a different location. Sometimes, data redundancy is done on purpose in order to improve security by placing information in multiple locations or by providing an alternative source to backup information if it is lost. Regardless, databases can minimize data redundancy by keeping related information in separate tables and specifying the relationship between them. This relationship explains how information in one table relates to information in another table.

Spreadsheets

Spreadsheets are an excellent way to organize large amounts of data. For example, organizations can use spreadsheets to keep track of monthly sales or organize employee data. Many spreadsheet programs are also able to analyze this data using built-in formulas. Spreadsheets are also useful because the data can be transferred into another program to do more sophisticated analysis.

Two of the most popular spreadsheet programs are Microsoft Excel and Google Sheets. Both function similarly. After opening the program, users will see a screen with boxes in it. These boxes are where users enter information, like numbers or text. The options on the top of the screen are similar to those of a word processor. Users can still use the "File" option to open, save, and edit documents, and "Format" changes how the page looks.

One click on a box selects it, while double-clicking it lets users enter information. On the top of the page is a list of the columns. On the side of the page is the list of rows. Clicking a column or row selects all of the information in it. Users can sort information in a column or row by right-clicking it and choosing what to do from there. While right-clicking, users can cut, copy, and paste information and also edit columns and rows.

Cell formatting is similar to customizing text in a word processor. All of the text and information can be customized with different fonts, sizes, colors, and alignments. Data can be displayed as a percent, decimal, and many other ways by selecting this option in the formatting section. Cells can be highlighted a different color to help differentiate them from other sections of the table. The borders can also be customized. Border options include having an outline or having no outline. Most spreadsheet applications will have a small preview of what the new borders and data will look like when cells are being formatted.

Excel can automate tasks such as calculations and data input. In Excel, formulas can be added to individual cells to calculate a mathematical formula. Excel already has several pre-built formulas. First, users will need to select the cell that they want to put the formula in. After this, they will enter an equal sign into the cell. A formula can be added either by manually typing it directly after the equal sign or by selecting a formula under the "Formulas" tab. The "Formulas" tab breaks down the different pre-built formulas into categories for easier viewing. Some of the many useful formulas that users can enter include SUM, MIN, MAX, and AVERAGE.

Users need to tell the program how to calculate their desired value. After choosing a formula, users will see a set of parentheses. This is where users will tell the program what cells they want to use in the formula. Each cell is labeled by a code, such as A1, B2, and C3. This code can be found by matching the row and column name shown at the top and side of the screen. Selecting an individual cell will show its code in a bar on the upper part of the screen.

In the parentheses of the formula, users can either manually type which cells are to be used in the calculation or click on each cell individually. Users can choose multiple cells by holding down the CTRL button on the keyboard while selecting the cells. Users can place a comma individually after each cell in the formula and also add symbols like a plus sign or division sign to complete mathematical operations. If users click on the lower corner of each cell containing a formula and drag and highlight additional boxes, the same formula will be repeated in each of the boxes.

PowerPoint

Microsoft PowerPoint is the premier software for making presentations. Google has its own version of PowerPoint called Google Slides. Both of these programs create a slideshow in which information can be easily displayed. Each slide is focused on a particular topic, and together they help to simplify complex topics. Users have the opportunity to add visuals, different fonts, and even audio and video to customize their presentations.

PowerPoint is similar to word-processing software in that each slide can be customized with text. Users can customize slides with several pre-built layouts, such as a title slide or a blank slide, and then add text, images, video, or audio to their presentation. The software also has pre-built themes, which changes how the presentation looks. This can create a clean, professional look for the presentation.

On the left side of the screen is a preview of all of the slides in the presentation. On the top of the page is an option to add a new slide. Users can also right-click on the slide previews to add a new slide. Right-clicking also gives the option of cutting, copying, and pasting text. Users can also duplicate slides, change the theme, and add transitions between each slide.

Users can save their work by clicking "File," then "Save" or "Save As." The top part of the screen contains similar tools to word-processing software. Users can edit text, insert images, format the presentation, and access other tools. All PowerPoint software has a "Slide Show" option which will maximize the screen and allow users to begin their presentations.

Preparing and Using Email

Email is how most companies communicate and send messages to each other. Before sending an email, users will need to register with a preferred email address and log in. There are numerous email service providers, such as Gmail, Outlook, AOL, and iCloud. Email can be paid or free. Free email services are free because they have fewer features and more advertisements. Paid email services offer more customization and can have a more professional appearance overall.

After creating an account and logging in, users first see their inbox. The inbox is where all emails are stored and received. In general, unread emails are bolded and more noticeable than emails that users have already opened. Emails are usually organized by newest first, but users can also choose to sort their emails by alphabetical order, unread, or important.

One of the most important features to understand is how to create an email. The button is generally located somewhere near the top of the page. Clicking on the button will take users to a blank email, where they first need to specify to whom the email is addressed. Then they will write a subject line and write the email in the main body of the text. The main body is just like a word-processor document, with all of the same features. Users can also send documents through email by attaching them. The attachment feature looks like a paper clip, and clicking this will open a list of files on the computer that can be sent.

Every email must have a recipient with a valid email address. The page will notify users if the email is invalid or if you attempt to send a message without a recipient. If users need to send an email to more than one recipient, there are several ways to do this. First, additional email addresses can be added to the recipient list by placing a comma after each address. This creates a list of who will receive the email.

Another option to notify multiple recipients is by using the CC and BCC features. Some emails have a separate line for adding email addresses to CC or BCC. CC stands for "carbon copy," while BCC stands for

20

"blind carbon copy." They work similarly. The biggest difference between these two features is privacy. In a CC email, recipients can see who else the email has been sent to. This is useful when users want all recipients to be aware of who is receiving the message and helps to create a common thread where people can discuss the issue at hand. In a BCC email, all recipients are kept private. Recipients will not know if other people have received an email. This is useful when emails need to be sent to large numbers of people, such as with a mass email campaign or company-wide email lists.

In the "Contacts" section, users can add, edit, and manage the contacts on the list. Contacts can be imported or exported into another email or location by clicking on the "Export" or "Import" button usually located on the left side of the screen.

Folders help organize emails. Users can add new folders and rename them. All emails will usually be sent to the inbox first. From here, users can select where to put these new emails. This can usually be done by clicking on the box located next to each email. This selects the email. On the top of the screen are several options, including the "Move" option. This option opens up a list of locations where the email can be sent. To move an email to a folder, users will click on the desired location. From here, the email can be found by opening the folder.

There are other useful buttons on the email page. "Trash" is where unwanted emails that the user wants to delete go. "Spam" is for messages that are repeated too frequently and may be trying to harm users. An "Archive" is where old emails are stored. "Junk" is usually for unsolicited advertisements or donation requests.

Web Browsers

Web browsers allow us to access the internet. There are numerous popular web browsers that people use. These include Google Chrome, Firefox, Microsoft Edge, Internet Explorer, and Safari. They are simple to understand and function similarly. Computers have web browsers built in already, but users can download their favorite web browser and use it instead.

At the top of the screen of any web browser will be a long box. This is where users will enter the website that they want to go to. Web browsers will connect to the website and then show it on the screen. Also on the top of the screen are various tools with numerous useful features. There will be left and right arrows, a symbol that looks like a house, and a curved arrow. The left arrow takes users back to the previous page that they visited, while the right arrow goes forward to the next page visited. The home button takes users to their homepage, where they can add their most used sites to make accessing them easier. The curved arrow is the "Refresh" button, which will load the page again if there is an issue. All web browsers can also add bookmarks or denote favorite websites. These bookmarks will appear as shortcuts on the page and can be easily accessed from there.

On the top right corner are three buttons that will control how the web browser appears. These buttons are "Minimize," "Restore Down," and "Close." "Minimize will shrink the web browser to the taskbar, or the bottom of the screen. "Restore Down" will make the screen smaller, like a window. When the screen is smaller, the middle button will change to "Maximize," which will make the screen full-size again. The "Close" button will close, or exit, the web browser.

Practice Quiz

1. What is the function of the CTRL + K command shortcut?
    a. Select all content on the document.
    b. Copy the selected text.
    c. Undo the previous action.
    d. Insert a hyperlink.

2. Under what tab in Word can users save and print their document?
    a. File
    b. Review
    c. Insert
    d. Page Layout

3. What kind of file format are Word documents usually saved as?
    a. .jpeg
    b. .doc
    c. .pdf
    d. .exe

4. Which shortcut in Word saves the document?
    a. CTRL + P
    b. CTRL + S
    c. CTRL + C
    d. CTRL + N

5. What does the justify option in Word do?
    a. It prints the document.
    b. It aligns text to the center.
    c. It gives the text straight edges on each side.
    d. It bolds the text.

See next page for answer explanations.

Answer Explanations

1. D: The CTRL + K command inserts a hyperlink, which is a link to an external location of a file, picture, website, or other text. Choice *A* is the function of CTRL + A. Choice *B* is the function of CTRL + C. Choice *C* is the function of CTRL + Z.

2. A: The "File" tab is where many useful features can be found, including printing and saving. Choice *B* is used primarily for editing documents, such as by adding comments or fixing spelling and grammar. Choice *C* is used for inserting or adding pictures, graphs, and other visuals. Choice *D* changes how the page looks and adjusts page orientation, margins, and more.

3. B: By default, documents made in Word come in a .doc file. This can be changed in the "Save As" screen. Choice *A* is a picture file. Choice *C* is used for PDFs and looks like a printed image of the document. Choice *D* is an executable file.

4. B: The CTRL + S shortcut saves the document and allows users to work on it later. Choice *A* brings up the printing menu. Choice *C* copies the selected text. Choice *D* opens a new document.

5. C: The "justify" option makes text look cleaner by creating uniform straight edges on both sides of the text. Spacing between words may change to achieve this look. Choices *A*, *B*, and *D* are not functions of the justify option.

Economics

Fundamental Economic Concepts

Economists study the production, distribution, and consumption of wealth as expressed through commodities, goods, and services. **Commodities** are raw materials or agricultural products—gold, silver, gas, oil, corn, barley, etc. Goods are physical, tangible items, such as computers, bathing suits, refrigerators, televisions, etc. Services are activities based on labor and/or skills, like the work of lawyers, waiters, engineers, computer programmers, etc.

The government's role is to implement an economic system to distribute resources. In a centrally planned economic system, the government makes all decisions related to production and distribution. In addition, price controls are common, if not pervasive. Communist countries have a centrally planned economic system, and they attempt to abolish private property, transfer the means of production to the public, and distribute profits on an equitable basis.

In contrast, **capitalism** is a market economic system. The **free market** is what sets prices based on the existing supply and demand, and private firms make all decisions related to production and distribution. Market economic systems are based on merit, meaning that resources are distributed unequally. Under a pure laissez-faire free-market system, the government can't regulate, tax, subsidize, or otherwise interfere with the free market. The only rule in laissez-faire economics is *caveat emptor* (buyer beware).

Nearly all economies are mixed economic systems where the public and private sectors share the means of production and profits. As such, all governments with a mixed economic system collect taxes, set tariffs, and spend resources on public projects; however, they differ on the amount of control over the free market. For example, some governments implement price controls to regulate certain economic sectors for a designated period.

When a free market is present, the price and quantity are based on supply and demand. **Supply** is the amount of a commodity, good, or service that's available for consumption, and **demand** is the desire of buyers to acquire the commodity, good, or service. **Money** refers to the method of payment, whether it's a government currency, credit, digital currency, or precious metal.

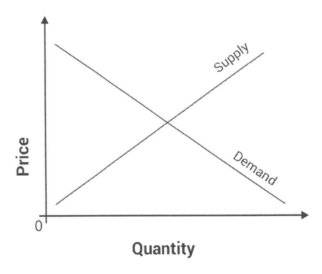

Government Involvement in the Economy

Governments can create their own currencies, and they can typically control the amount of currency in circulation, as well as the cost of short-term borrowing. Most countries designate a central bank or government agency to set and enforce monetary policies to control inflation and interest rates. **Inflation** is a period of increased prices and decreased currency values. **Interest rates** are what lenders charge borrowers to receive loans or credit. For example, governments sell bonds to borrow money for a designated period, and when the period ends, the buyer receives an interest payment plus the amount of the original debt.

In general, economics is a source of domestic and foreign conflict due to the scarcity (shortage) of resources like money, raw materials, and skills. Within a country, the needs and wants of the population are unlimited, while many resources are scarce. The same is also true in the context of international resources—the supply of resources is limited, while demand is unlimited.

Countries' domestic economic policy agendas involve raising revenue through taxes and spending money to enact and enforce policy decisions. Foreign economic policy agendas involve tariffs for imported goods. **Tariffs** are mostly used to protect industries with a special value to the homeland or to punish foreign countries.

Governments make production and trade policy decisions based on **comparative advantage**—the principle that countries produce the goods and services that have the least **opportunity cost**. Opportunity cost measures the loss of potential gain if the country had produced some other good or service. As such, in a free market, countries specialize at what they can do most efficiently relative to their competitors.

Most governments sign free-trade agreements with close allies and major trading partners. **Free-trade agreements** lower or eliminate tariffs. The agreements can be bilateral (2 countries) or multilateral (3+ countries). For example, the Gulf Cooperation Council is a multilateral free-trade agreement between Arab states in the Persian Gulf. In addition, many countries join intergovernmental organizations to borrow money, donate aid, or settle disputes. The **World Trade Organization** provides structural support for trade negotiations and offers dispute resolution services. The International Money Fund tries to increase global economic cooperation. The **World Bank** attempts to alleviate poverty by loaning money to developing countries for large projects.

Income inequality and perceptions of unfairness stir domestic unrest. In effect, worsening economic conditions cause political conflicts. The public might object to tax policies, stagnant or falling incomes, shortages of resources, underfunded social services, or any other specific policy. If the economic situation continues to deteriorate, the public might seek to overthrow the government. For example, during the French Revolution (1789-1799), King Louis XVI was executed after the monarchy amassed enormous war debts, enforced regressive taxes on their poorest citizens, and publicly flaunted their wealth in front of an increasingly poor public.

Technological innovation can both drive economic growth and send economies spiraling into a depression. Throughout history, technology has increased the efficiency of human labor. If the excess labor migrates to a different economic sector, the economy will grow. Many emerging technologies create new economic sectors, but some economic sectors are hurt by this transition. For example, the printing press expanded the markets for writers, records-keepers, and librarians. On the other hand, the printing press destroyed the market for scribes. Typically, free-market economic systems generate more

25

technological advancements since the private firms are incentivized to pursue profits, which drives innovation. However, public spending can also lead to groundbreaking advances. For example, the Space Race revolutionized the computer-based economic sector, and the American military created **ARPANET**, the foundation for what would later become the Internet.

Due to comparative advantage in the free market, developing countries handle most of the world's labor-intensive work, like manufacturing. Developed countries benefit from the cheaper labor in lower costs, but there are fewer jobs for blue-collar workers. These workers often don't have the necessary skills to smoothly transition into a new field, especially as fields become increasingly specialized. Automation has a similar impact—decreased costs, increased unemployment, and a skills gap in the labor market. Consequently, governments must enact economic policies that maximize the advantages of cheaper labor and lower costs, while also protecting the economic system's legitimacy. The legitimacy of an economic system is context-specific, depending on historical and cultural forces. However, systems with higher standards of living and less income disparity enjoy more widespread legitimacy with the public.

Consumer Economics

Consumer economics focuses on the ways in which individuals (consumers) interact with the market economy at the local, regional, national, and global level. Consumer economics became more embedded within global systems following the market revolution of the early 1700s. This consumer turn that occurred only became catalyzed by the broader Industrial Revolution, which took hold across the globe from the mid-1700s to early 1900s. Both of these revolutions allowed for previously self-sustaining economies to be thrust into the consumer frameworks of the so-called market. People transitioned out of their traditionally self-sufficient agrarian lifestyles and into highly dependent consumer economies. Today, consumerism refers to the practice of buying and selling goods that exist within this larger international market, which was once industrialized but is swiftly becoming deindustrialized. Consumer habits affect our everyday lives, so economists, economics teachers, and students of economics spend a lot of their time analyzing consumer trends. These trends can focus on local consumer economies, regional consumer economies, national consumer economies, or international consumer economies.

Below are some key concepts for understanding consumer economics:

Free Enterprise Economy: A free enterprise economy—sometimes referred to simply as a market economy—helps producers determine what to produce, how to produce, how much to produce, and for whom to produce based on supply, demand, and competition. In a market economy, profit drives decisions; government does not control resources, goods, or any other major sector of a market economy. Businesses run by the people determine the economic structure, supply, and demand of a market economy. A free enterprise economy has five distinctive characteristics: 1) private property, 2) economic freedom, 3) economic incentives, 4) competitive markets, and 5) limited government interference.

Supply and Demand: In free enterprise systems, such as the US market economy, people are free to buy the goods and services they want/need. Since the consumer often dictates purchases/consumption in this free enterprise system, pricing and production often ebbs and flows with the economic principles of supply and demand. Supply refers to the amount of goods and services a business is willing to produce and distribute. Supply rises when businesses can sell products and services at a higher price. Supply decreases when prices are low. Demand refers to how many products and services consumers are willing to buy. When prices rise, demand tends to drop. When prices drop, demand tends to rise. Supply and demand, therefore, work together to dictate prices. The effects of supply and demand on prices can be seen, for instance, during times of national disaster. Drought can, for example, raise water rates for communities.

Competition: Competition refers to economic rivalries between companies. Competition can also affect supply and demand, and, in turn, production, pricing, distribution, and consumption. Competition can often force companies to lower their prices or strengthen the quality of their product or service.

Scarcity: The consumer economy is built upon the foundation and notion of scarcity, the limited availability of a particular commodity. Scarcity affects all economic agents within the consumer economy; it affects laborers, businesses, households, consumers, banks and other financial institutions, and creditors. Scarcity demands that all economic agents in the consumer economy must make difficult decisions about the ways in which they obtain resources, budget, save, and take on credit.

Budgeting: Buying one good or service means that these economic agents will have to sacrifice another good or service. Saving money entails sacrificing spending. Budgeting entails sacrificing excessive expenditures, savings accounts, or credits. Budgeting in a consumer economy mean that households, businesses, and governments must constantly make educated decisions about the necessity, quality, and satisfaction of the goods and services they choose to produce or purchase. There are only so many dollars available for each household, business, and government. All economic agents must, therefore, decide how to adequately spend their time and money.

Practice Quiz

1. Which of the following indicators is one of the best ways to measure a country's economic growth?
   a. Unemployment rate
   b. Gross Domestic Product (GDP)
   c. Consumer Price Index (CPI)
   d. Producer Price Index (PPI)

2. In a command economy, what influences the economy the most?
   a. Government
   b. Competition
   c. Supply
   d. Demand

3. Which of the following is an example of a price ceiling?
   a. Minimum wage
   b. Agricultural product prices
   c. Alcohol prices
   d. Prescription drug prices

4. Fresh water is best characterized as what kind of a good?
   a. Public goods
   b. Private goods
   c. Club goods
   d. Common resources

5. Which of these goods is excludable and rival?
   a. Toll roads
   b. Law enforcement
   c. Houses
   d. Fresh air

See next page for answer explanations.

Answer Explanations

1. B: The GDP is one of the best and most common ways of measuring a country's economic growth. It is the measure of the total value of all goods and services that a country produces. Choice *A* measures the proportion of people who are not currently working, but it does not measure how long they have not been working. Choice *C* is one of the best measures for inflation because it tracks the change over time that people pay for goods and services. Choice *D* measures inflation at the wholesale level and is related to the CPI.

2. A: A command economy is where a powerful central government controls business, production, and prices. Choices *B, C,* and *D* are examples of free-market economies, where supply, demand, and individuals determine market forces.

3. D: A price ceiling is the legally allowed maximum amount that can be charged for a good or service. Many prescription drugs have a price ceiling in order to make sure that everyone is able to afford them. Choices *A, B,* and *C* are examples of a price floor. A price floor is the minimum price that a good or service can be sold for.

4. D: Fresh water is a common resource, meaning that anyone can use it, but it cannot be used by everyone at the same time. Choice *A* is something that everyone benefits from and is usually provided for free. Choice *B* are goods that individuals must pay for themselves, and using them reduces their availability for others. Choice *C* are goods that people can be prevented from using, but using them does not make them less available to others.

5. C: Houses are excludable and rival goods. Consumers must pay for houses, and buying a house reduces the availability of houses for others. Choice *A* is a club good. Choices *B* and *D* are common resources.

Management

Part of being a foreign service officer means you may be leading a team of colleagues or other staff members. Therefore, it is important to have a solid grasp of management and leadership skills. Having knowledge of the psychology of management can help you better understand how different management styles affect people. Regardless of how you choose to lead, all coworkers deserve respect.

The Psychology of Management

The psychology of the workplace is typically referred to as **industrial and organizational (I/O) psychology**. When managing your staff, remember the following considerations.

- **How are decisions made?** The way your team makes decisions can significantly impact staff members' morale. Are all the decisions made only by the team lead? Are decisions made by a vote during group meetings? Is everyone's input valued equally when making decisions, or do some members have greater sway than others? Leaders' decision-making can keep things moving quickly and avoid delays, but involving everyone in the decision-making can offer new perspectives. Team members will also be more accepting of decisions if they feel they were an active part of making them.

- **How does the team communicate?** From emails to meetings, there are a lot of ways for a team to stay in touch with each other. While digital communications like email and instant messaging can be speedy and efficient, in-person discussion and meetings still provide an important social benefit. When team members are present with each other and working together on a goal, there is a greater sense of synergy between everyone. When the team is working remotely, conversations can move more slowly and tone is harder to convey, but for some people delayed or remote communication is more convenient than face-to-face communication. In-person communication is great for positive news, but negative news is typically received better through email or other delayed messaging. Considering the ways the team communicates information can help understand how they will respond to it.

- **How often does the team work together or individually?** A team working together on a project will be more social and feel more unified in pursuit of success. This can lead to positive psychological benefits for team members, but not all types of work are suitable for this kind of team effort. Most work will instead need to be done individually, so finding ways for the team to take breaks and socialize is important to keeping morale strong. It's also often easier for team members to ask for help when actively working together with others, so consider how individuals working on their own can receive support from team members, too.

There is no perfect answer to these questions, as it strongly depends on the workplace, type of work, and situation. Keeping these questions in mind, however, will provide the context you need as a manager to evaluate and improve team performance.

General Leadership Advice

A basic piece of advice you may hear about leadership is to always listen to your team members, and the reasons are obvious. Team members who feel like their voice is heard and their opinion is valued will perform better and feel more positively about their role on the team. Team members will also be more accepting of team decisions when they feel that their opinion was fairly considered.

Another good tip is to encourage a good work-life balance for your team. Many leaders often think this means that employees should keep their personal drama away from work, and while that's true, it's equally important that they keep their work responsibilities out of their personal lives. People need time to recharge and live their own lives, so keeping them constantly on edge about their job or a project is extremely detrimental in the long run and can lead to burnout. Some positions may require increased availability, and requesting people to work additional hours to meet tight deadlines may be necessary. To keep up staff morale, make sure these situations are framed as requests. Asking people to help gets a very different response versus demanding that they help.

Another strategy that helps improve morale is an open-door policy where team members can freely ask questions and share concerns, which can help them all work together on even small tasks. It also helps them feel more at ease around their manager and more comfortable with sharing their input during work. Another option is to provide the opportunity for regular team-building activities. This can be anything from going out as a team for a weekly happy hour, a team vacation, or a semi-regular game night. The goal is to provide your staff with an opportunity to work together in different and fun ways, allowing them to strengthen communication and problem-solving skills as a unit.

Another tip is to provide opportunities for career advancement. Give team members access to mentorship or on-the-job training opportunities and help them pursue their personal career goals. Training and development courses help employees get better at their skills or learn new ones. More skilled employees can perform higher-quality work. Mentorship programs give newer or younger employees an opportunity to learn from more experienced ones, helping them catch up to the quality of the rest of the team. Even if the employee is wanting to learn a skill that will allow them to move into a new position that is not a part of your team, helping your team members pursue their personal career development goals will increase their satisfaction with you and the job they hold. A happy employee is more likely to stay on the team until a replacement is found and trained before departing for a new job, rather than simply quitting.

As a supervisor you will also have to evaluate your team members and decide who to assign work to. Performance evaluations should be done in regular intervals, whether that's monthly, every six months, after every major project, or whatever frequency you choose. You can perform evaluations yourself or choose to have team members evaluate each other. Employees should be evaluated on both the quantity of work they complete as well as the quality of employee they are. Consider how you can measure how much work each team member completes; this may be different depending on the type of work your team is doing or the overall amount of work your team takes on each evaluation period. For example, for a customer support team, a simple metric would be how many support calls or tickets each employee has completed. However, for a product development team that may only put out a new product every few months, it may be better to measure how much work each team member completed compared to the total work the whole team completed. On the quality front, consider different ways to gauge employee cooperation and engagement. This is a good opportunity to ask employees to rate each other in terms of their attitude or behavior. Alternatively, a system where poor behavior is reported to the manager and tallied later may work best. However you choose to approach these evaluation metrics, you still want to consider both aspects of the employees' work and determine which is more important. If your most productive employee is also the one causing the most trouble, examine the situation and determine whether productivity or employee morale is more important.

However, you should avoid any subjective analysis of employees. Keep the evaluation objectively focused on the quality of their work and their job performance, and avoid allowing how you or others feel personally about an employee to affect your evaluation. Keeping these evaluations honest and accurate allows you as a supervisor to accurately assign work to team members. Try to focus on each employee's skills and assign work that you believe is best suited to someone's strengths. Follow up with employees later, ask how they're handling the work, and assess if your judgment is correct. By assigning work based on team members' strengths, you can maximize the productivity of the team and avoid slowdowns caused by mistakes or extra learning curves.

In general, focus on keeping things positive no matter how you approach leading your staff. Keep team members feeling appreciated and valued. Keep them engaged with their work and the team, and appropriately credit them to make sure they feel accomplishment with every success.

Autocratic Management Styles

An **autocratic management** style is focused on control. Higher-ups dictate what their subordinates do, and they must comply. Employees rarely communicate with each other, and the focus is simply on obeying orders. Autocratic management can be effective in crisis situations, minimizing decision-making time and keeping things extremely clear and simple for everyone. However, autocratic management also fosters the most resentment among staff, so outside of emergency situations these management styles are not recommended.

- **Authoritative:** Authoritative management is by far the strictest and most straightforward. Bosses and leaders tell their team what to do, and the employees are meant to complete assigned tasks without question or variation. Bosses will also often micromanage their employees, watching over them and detailing every step they should perform, such as what they are doing, what reports they are submitting, and so on. Authoritative management allows for quick decision-making and clear roles, but it also creates the most frustration among employees and creates a very adversarial relationship. It can also prevent increases in efficiency since employees will rarely change how they do their work in order to keep their bosses satisfied.

- **Persuasive:** Persuasive management is similar to authoritative management, but it is more open to input from employees. However, rather than opening discussion or accepting changes, these questions serve the purpose of allowing the boss to explain to their staff the reasons for their one-sided decisions. This can create slightly less resentment than authoritative management, but team members may still feel frustrated at being unable to meaningfully contribute to the overall improvement of the team.

- **Paternalistic:** Paternalistic management tries to establish a strong sense of family among the team. Bosses will explain their decisions to the team members, but generally leave no room for questions, instead relying on trust and loyalty from staff. These managers make unilateral decisions based on the wellbeing of the whole team and make sure everyone has the resources and skills they need to conduct the work they have been assigned. This can be especially effective in smaller organizations where the familial approach can be comforting and accepting. However, any employees who aren't on board with this approach will be irritated by the platitudes or even find it condescending and rude.

Democratic Management Styles

Democratic management is a balanced style of management, featuring a leader who determines the direction and pace while focusing on the input and skills of the whole team. Democratic management is much more open to two-way communication where bosses assign work but also receive feedback from their staff. With more communication comes a more diverse range of skills and opinions.

- **Consultative:** A manager using consultative management will talk to each member of their team, get everyone's thoughts and opinions, and use all that information to make the final decision on behalf of the team. This style is helpful for building trust within the team and focusing on growth and innovation, both for employees and for management. However, constantly consulting every team member can be a very slow process without good time-management. The manager will also want to avoid any appearance of favoring some team members over others, which may lead to discouragement or resentment.

- **Participative:** Participative management gives team members a more active role in the decision-making process. Managers share information about the goals of the company while getting team members' opinions about how to proceed or ideas for new innovations. This creates increased engagement, innovation, and a strong connection between the company and the team. However, this style carries two notable risks. First, if the company is in an industry that typically has trade secrets, then giving all staff access to these trade secrets is risky. Second, some team members may have strong personalities that overpower less assertive employees, which can lead to these less assertive employees feeling like they aren't being given an equal opportunity, and this can create conflicts between team members.

- **Collaborative:** Collaborative managers choose to make all decisions based on a majority vote from the team. All team members are encouraged to share their opinions and take ownership of the team's decisions as well. Management focuses only on facilitating communication between team members and assisting when needed. When this style is at its best, the team will feel completely engaged, trusted, and valued by the company. Diverse opinions are both submitted and considered by every team member, leading to open communication and creative solutions. Sometimes decisions may not be in the best interest of the company, though, and if management must frequently step in, then team members may become frustrated.

- **Transformational:** Transformational management is focused on team growth and new achievements. Managers often work alongside the team to motivate them into pushing past their comfort zones and achieving greater and greater accomplishments. This style of management encourages creative thinking, leading to all team members improving their problem-solving skills. However, exercising transformational management for too long or without appropriate caution will lead to burnout and exhaustion. Be sure to balance growth with time for relaxation.

Laissez-faire Management Styles

If autocratic management is on one end of the scale focused on control, then **laissez-faire management** is its opposite. Managers offer very little direction, typically only assigning work at the beginning of projects and collecting it upon completion. This puts almost all the responsibility on the team members themselves, leaving it up to them to determine their workflow and decide when to ask for help. While some people will thrive in this kind of environment, others may struggle without clear guidance. However, giving the team the freedom to decide how they work generates the highest levels of employee satisfaction.

- **Delegative:** Delegative managers only assign tasks to team members and give reviews and feedback on the work when it's complete. Managers may or may not be available to help with problems when asked, depending on the company. Team members are solely responsible for how the work gets completed and dealing with problems that arise during the process. Some staff may prefer the freedom to dictate their workflow, and productivity is often increased in fields with highly skilled workers. The lack of leadership presence may prove problematic for other staff who prefer more direction, though, leading to reduced productivity or lack of focus. Some employees may even become extremely resentful of management, feeling that their boss doesn't contribute anything useful.

- **Visionary:** Visionary management focuses on managers serving as an inspiration for their team. Managers will work hard to motivate the team toward a specific goal using praise and positive reinforcement. They will often check in to provide feedback and make sure things are progressing, but otherwise they trust that the team is moving along in accordance with this vision. When employees are motivated and in agreement with this vision, they will be at peak engagement and satisfaction. However, this management style is very situational. Not all managers are good at inspiring others, and this can't be faked, so this style is only successful in certain situations.

Government-required practices – Equal Employment Opportunity (EEO)

There are many ways to go about managing employees and staff. However, as a foreign service officer, you are essentially an employee of the federal government. This means that regardless of the style you choose to implement, certain practices must be observed in accordance with federal law. Many of these practices involve monitoring and reporting on performance milestones and supporting the goals of your agency. The US Government Accountability Office (GAO) has a webpage where these requirements are explained in detail at https://www.gao.gov/leading-practices-managing-results-government.

To summarize, you will be required to prepare clear strategic and performance plans for your agency. You will need to have agency-wide goals and perform quarterly performance reviews to determine and report on the success and efficiency of your agency. If you work with other government agencies or become a leader for several smaller agencies, you must consider plans for all of them. These strategic plans need to include a mission statement and description of goals, as well as how those goals are affected by inter-agency collaboration, congressional consultation, and external factors. The agency must have a plan for quarterly performance reviews and a plan for how performance impacts agency goals. These plans generally need to be reissued every four years in the middle of a presidential term, and every plan covers at least four years. Every two years the agency needs to consult with all relevant congressional committees for opinions on the agency's performance.

Additionally, as a foreign service officer you must comply with all laws related to **Equal Employment Opportunity (EEO)**. EEO laws are enforced to prevent discriminatory hiring practices for any reason. In general, you should only allow a potential or current employee's skill or experience to be the reasons for rejection or termination. Personal factors such as race, gender, sex, age, disability, religion, or national origin are not allowed to be factored into these types of decisions. Several laws that have been passed over the years have built the foundation of and progressed EEO, as described below.

- The **Equal Pay Act of 1963** made it illegal to pay men and women different wages if they perform equal work.

- **Title VII of the Civil Rights Act of 1964** made it illegal to discriminate based on race, color, religion, national origin, or sex; made it illegal to retaliate against any employees who have complained of discrimination or participated in a discrimination investigation or lawsuit; and requires employers to reasonably accommodate employees' religious practices unless doing so would impose undue hardship upon business operations.

- The **Age Discrimination in Employment Act of 1967** protects people aged 40 or older from age-based discrimination.

- **Sections 501 and 505 of the Rehabilitation Act of 1973** made it illegal to discriminate against a person who qualifies as having a disability and is employed by the federal government.

- The **Pregnancy Discrimination Act of 1978** amended Title VII to include discrimination on the basis of pregnancy or childbirth status.

- **Title I of the Americans with Disabilities Act of 1990** made it illegal to discriminate against a person who qualifies as having a disability and works in private sector, state government, or local government positions.

- The **Genetic Information Nondiscrimination Act of 2008** made it illegal to discriminate based on genetic information, such as disease, disorder, or medical history, including that of the employee or applicant's family members.

Administrative Methods and Procedures

Federal law requires all federal government agencies to abide by certain procedures for both day-to-day operations and public transparency. An embassy in a foreign country is considered a federal government agency, so you must be aware of these procedures. There are too many rules to cover in depth in this study guide. However, most of them come from the **Administrative Procedure Act (APA)** of 1946. This study guide will cover Section 552 of the APA, which addresses many basic agency rules and proceedings as well as information that needs to be publicly available.

Section 552 of the APA outlines what information will need to be publicly available. Some of this information needs to be available upon request, while other information needs to be printed in the **Federal Register**, which is an officially published journal of the US federal government that describes new rules, regulations, agency notices or reports, and executive orders. The Register is published every weekday except federal holidays and is also available to the general public. The information specified by Section 552 of the APA includes the following:

- Descriptions of places and employees from which a member of the public may request information
- A general statement of the agency's purpose and methods, including the nature of those methods
- Procedures to obtain forms available to the public and what those forms cover
- Laws or policies that are created by the agency, and well as any amendments or repeals to them
- All final opinions and orders in the adjudication of cases
- Staff manuals and instructions that affect members of the public
- All final votes made by all members of any agency voting proceedings
- Any records that have been previously requested that have been determined to be likely to be requested again

Any of the above information requested from the public must be provided promptly and in the requested format. The agency will need to provide information about all applicable fees for document search and duplication, including under what circumstances those fees are reduced or waived.

Some information may not be publicly requested, in which case the agency may deny the request. Agencies must determine within twenty days of the request whether they will comply with the request. They must provide the reasons for denial if they do not intend to comply, and how the request may be appealed to the head of the agency. Any records containing protected information must be effectively scrubbed or deleted of such information before it can be presented to the public. The information that is not subject to public requests is as follows:

- Any information to be kept secret by executive order as a matter of national defense or foreign policy.
- Information related only to the internal rules and practices of an agency.
- Any information specifically exempt from disclosure by another statute.
- Confidential commercial or financial information.
- Inter- or intra-agency memos which would only be otherwise available to a party in litigation with the agency.
- Personnel or medical files that would constitute an invasion of personal privacy.
- Any information being compiled for a criminal investigation where the disclosure would interfere with police and legal proceedings.

Additionally, the agency must file a report with the Attorney General of the United States that discusses how many requests for information were denied, the reasons for their denial, how many denied requests were appealed, the results of those appeals, and a complete list of the statutes used as reasons for denial. The report must also include the total number of requests received and processed, the median number of days taken to process, total fees collected, total number of full-time employees devoted to processing requests, and total amount expended in processing requests. This report must also be made publicly available.

Other Requirements

Taxes: Federal employees are not exempt from paying taxes. The entity or organization they work for is responsible for paying the same federal income, social security, and Medicare taxes as private sector employees, usually by withholding a portion of the employee's paycheck to pay the taxes.

Health and Safety: To ensure a safe working environment, all federal agencies are required to comply with Section VI of the Occupational Safety and Health Act. The Act sets requirements related to worker health and safety in different kinds of working environments and is enforced by the **Occupational Safety and Health Administration (OSHA)**. OSHA also performs periodic inspections of federal agencies to examine their health and safety programs. These requirements are extremely detailed and are beyond the scope of this study guide, so supervisors will need to familiarize themselves with the specific regulations that apply to whatever workplace or workplaces they supervise.

Retirement: As of January 1, 1987, federal employees are covered by the **Federal Employees Retirement System (FERS)**. FERS provides three sources of retirement income: Social Security, Basic Benefit Plan, and Thrift Savings Plan. **Social Security** is a system where a portion of your paycheck is held and paid to Social Security instead, and upon retirement you gain access to various benefits. Social Security is also available for most private sector and some state or local government employees. The **Basic Benefit Plan** provides an additional set of defined retirement benefits that vary depending on your pay and how many years you worked for the federal government. Depending on when you leave federal service, you can choose either immediate, early, or deferred retirement benefits. The **Thrift Savings Plan** is similar to a 401k Plan provided by private employers. You can choose how much and how often to deposit into your

Thrift Savings Plan, and when you retire you will receive the benefits as either a life annuity, a single lump payment, or a set of monthly payments.

Practice Quiz

1. As a manager you must be aware of a variety of techniques relating to the psychology of the workplace. What is the official name for this type of psychology?
    a. Coworker psychology
    b. Hierarchy psychology
    c. Workplace psychology
    d. Industrial and organizational psychology

2. Which of the following methods of decision-making most effectively gives everyone in the team an opportunity to contribute?
    a. Discussing decisions in private meetings with select team members
    b. Discussing decisions during a team meeting
    c. Making all the decisions yourself as team lead
    d. Letting everyone make their own individual decisions

3. During the morning hours of the workday, you receive an email from your boss requesting changes to the parameters of a project that your team is about to begin. You need to quickly and clearly transmit this information to the rest of the team before they get too far ahead and must throw out redundant work. What would be the best method to do this?
    a. Walk down the hall and tell your team in person immediately.
    b. Compose and send an email to the team for them to review.
    c. Call a meeting over lunch and discuss the changes.
    d. Tell the first employee who passes your door to spread the word.

4. After a long period of time in forced remote work, your team is finally reconvening in the office to resume work in person. Many team members have adjusted to working on their own with little communication, and a couple have privately told you they're struggling to get used to the office routine again after preferring their work-from-home situation. Which of the following is the best method of boosting team morale in this situation?
    a. Tell everyone you understand the transition back is tough, but necessary for productivity.
    b. Support cooperative work and encourage everyone to ask for help from each other if they need it.
    c. Shift everyone into an open office floor plan so they can all talk to each other at any time.
    d. Allow anyone who wants to work from home again to do so, against the company's request.

5. The deadline for your team's project has been shifted, and your team has less time to complete it. You realize you may need to ask team members to work overtime to finish the project on time. What is the best way to approach this situation?
    a. Negotiate with your superiors to try to extend the deadline.
    b. Send an email to the team informing them and requiring everyone work overtime.
    c. Inform the team and make an open request for overtime volunteers.
    d. Take on the overtime work yourself to save your team the trouble.

See next page for answer explanations.

Answer Explanations

1. D: Industrial and organizational psychology, often abbreviated to I/O psychology, is the type of psychology that relates to the workplace environment. *Coworker psychology*, *hierarchy psychology*, and *workplace psychology* are all false terms, so Choices *A*, *B*, and *C* are all incorrect.

2. B: An open meeting with all team members is the best way to let everyone feel like they have a voice in decision-making. Private meetings with select team members will foster resentment in those excluded from the group, so Choice *A* is incorrect. Making all decisions yourself fosters even more resentment since nobody else has any influence, so Choice *C* is incorrect. Choice *D* does offer the most freedom for everyone, but also may lead to team members making contradictory decisions and causing confusion, so it is incorrect compared to Choice *B*.

3. A: The quickest way to convey the change in parameters would be to get up and physically visit your team to inform them of the changes. Composing an email is convenient, but it may take longer and/or not be read by some employees in a timely manner, so Choice *B* is incorrect. Calling a meeting over lunch may be too late to convey these changes, which may lead to redundant work, so Choice *C* is incorrect. Telling the first team member you see to spread the word is risky because the message may not be communicated accurately, and it may also make you seem incapable of spreading the news yourself, so Choice *D* is incorrect.

4. B: It's important to show compassion for your team's struggles while helping them find a solution, so offering to support team members and encouraging them to work together is the best solution here. Simply sending a message of sympathy does little to physically help your team, so Choice *A* is incorrect. Sudden changes to the floor plan could throw off many employees' workflow, so Choice *C* is incorrect. Disobeying the company's requirements will put you in a compromising position, so Choice *D* is incorrect.

5. C: The best approach in this situation is to inform your team and ask for overtime volunteers, but make sure to frame it as a voluntary situation to avoid forcing an unfair work-life balance on your team. Choice *A* is incorrect as the deadline extension may be non-negotiable if it was advanced forward from the original deadline. Choice *B* is incorrect because forcing extended overtime on the team can disrupt work-life balance and cause frustrations. Choice *D* is incorrect because it is equally unfair to fully take on the overtime yourself, and this may cause other problems if you can't handle the workload alone.

Mathematics and Statistics

This knowledge area encompasses a general understanding of basic mathematical and statistical procedures. It may include calculations.

Rational and Irrational Numbers

Rational numbers are those that can be written as a fraction, including **whole** or **negative** numbers, **fractions**, or **repeating decimals**. Examples of rational numbers include $\frac{1}{2}$, $\frac{5}{4}$, 2.75, and 8. Whole numbers can be written as fractions by putting the number itself as the numerator and 1 as the denominator; for example, 25 and 17 can be written as $\frac{25}{1}$ and $\frac{17}{1}$, respectively. One way of interpreting these fractions is to say that they are **ratios**, or comparisons of two quantities. The fractions given may represent 25 students to 1 classroom, or 17 desks to 1 computer lab.

Repeating decimals can also be written as fractions; 0.3333 and 0.6666667 can be written as $\frac{1}{3}$ and $\frac{2}{3}$. Fractions can be described as having a part-to-whole relationship. The $\frac{1}{3}$ may represent 1 piece of pizza out of the whole cut into 3 pieces. The fraction $\frac{2}{3}$ may represent 2 pieces of the same whole pizza. Rational numbers, including fractions, can be added together. When the denominators of two fractions are the same, you can simply add the numerators. For example, adding the fractions $\frac{1}{3}$ and $\frac{2}{3}$ is as simple as adding the numerators, 1 and 2. The result is $\frac{3}{3}$, which equals 1. Both of these numbers are rational and represent a whole.

In addition to fractions, rational numbers also include whole numbers and negative integers. When whole numbers are added, the result is always greater than the addends (unless 0 is added to the number, in which case its value would remain the same). For example, the equation:

$$4 + 18 = 22$$

4 increased by 18 results in 22. When subtracting rational numbers, sometimes the result is a negative number. For example, the equation:

$$5 - 12 = -7$$

Taking 12 away from 5 results in a negative answer (-7) because the starting number (5) is smaller than the number taken away (12). For multiplication and division, similar results are found. Multiplying rational numbers may look like the following equation:

$$5 \times 7 = 35$$

Both numbers are positive and whole, and the result is a larger number than the factors. The number 5 is counted 7 times, which results in a total of 35. Sometimes, the equation looks like:

$$-4 \times 3 = -12$$

The result is negative because a positive number times a negative number gives a negative answer. The rule is that any time a negative number and a positive number are multiplied or divided, the result is negative.

Operations with Rational Numbers

Basic Operations

The four basic operations include addition, subtraction, multiplication, and division. The result of addition is a **sum**, the result of subtraction is a **difference**, the result of multiplication is a **product**, and the result of division is a **quotient**. Each type of operation can be used when working with rational numbers.

These operations should first be learned using whole numbers. Addition needs to be done column by column. To add two whole numbers, add the ones column first, then the tens columns, then the hundreds, etc. If the sum of any column is greater than 9, a one must be carried over to the next column.

For example, the following is the result of 482 + 924:

$$\begin{array}{r} 1 \\ 482 \\ +924 \\ \hline 1406 \end{array}$$

Notice that the sum of the tens column was 10, so a one was carried over to the hundreds column. Subtraction is also performed column by column. Subtraction is performed in the ones column first, then the tens, etc. If the number on top is smaller than the number below, a one must be borrowed from the column to the left. For example, the following is the result of 5,424 − 756:

$$\begin{array}{r} 4\ 13\ 11\ 14 \\ \cancel{5}\ \cancel{4}\ \cancel{2}\ \cancel{4} \\ -\ 7\ \ 5\ \ 6 \\ \hline 4\ \ 6\ \ 6\ \ 8 \end{array}$$

Notice that a one is borrowed from the tens, hundreds, and thousands place. After subtraction, the answer can be checked through addition. A check of this problem would be to show that:

$$756 + 4{,}668 = 5{,}424$$

In multiplication, the number on top is known as the **multiplicand**, and the number below is the **multiplier**. Complete the problem by multiplying the multiplicand by each digit of the multiplier. Make sure to place the ones value of each result under the multiplying digit in the multiplier. The final product is found by adding each partial product. The following example shows the process of multiplying 46 times 37:

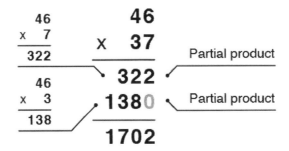

Division can be performed using long division. When dividing, the first number is known as the **dividend**, and the second is the **divisor**. For example, with $a \div b = c$, a is the dividend, b is the divisor, and c is the quotient. For long division, place the dividend within the division bar and the divisor on the outside. For example, with $8,764 \div 4$, refer to the first problem in the diagram below. The first digit, 8, is divisible by 4 two times. Therefore, 2 goes above the division bar over the 8. Then, multiply 4 times 2 to get 8, and that product goes below the 8. Subtract to get 0, and then carry down the second digit, 7. 4 goes into 7 one time, with 3 left over. The 1 goes above the division bar over the 7. Then subtract the product of 4 times 1 (4) from 7 to get 3 and carry down the 6. Continuing this process for the next two digits results in a 9 and a 1. The final subtraction results in a 0, which means that 8,764 is evenly divisible by 4 with no remaining numbers.

The second example shows that:
$$4,536 \div 216 = 21$$

The steps are a little different because 216 cannot be contained in 4 or 5, so the first step is placing a 2 above the 3 because there are two 216's in 453.

Finally, the third example shows that:
$$546 \div 31 = 17 \, R \, 19$$

The 19 is a remainder. Notice that the final subtraction does not result in a 0, which means that 546 is not evenly divisible by 31. The remainder can also be written as a fraction over the divisor:

$$546 \div 31 = 17\frac{19}{31}$$

```
  2191            21            17 r 19
4 8764       216 4536       31 546
  8              432            31
  07             216            236
  4              216            217
  36               0             19
  36
    04
     4
     0
```

A remainder can have meaning in a division problem with real-world application. Consider the third example above:

$$546 \div 31 = 17 \text{ R } 19$$

Let's say that we had $546 to spend on calculators that cost $31 each, and we wanted to know how many we could buy. The division problem would answer this question. The result states that 17 calculators could be purchased with $19 left over. Note that the remainder will never be greater than or equal to the divisor.

Operations and Negative Numbers

Once the operations are understood with whole numbers, they can be used with negative numbers. There are many rules surrounding operations with negative numbers. First, consider addition. The sum of two numbers can be shown using a number line. For example, to add $-5 + (-6)$, plot the point –5 on the number line. Adding a negative number is the same as subtracting, so move 6 units to the left. This process results in landing on –11 on the number line, which is the sum of –5 and –6. If adding a positive number, move to the right on the number line. While visualizing this process using a number line is useful for understanding, it is more efficient to learn the rules of operations. When adding two numbers with the same sign, add the absolute values of both numbers, and use the common sign of both numbers for the sum. The absolute value simply means the positive form of the number. For example, to add $-5 + (-6)$, add their absolute values:

$$5 + 6 = 11$$

Then, introduce a negative symbol because both addends are negative. The result is –11. To add two integers with unlike signs, subtract the lesser absolute value from the greater absolute value, and apply the sign of the number with the greater absolute value to the result. For example, the sum $-7 + 4$ can be computed by finding the difference $7 - 4 = 3$ and then applying a negative because the value with the larger absolute value is negative. The result is –3. Similarly, the sum $-4 + 7$ can be found by computing the same difference but leaving it as a positive result because the addend with the larger absolute value is positive. Also, recall that any number plus 0 equals that number. This is known as the **Addition Property of 0**.

Subtracting two integers with opposite signs can be computed by changing to addition to avoid confusion. The rule is to add the first number to the opposite of the second number. The opposite of a number is the number with the same value on the other side of 0 on the number line. For example, −2 and 2 are opposites. Consider $4 - 8$. Change this to adding the opposite as follows: $4 + (-8)$. Then, follow the rules described above to obtain −4. Now consider $-8 - (-2)$. Change this problem to adding the opposite as $-8 + 2$, which equals −6. Notice that subtracting a negative number is really adding a positive number.

The operations of multiplication and division are actually less confusing than addition and subtraction because the rules are simpler to understand. If two factors in a multiplication problem have the same sign, the product is positive. If one factor is positive and one factor is negative, the product is negative. For example,

$$(-9)(-3) = 27$$

and

$$9(-3) = -27$$

Also, a number multiplied by 0 always results in 0. If a problem consists of several multipliers, the result is negative if it contains an odd number of negative factors, and the result is positive if it contains an even number of negative factors. For example,

$$(-1)(-1)(-1)(-1) = 1$$

and

$$(-1)(-1)(-1)(-1)(-1) = -1$$

These two problems also display repeated multiplication, which can be written in a more compact notation using exponents. The first example can be written as $(-1)^4 = 1$, and the second example can be written as $(-1)^5 = -1$. Both are exponential expressions; −1 is the base in both instances, and 4 and 5 are the respective exponents. Note that a negative number raised to an odd power is always negative, and a negative number raised to an even power is always positive. Also, $(-1)^4$ is not the same as -1^4. In the first expression, the negative is included in the parentheses, but it is not in the second expression. The second expression is found by evaluating 1^4 first to get 1 and then applying the negative sign to obtain −1.

Similar rules apply within division. If two numbers in a division problem have the same sign, the quotient is positive. If two numbers in a division problem have different signs, the quotient is negative. For example:

$$14 \div (-2) = -7$$

and

$$-14 \div (-2) = 7$$

To check division, multiply the quotient by the divisor to obtain the dividend. Also, remember that 0 divided by any number is equal to 0. However, any number divided by 0 is undefined. It just does not make sense to divide a number by 0 parts.

Order of Operations

If more than one operation is to be completed in a problem, follow the **order of operations**. The mnemonic device, **PEMDAS**, states the order in which addition, subtraction, multiplication, and division need to be done. It also includes when to evaluate operations within grouping symbols and when to incorporate exponents. PEMDAS, which some remember by thinking "please excuse my dear Aunt Sally," refers to *parentheses, exponents, multiplication, division, addition*, and *subtraction*. First, complete any operation within parentheses or any other grouping symbol like brackets, braces, or absolute value symbols. Note that this does not refer to when parentheses are used to represent multiplication like $(2)(5)$. Then, any exponents must be computed. Next, multiplication and division are performed from left to right. Finally, addition and subtraction are performed from left to right. The following is an example in which the operations within the parentheses need to be performed first:

$$9-3(3^2-3+4\cdot3)$$

$$9-3(3^2-3+4\cdot3) \quad \text{Work within the parentheses first}$$
$$= 9-3(9-3+12)$$
$$= 9-3(18)$$
$$= 9-54$$
$$= -45$$

Operations and Decimals

Operations can be performed on rational numbers in decimal form. To write a fraction as an equivalent decimal expression, divide the numerator by the denominator. For example:

$$\frac{1}{8} = 1 \div 8 = 0.125$$

With the case of decimals, it is important to keep track of place value. To add decimals, make sure the decimal places are in alignment and add vertically. If the numbers do not line up because there are extra or missing place values in one of the numbers, then zeros may be used as placeholders. For example, $0.123 + 0.23$ becomes:

$$\begin{array}{r} 0.123 \\ +\ 0.230 \\ \hline 0.353 \end{array}$$

Subtraction is done the same way. Multiplication and division are more complicated. To multiply two decimals, place one on top of the other as in a regular multiplication process and do not worry about lining up the decimal points. Then, multiply as with whole numbers, ignoring the decimals. Finally, in the solution, insert the decimal point as many places to the left as there are total decimal values in the original problem. Here is an example of decimal multiplication:

$$0.52 \quad \textit{2 decimal places}$$
$$\times \quad 0.2 \quad \textit{1 decimal place}$$
$$\overline{0.104} \quad \textit{3 decimal places}$$

The answer to 52 times 2 is 104, and because there are three decimal values in the problem, the decimal point is positioned three units to the left in the answer.

The decimal point plays an integral role throughout the whole problem when dividing with decimals. First, set up the problem in a long division format. If the divisor is not an integer, move the decimal to the right as many units as needed to make it an integer. The decimal in the dividend must be moved to the right the same number of places to maintain equality. Then, complete division normally. Below is an example of long division with decimals using the problem $12.72 \div 0.06$:

Long division with decimals

$$
\begin{array}{r}
2\,1\,2 \\
6\,\overline{)\,1\,2\,7\,2} \\
1\,2 \\
0\,7 \\
6 \\
1\,2
\end{array}
$$

The decimal point in 0.06 needed to move two units to the right to turn it into an integer (6), so it also needed to move two units to the right in 12.72 to make it 1,272. The quotient is 212. To check a division problem, multiply the answer by the divisor to see if the result is equal to the dividend.

Operations and Fractions

When adding and subtracting fractions, the first step is to find the least common denominator. For example, the problem $\frac{3}{5} + \frac{6}{7}$ requires that a common multiple be found between 5 and 7. The smallest number that divides evenly by both 5 and 7 is 35. For the denominators to become 35, the first fraction must be multiplied by 7 and the second by 5. When $\frac{3}{5}$ is multiplied by 7, it becomes $\frac{21}{35}$. When $\frac{6}{7}$ is multiplied by 5, it becomes $\frac{30}{35}$. Once the fractions have the same denominator, the numerators can be added. The answer to the addition problem becomes:

$$\frac{3}{5}+\frac{6}{7}=\frac{21}{35}+\frac{30}{35}=\frac{41}{35}$$

The same technique can be used to subtract fractions. Multiplication and division may seem easier to perform because finding common denominators is unnecessary. If the problem reads $\frac{1}{3}\times\frac{4}{5}$, then the numerators and denominators are multiplied by each other and the answer is found to be $\frac{4}{15}$. For division, the problem must be changed to multiplication before performing operations. To complete a fraction division problem, you need to leave, change, and flip before multiplying. If the problem reads $\frac{3}{7}\div\frac{3}{4}$, then the first fraction is *left* alone, the operation is *changed* to multiplication, and the last fraction is *flipped*. The problem becomes $\frac{3}{7}\times\frac{4}{3}=\frac{12}{21}$.

Interpreting Categorical and Quantitative Data

Tables are a good way of showing a lot of information in a small space. The information in a table is organized in columns and rows. For example, a table may be used to show the number of votes each candidate received in an election. By interpreting the table, one may observe which candidate won the election and which candidates came in second and third. In using a bar chart to display monthly rainfall amounts in different countries, rainfall can be compared between countries at different times of the year. Graphs are also a useful way to show change in variables over time, as in a line graph, or percentages of a whole, as in a pie graph.

The table below relates the number of items to the total cost. The table shows that one item costs $5. By looking at the table further, five items cost $25, ten items cost $50, and fifty items cost $250. This cost can be extended for any number of items. Since one item costs $5, then two items would cost $10. Though this information is not in the table, the given price can be used to calculate unknown information.

Number of Items	1	5	10	50
Cost ($)	5	25	50	250

A **bar graph** is a graph that summarizes data using bars of different heights. It is useful when comparing two or more items or when seeing how a quantity changes over time. It has both a horizontal and vertical axis. To interpret bar graphs, recognize what each bar represents and connect that to the two variables. The bar graph below shows the scores for six people during three different games. The different colors of the bars distinguish between the three games, and the height of the bar indicates their score for that game. William scored 25 on game 3, and Abigail scored 38 on game 3. By comparing the bars, it is obvious that Williams scored lower than Abigail.

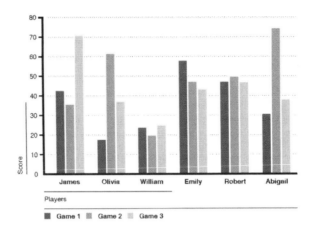

A **line graph** is a way to compare two variables that are plotted on opposite axes of a graph. The line indicates a continuous change as it rises or falls. The line's rate of change is known as its slope. The horizontal axis often represents a variable of time. Readers can quickly see if an amount has grown or decreased over time. The bottom of the graph, or the x-axis, shows the units for time, such as days, hours, months, etc. If there are multiple lines, a comparison can be made between what the two lines represent. For example, the following line graph, shown previously, displays the change in temperature over five days. The top line represents the high, and the bottom line represents the low for each day. Looking at the top line alone, the high decreases for a day, then increases on Wednesday. Then it decreases on Thursday and increases again on Friday. The low temperatures have a similar trend, shown in the bottom line. The range in temperatures each day can also be calculated by finding the difference between the top line and bottom line on a particular day. On Wednesday, the range was 14 degrees, from 62 to 76° F.

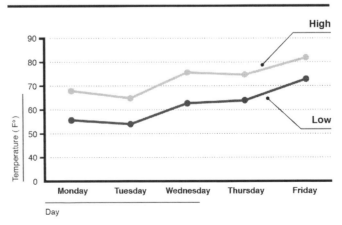

Pie charts show percentages of a whole; they are circular representations of data used to highlight numerical proportions. Each category represents a piece of the pie, and together, all of the pieces make up a whole. The size of each pie slice is proportional to the amount it represents; therefore, a reader can quickly make comparisons by visualizing the sizes of the pieces. They can be useful for comparison between different categories. The following pie chart is a simple example of three different categories shown in comparison to each other.

Light gray represents cats, dark gray represents dogs, and the medium shade of gray represents other pets. These three equal pieces each represent just more than 33 percent, or $\frac{1}{3}$ of the whole. Values 1 and 2 may be combined to represent $\frac{2}{3}$ of the whole. In an example where the total pie represents 75,000 animals, then cats would be equal to $\frac{1}{3}$ of the total, or 25,000. Dogs would equal 25,000 and other pets also equal 25,000.

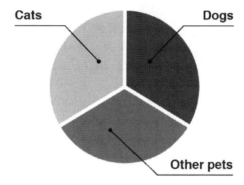

Since circles have 360 degrees, they are used to create pie charts. Because each piece of the pie is a percentage of a whole, that percentage is multiplied times 360 to get the number of degrees each piece represents. In the example above, each piece is $\frac{1}{3}$ of the whole, so each piece is equivalent to 120 degrees. Together, all three pieces add up to 360 degrees.

Stacked bar graphs are also used fairly frequently when comparing multiple variables at one time. They combine some elements of both pie charts and bar graphs, using the organization of bar graphs and the proportionality aspect of pie charts. The following is an example of a stacked bar graph that represents the number of students in a band playing drums, flute, trombone, and clarinet. Each bar graph is broken up further into girls and boys.

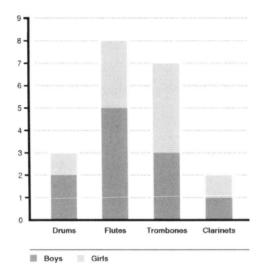

As mentioned, a **scatterplot** is another way to represent paired data. It uses Cartesian coordinates, like a line graph, meaning it has both a horizontal and vertical axis. Each data point is represented as a dot on the graph. The dots are never connected with a line. For example, the following is a scatterplot showing the connection between people's ages and heights.

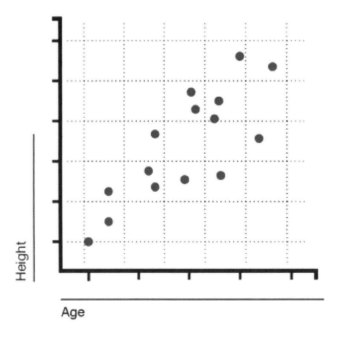

50

A scatterplot, also known as a **scattergram,** can be used to predict another value and to see if a correlation exists between two variables in a set of data. If the data resembles a straight line, then it is associated, or correlated. The following is an example of a scatterplot in which the data does not seem to have an association:

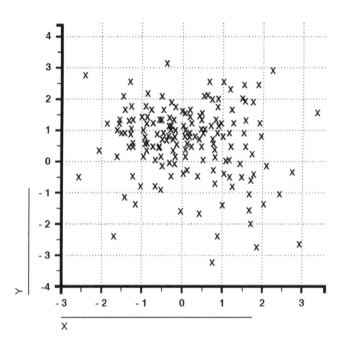

Sets of numbers and other similarly organized data can also be represented graphically. Venn diagrams are a common way to do so. A **Venn diagram** represents each set of data as a circle. The circles overlap, showing that each set of data is overlapping. A Venn diagram is also known as a **logic diagram** because it visualizes all possible logical combinations between two sets. Common elements of two sets are represented by the area of overlap. The following is an example of a Venn diagram of two sets A and B:

Parts of the Venn Diagram

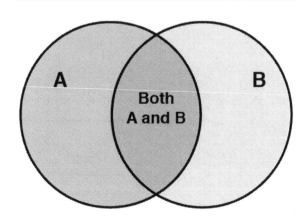

Another name for the area of overlap is the **intersection.** The intersection of A and B, written $A \cap B$, contains all elements that are in both sets A and B. The **union** of A and B, $A \cup B$, contains all elements in both sets A and B. Finally, the **complement** of $A \cup B$ is equal to all elements that are not in either set A or set B. These elements are placed outside of the circles.

Venn diagrams are typically not drawn to scale; however, if they are, and if each circle's area is proportional to the amount of data it represents, then it is called an area-proportional Venn diagram.

Describing Distributions

One way information can be interpreted from tables, charts, and graphs is through statistics. The three most common calculations for a set of data are the mean, median, and mode. These three are called **measures of central tendency**, which are helpful in comparing two or more different sets of data. The **mean** refers to the average and is found by adding up all values and dividing the total by the number of values. In other words, the mean is equal to the sum of all values divided by the number of data entries. For example, if you bowled a total of 532 points in 4 bowling games, your mean score was $\frac{532}{4} = 133$ points per game. Students can apply the concept of mean to calculate what score they need on a final exam to earn a desired grade in a class.

The **median** is found by lining up values from least to greatest and choosing the middle value. If there is an even number of values, then calculate the mean of the two middle amounts to find the median. For example, the median of the set of dollar amounts $5, $6, $9, $12, and $13 is $9. The median of the set of dollar amounts $1, $5, $6, $8, $9, $10 is $7, which is the mean of $6 and $8. The **mode** is the value that occurs the most. The mode of the data set {1, 3, 1, 5, 5, 8, 10} actually refers to two numbers: 1 and 5. In this case, the data set is **bimodal** because it has two modes. A data set can have no mode if no amount is repeated. Another useful statistic is range. The **range** for a set of data refers to the difference between the highest and lowest value.

In some cases, numbers in a list of data might have weights attached to them. In that case, a **weighted mean** can be calculated. A common application of a weighted mean is GPA. In a semester, each class is assigned a number of credit hours, its weight, and at the end of the semester each student receives a grade. To compute GPA, an A is a 4, a B is a 3, a C is a 2, a D is a 1, and an F is a 0. Consider a student that takes a 4-hour English class, a 3-hour math class, and a 4-hour history class and receives all B's. The weighted mean, GPA, is found by multiplying each grade times its weight, number of credit hours, and dividing by the total number of credit hours. Therefore, the student's GPA is:

$$\frac{3 \times 4 + 3 \times 3 + 3 \times 4}{11} = \frac{33}{11} = 3.0.$$

The following bar chart shows how many students attend a cycle class on each day of the week. To find the mean attendance for the week, add each day's attendance together:

$$10 + 7 + 6 + 9 + 8 + 14 + 4 = 58$$

Then divide the total by the number of days:

$$58 \div 7 = 8.3.$$

The mean attendance for the week was 8.3 people. The median attendance can be found by putting the attendance numbers in order from least to greatest: 4, 6, 7, 8, 9, 10, 14, and choosing the middle number:

8 people. This set of data has no mode because no numbers repeat. The range is 10, which is found by finding the difference between the lowest number, 4, and the highest number, 14.

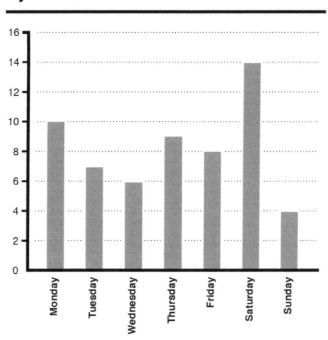

Cycle class attendance

A **histogram** is a bar graph used to group data into "bins" that cover a range on the horizontal, or x-axis. Histograms consist of rectangles whose heights are equal to the frequency of a specific category. The horizontal axis represents the specific categories. Because they cover a range of data, these bins have no gaps between bars, unlike the bar graph above. In a histogram showing the heights of adult golden retrievers, the bottom axis would be groups of heights, and the y-axis would be the number of dogs in each range. Evaluating this histogram would show the height of most golden retrievers as falling within a certain range. It also provides information to find the average height and range for how tall golden retrievers may grow.

The following is a histogram that represents exam grades in a given class. The horizontal axis represents ranges of the number of points scored, and the vertical axis represents the number of students. For example, approximately 33 students scored in the 60 to 70 range.

Results of the exam

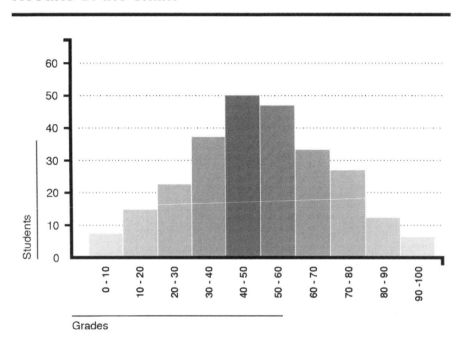

Certain measures of central tendency can be easily visualized with a histogram. If the points scored were shown with individual rectangles, the tallest rectangle would represent the mode. A bimodal set of data would have two peaks of equal height. Histograms can be classified as having data **skewed to the left, skewed to the right**, or **normally distributed**, which is also known as **bell-shaped**.

These three classifications can be seen in the following chart:

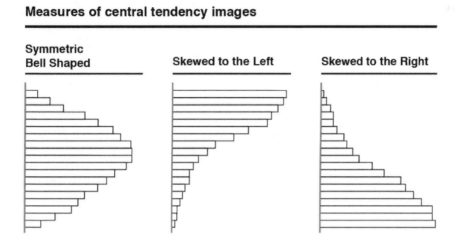

Measures of central tendency images

| Symmetric Bell Shaped | Skewed to the Left | Skewed to the Right |

When the data is normal, the mean, median, and mode are very similar because they all represent the most typical value in the data set. In this case, the mean is typically considered the best measure of central tendency because it includes all data points. However, if the data is skewed, the mean becomes less meaningful because it is dragged in the direction of the skew. Therefore, the median becomes the best measure because it is not affected by any outliers.

The measures of central tendency and the range may also be found by evaluating information on a line graph.

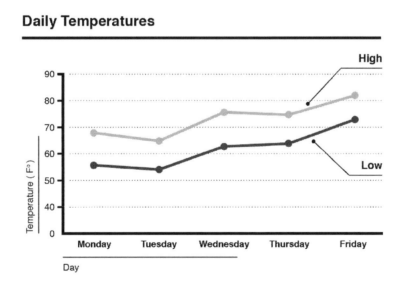

Daily Temperatures

In the line graph above that shows the daily high and low temperatures, the average high temperature can be found by gathering data from each day on the triangle line. The days' highs are 69, 65, 75, 74, and 81. To find the average, add them together to get 364, then divide by 5 (because there are 5 temperatures). The average high for the five days is 72.8. If 72.8 degrees is found on the graph, it will fall in the middle of all the values. The average low temperature can be found in the same way.

Given a set of data, the **correlation coefficient**, r, measures the association between all the data points. If two values are **correlated**, there is an association between them. However, correlation does not necessarily mean causation, or that one value causes the other. There is a common mistake made that assumes correlation implies causation. Average daily temperature and number of sunbathers are both correlated and have causation. If the temperature increases, that change in weather causes more people to want to catch some rays. However, wearing plus-size clothing and having heart disease are two variables that are correlated but do not have causation. The larger someone is, the more likely he or she is to have heart disease. However, being overweight does not cause someone to have the disease.

The value of the correlation coefficient is between −1 and 1, where −1 represents a perfect negative linear relationship, 0 represents no relationship between the two data sets, and 1 represents a perfect positive linear relationship. A negative linear relationship means that as x-values increase, y-values decrease. A positive linear relationship means that as x-values increase, y-values increase. The formula for computing the correlation coefficient is:

$$r = \frac{n \sum xy - (\sum x)(\sum y)}{\sqrt{n(\sum x^2) - (\sum x)^2}\sqrt{n(\sum y^2) - (y)^2}}$$

where n is the number of data points. The closer r is to 1 or −1, the stronger the correlation. A correlation can be seen when plotting data. If the graph resembles a straight line, there is a correlation.

Solving Problems Involving Measures of Center and Range
As mentioned, a data set can be described by calculating the mean, median, and mode. These values allow the data to be described with a single value that is representative of the data set.

The most common measure of center is the **mean,** also referred to as the **average.**

To calculate the mean:

- Add all data values together.
- Divide by the sample size (the number of data points in the set).

The **median** is middle data value, so that half of the data lies below this value and half lies above it.

To calculate the median:

- Order the data from least to greatest.
- The point in the middle of the set is the median.
- If there is an even number of data points, add the two middle points and divide by 2.

The **mode** is the data value that occurs most often.

To calculate the mode:

- Order the data from least to greatest.
- Find the value that occurs most often.

Example: Amelia is a leading scorer on the school's basketball team. The following data set represents the number of points that Amelia has scored in each game this season. Use the mean, median, and mode to describe the data.

16, 12, 26, 14, 28, 14, 12, 15, 25

Solution:

Mean:

$$16 + 12 + 26 + 14 + 28 + 14 + 12 + 15 + 25 = 162$$

$$162 \div 9 = 18$$

Amelia averages 18 points per game.

Median:

12, 12, 14, 14, **15**, 16, 25, 26, 28

Amelia's median score is 15.

Mode:

12, 12, 14, 14, 15, 16, 25, 26, 28

The numbers 12 and 14 each occur twice, so this data set has 2 modes: 12 and 14.

The **range** is the difference between the largest and smallest values in the set. In the example above, the range is:

$$28 - 12 = 16$$

Determining How Changes in Data Affect Measures of Center or Range

An **outlier** is a data point that lies an unusual distance from other points in the data set. Removing an outlier from a data set will change the measures of central tendency. Removing a large outlier (a high number) from a data set will decrease both the mean and the median. Removing a small outlier (a number much lower than most in the data set) from a data set will increase both the mean and the median. For example, in data set {3, 6, 8, 12, 13, 14, 60}, the data point 60, is an outlier because it is unusually far from the other points. In this data set, the mean is 16.6. Notice that this mean number is even larger than all other data points in the set except for 60. Removing the outlier changes the mean to 9.3, and the median goes from 12 to 10. Removing an outlier will also decrease the range. In the data set above, the range is 57 when the outlier is included, but it decreases to 11 when the outlier is removed.

Adding an outlier to a data set will also affect the measures of central tendency. When a larger outlier is added to a data set, the mean and median increase. When a small outlier is added to a data set, the mean and median decrease. Adding an outlier to a data set will increase the range.

This does not seem to provide an appropriate measure of center when considering this data set. What will happen if that outlier is removed? Removing the extremely large data point, 60, is going to reduce the mean to 9.3. The mean decreased dramatically because 60 was much larger than any of the other data values. What would happen with an extremely low value in a data set like this one, {12, 87, 90, 95, 98,

100}? The mean of the given set is 80. When the outlier, 12, is removed, the mean should increase and fit more closely to the other data points. Removing 12 and recalculating the mean show that this is correct. After removing the outlier, the mean is 94. So, removing a large outlier will decrease the mean while removing a small outlier will increase the mean.

Statistical Measures

Statistics is the branch of mathematics that deals with the collection, organization, and analysis of data. A statistical question is one that can be answered by collecting and analyzing data. When collecting data, expect variability. For example, "How many miles of railroad track are laid in Texas?" is not a statistical question because it can be answered in one way. "How many miles of railroad track are laid in each State of the United States?" is a statistical question because, to determine this answer, one would need to collect data from each State in the country, and it is reasonable to expect the answers to vary.

Identify these as statistical or not statistical:

- How old is the President?
- What is the average age of the people in Congress?

The first question is not statistical, but the last question is.

Data collection can be done through surveys, experiments, observations, and interviews. A **census** is a type of survey that is done with a whole population. Because it can be difficult to collect data for an entire population, sometimes a **sample** is used. In this case, one would survey only a fraction of the population and make inferences about the data. Sample surveys are not as accurate as a census, but they are an easier and less expensive method of collecting data. An **experiment** is used when a researcher wants to explain how one variable causes changes in another variable. For example, if a researcher wanted to know if a particular drug affects weight loss, he or she would choose a **treatment group** that would take the drug, and another group, the **control group**, that would not take the drug. Special care must be taken when choosing these groups to ensure that bias is not a factor.

Bias occurs when an outside factor influences the outcome of the research. In observational studies, the researcher does not try to influence either variable but simply observes the behavior of the subjects. Interviews are sometimes used to collect data as well. The researcher will ask questions that focus on her area of interest in order to gain insight from the participants. When gathering data through observation or interviews, it is important that the researcher is well trained so that he or she does not influence the results and the study remains reliable. A study is reliable if it can be repeated under the same conditions and the same results are received each time.

Random Processes Underlying Statistical Experiments

For researchers to make valid conclusions about population characteristics and parameters, the sample used to compare must be random. In a **random sample**, every member of the population must have an equal chance of being selected. In this situation, the sample is **unbiased** and is said to be a good representation of the population. If a sample is selected in an inappropriate manner, it is said to be **biased.** A sample can be biased if, for example, some subjects were more likely to be chosen than others. In order to have unbiased samples, the four main sampling methods used tend to be random, systematic, stratified, and cluster sampling.

Random sampling occurs when, given a sample size n, all possible samples of that size are equally likely to be chosen. Random numbers from calculators are typically used in this setting. Each member of a population is paired with a number, and then a set of random numbers is generated. Each person paired with one of those random numbers is selected. A **systematic sample** is when every fourth, seventh, tenth, etc., person from a population is selected to be in a sample. A **stratified sample** is when the population is divided into subgroups, or **strata**, using a characteristic, and then members from each stratum are randomly selected. For example, university students could be divided into age groups and then selected from each age group. Finally, a **cluster sample** is when a sample is used from an already selected group, like city block or zip code. These four methods are used most frequently because they are most likely to yield unbiased results.

Once an unbiased sample is obtained, data need to be collected. Common data collection methods include surveys with questions that are unbiased, contain clear language, avoid double negatives, and do not contain compound sentences that ask two questions at once. When formulating these questions, the simpler verbiage, the better.

Using Random Sampling to Draw Inferences About a Population

In statistics, a **population** contains all subjects being studied. For example, a population could be every student at a university or all males in the United States. A **sample** consists of a group of subjects from an entire population. A sample would be 100 students at a university or 100,000 males in the United States. **Inferential statistics** is the process of using a sample to generalize information concerning populations. **Hypothesis testing** is the actual process used when evaluating claims made about a population based on a sample.

A **statistic** is a measure obtained from a sample, and a **parameter** is a measure obtained from a population. For example, the mean SAT score of the 100 students at a university would be a statistic, and the mean SAT score of all university students would be a parameter.

The beginning stages of hypothesis testing starts with formulating a **hypothesis**, a statement made concerning a population parameter. The hypothesis may be true, or it may not be true. The test will answer that question. In each setting, there are two different types of hypotheses: the **null hypothesis**, written as H_0, and the **alternative hypothesis**, written as H_1. The null hypothesis represents verbally when there is not a difference between two parameters, and the alternative hypothesis represents verbally when there is a difference between two parameters. Consider the following experiment: A researcher wants to see if a new brand of allergy medication has any effect on drowsiness of the patients who take the medication. He wants to know if the average hours spent sleeping per day increases. The mean for the population under study is 8 hours, so $\mu = 8$. In other words, the population parameter is μ, the mean. The null hypothesis is $\mu = 8$ and the alternative hypothesis is $\mu > 8$. When using a smaller sample of a population, the null hypothesis represents the situation when the mean remains unaffected and the alternative hypothesis represents the situation when the mean increases. The chosen statistical test will apply the data from the sample to actually decide whether the null hypothesis should or should not be rejected.

Probabilistic Reasoning

Chance Processes and Probability Models

Probability describes how likely it is that an event will occur. Probabilities are always a number from zero to 1. If an event has a high likelihood of occurrence, it will have a probability close to 1. If there is only a small chance that an event will occur, the likelihood is close to zero. A fair six-sided die has one of the numbers 1, 2, 3, 4, 5, and 6 on each side. When this die is rolled there is a one in six chance that it will land on 2. This is because there are six possibilities and only one side has a 2 on it. The probability then is $\frac{1}{6}$ or 0.167. The probability of rolling an even number from this die is three in six, which is $\frac{1}{2}$ or 0.5. This is because there are three sides on the die with even numbers (2, 4, 6), and there are six possible sides. The probability of rolling a number less than 10 is 1; since every side of the die has a number less than 6, it would be impossible to roll a number 10 or higher. On the other hand, the probability of rolling a number larger than 20 is zero. There are no numbers greater than 20 on the die, so it is certain that this will not occur, thus the probability is zero.

If a teacher says that the probability of anyone passing her final exam is 0.2, is it highly likely that anyone will pass? No, the probability of anyone passing her exam is low because 0.2 is closer to zero than to 1. If another teacher is proud that the probability of students passing his class is 0.95, how likely is it that a student will pass? It is highly likely that a student will pass because the probability, 0.95, is very close to 1.

A probability experiment is a repeated action that has a specific set of possible results. The result of such an experiment is known as an **outcome,** and the set of all potential outcomes is known as the **sample space.** An **event** consists of one or more of those outcomes. For example, consider the probability experiment of tossing a coin and rolling a six-sided die. The coin has two possible outcomes—a heads or a tails—and the die has six possible outcomes—rolling each number 1–6. Therefore, the sample space has twelve possible outcomes: a heads or a tails paired with each roll of the die.

A **simple event** is an event that consists of a single outcome. For instance, selecting a queen of hearts from a standard fifty-two-card deck is a simple event; however, selecting a queen is not a simple event because there are four possibilities.

Classical, or **theoretical, probability** is when each outcome in a sample space has the same chance to occur. The probability for an event is equal to the number of outcomes in that event divided by the total number of outcomes in the sample space. For example, consider rolling a six-sided die. The probability of rolling a 2 is $\frac{1}{6}$, and the probability of rolling an even number is $\frac{3}{6}$, or $\frac{1}{2}$, because there are three even numbers on the die. This type of probability is based on what should happen in theory but not what actually happens in real life.

Empirical probability is based on actual experiments or observations. For example, if a die is rolled eight times, and a 1 is rolled two times, the empirical probability of rolling a 1 is $\frac{2}{8} = \frac{1}{4}$, which is higher than the theoretical probability. The Law of Large Numbers states that as an experiment is completed repeatedly, the empirical probability of an event should get closer to the theoretical probability of an event.

The **addition rule** is necessary to find the probability of event A or event B occurring or both occurring at the same time. If events A and B are **mutually exclusive** or **disjoint,** which means they cannot occur at the same time:

$$P(A \text{ or } B) = P(A) + P(B)$$

If events A and B are not mutually exclusive:

$$P(A \text{ or } B) = P(A) + P(B) - P(A \text{ and } B)$$

where $P(A \text{ and } B)$ represents the probability of event A and B both occurring at the same time. An example of two events that are mutually exclusive are rolling a 6 on a die and rolling an odd number on a die.

The probability of rolling a 6 or rolling an odd number is:

$$\frac{1}{6} + \frac{3}{6} = \frac{4}{6} = \frac{2}{3}$$

Rolling a 6 and rolling an even number are not mutually exclusive because there is some overlap. The probability of rolling a 6 or rolling an even number is:

$$\frac{1}{6} + \frac{3}{6} - \frac{1}{6} = \frac{3}{6} = \frac{1}{2}$$

Conditional Probability

The **multiplication rule** is necessary when finding the probability that event A occurs in a first trial and event B occurs in a second trial, which is written as $P(A \text{ and } B)$. This rule differs if the events are independent or dependent. Two events A and B are **independent** if the occurrence of one event does not affect the probability that the other will occur. If A and B are not independent, they are **dependent**, and the outcome of the first event somehow affects the outcome of the second. If events A and B are independent:

$$P(A \text{ and } B) = P(A)P(B)$$

and if events A and B are dependent:

$$P(A \text{ and } B) = P(A)P(B|A)$$

where $P(B|A)$ represents the probability event B occurs given that event A has already occurred.

$P(B|A)$ represents **conditional probability**, or the probability of event B occurring given that event A has already occurred. $P(B|A)$ can be found by dividing the probability of events A and B both occurring by the probability of event A occurring using the formula $P(B|A) = \frac{P(A \text{ and } B)}{P(A)}$ and represents the total number of outcomes remaining for B to occur after A occurs. This formula is derived from the multiplication rule with dependent events by dividing both sides by $P(A)$. Note that $P(B|A)$ and $P(A|B)$ are not the same. The first quantity shows that event B has occurred after event A, and the second quantity shows that event A has occurred after event B. Incorrectly interchanging these ideas is known as **confusing the inverse**.

Consider the case of drawing two cards from a deck of fifty-two cards. The probability of pulling two queens would vary based on whether the initial card was placed back in the deck for the second pull. If the card is placed back in, the probability of pulling two queens is:

$$\frac{4}{52} \times \frac{4}{52} = 0.00592.$$

If the card is not placed back in, the probability of pulling two queens is:

$$\frac{4}{52} \times \frac{3}{51} = 0.00452$$

When the card is not placed back in, both the numerator and denominator of the second probability decrease by 1. This is due to the fact that, theoretically, there is one less queen in the deck, and there is one less total card in the deck as well.

Using Probability to Evaluate the Outcomes of Decisions

A **two-way frequency table** displays categorical data with two variables, and it highlights relationships that exist between those two variables. Such tables are used frequently to summarize survey results and are also known as **contingency tables**. Each cell shows a count pertaining to that individual variable pairing, known as a **joint frequency**, and the totals of each row and column are also in the table.

Consider the following two-way frequency table:

Distribution of the Residents of a Particular Village

	70 or older	69 or younger	Totals
Women	20	40	60
Men	5	35	40
Total	25	75	100

The table shows the breakdown of ages and sexes of 100 people in a particular village. The end of each row or column displays the number of people represented by the corresponding data, and the total number of people is shown in the bottom right corner. For example, there were 25 people aged 70 or older and 60 women in the data. The 20 in the first cell shows that out of 100 total villagers, 20 were women aged 70 or older. The 5 in the cell below shows that out of 100 total villagers, 5 were men aged 70 or older.

A two-way table can also show relative frequencies by indicating the percentages of people instead of the count. If each frequency is calculated over the entire total of 100, the first cell would be 20% or 0.2. However, the relative frequencies can also be calculated over row or column totals. If row totals were used, the first cell would be:

$$\frac{20}{60} = 0.333 = 33.3\%$$

If column totals were used, the first cell would be:

$$\frac{20}{25} = 0.8 = 80\%.$$

Such tables can be used to calculate **conditional probabilities**, which are probabilities that an event occurs, given another event. Consider a randomly selected villager. The probability of selecting a male 70 years old or older is $\frac{5}{100} = 0.05$ because there are 5 males over the age of 70 and 100 total villagers.

Practice Quiz

1. A study of adult drivers finds that it is likely that an adult driver wears their seatbelt. Which of the following could be the probability that an adult driver wears their seat belt?
    a. 0.90
    b. 0.05
    c. 0
    d. 1.5

2. Which of the statements below is a statistical question?
    a. What was your grade on the last test?
    b. What were the grades of the students in your class on the last test?
    c. What kind of car do you drive?
    d. What was Sam's time in the marathon?

3. The number of members of the House of Representatives varies directly with the total population in a state. If the state of New York has 19,800,000 residents and has 27 total representatives, how many should Ohio have with a population of 11,800,000?
    a. 10
    b. 16
    c. 11
    d. 5

4. From the chart below, which two are preferred by more men than women?

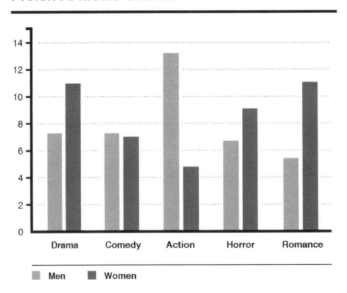

Preferred Movie Genres

    a. Comedy and Action
    b. Drama and Comedy
    c. Action and Horror
    d. Action and Romance

5. The following set represents the test scores from a university class: {35, 79, 80, 87, 87, 90, 92, 95, 95, 98, 99}. If the outlier is removed from this set, which of the following is true?

    a. The mean and the median will decrease.
    b. The mean and the median will increase.
    c. The mean and the mode will increase.
    d. The mean and the mode will decrease.

See next page for answer explanations.

Answer Explanations

1. A: The probability of 0.9 is closer to 1 than any of the other answers. The closer a probability is to 1, the greater the likelihood that the event will occur. The probability of 0.05 shows that it is very unlikely that an adult driver will wear their seatbelt because it is close to zero. A zero probability means that it will not occur. Choice D is wrong because probability must fall between 0 and 1.

2. B: This is a statistical question because to determine this answer one would need to collect data from each person in the class and it is expected the answers would vary. The other answers do not require data to be collected from multiple sources, therefore the answers will not vary.

3. B: The number of representatives varies directly with the population, so the equation necessary is $N = k \times P$, where N is number of representatives, k is the variation constant, and P is total population in millions. Plugging in the information for New York allows k to be solved for. This process gives $27 = k \times 19.8$, so $k \approx 1.36$. Therefore, the formula for number of representatives given total population in millions is:

$$N = 1.36 \times P$$

Plugging in $P = 11.8$ for Ohio results in $N \approx 16.05$, which rounds to 16 total representatives.

4. A: The chart is a bar chart showing how many men and women prefer each genre of movies. The dark gray bars represent the number of women, while the light gray bars represent the number of men. The light gray bars are higher and represent more men than women for the genres of Comedy and Action.

5. B: The outlier is 35. When a small outlier is removed from a data set, the mean and the median increase. The first step in this process is to identify the outlier, which is the number that lies away from the given set. Once the outlier is identified, the mean and median can be recalculated. The mean will be affected because it averages all of the numbers. The median will be affected because it finds the middle number, which is subject to change because a number is lost. The mode will most likely not change because it is the number that occurs the most, which will not be the outlier if there is only one outlier.

United States Government

Role of the Citizen in a Democratic Society

The rights enjoyed by Americans are rooted in the Bill of Rights, but no right is unconditional. In some specific circumstances, the government can restrict citizens' rights. The government is especially powerful during wartime. For example, President Abraham Lincoln suspended the right to due process during the Civil War. Other common limits are defamation laws and limits on "fighting words."

Following the Civil War, the concept of civil rights was added to rights enjoyed by Americans. The Thirteenth, Fourteenth, and Fifteenth Amendments prohibited slavery, provided for due process and equal protection under the law, and protected the right to vote based on race, color, or previous condition of servitude, respectively. Inspired by the Civil Rights Movement, activists have fought for equal rights and protection under the law based on gender and sexuality, culminating in the landmark Supreme Court decision *United States v. Windsor* (2013), which established the right to same-sex marriage.

Americans also have responsibilities. First and foremost, Americans are expected to obey the civil and criminal justice system, or else they will face what can be severe punishment. The United States imprisons more of its citizens, in both the total prison population and per capita, than any other country in the world by a wide margin. Civil disobedience has been used in the United States to great effect, but there's typically strong pushback from the establishment and the public.

The other major responsibility for citizens is to participate in the political system. Although voting, donating to candidates, running for office, and other forms of participation are not legally mandated, the United States is a representative democracy, and a lack of public participation undermines the government's legitimacy. Yet, voter turnout is low in the United States. Approximately 55 percent of registered Americans vote in presidential elections, and local elections have even lower turnout.

The Constitution of the United States of America

Since the Declaration of Independence was signed in 1776, the United States has implemented a perpetually innovating system of government to organize the country and maintain order. Over time, new agencies and departments have been added to the nation's government, each reflecting the momentous events and changes of their time.

The Constitution is the basis for how the United States government is run. It outlines the various rules, requirements, and rights associated with government. It created the three branches of government and is the ultimate law of the land. Over the years, additional rules and requirements, known as amendments, have been added to the Constitution.

Amendments may be proposed by Congress or if two-thirds of the States request it. After being proposed, the amendment must be ratified by three-fourths of the state legislatures or two-thirds of the states through a specific convention designed for this purpose. The first ten amendments are known as the Bill of Rights. The Bill of Rights outlines various basic rights granted to citizens of the United States. These are some of the most famous and well-known fundamental rights in the world. They include freedom of speech, guarantees to a fair trial, the right to bear arms, and more.

The Constitution, including its interpretation by the Supreme Court of the United States, divided the powers as follows:

Exclusive federal government powers

- Coin money
- Declare war
- Establish federal courts
- Sign foreign treaties
- Expand territories and admit new states
- Regulate immigration
- Regulate interstate commerce

Exclusive state government powers

- Establish local government
- Hold and regulate elections
- Implement welfare and benefit programs
- Create and oversee public education
- Establish licensing requirements
- Regulate state corporations
- Regulate commerce within the state

Concurrent powers (shared)

- Levy taxes
- Borrow money
- Charter corporations

Bill of Rights

The Bill of Rights is comprised of the first ten amendments to the Constitution.

- **First Amendment**: freedom of speech, freedom of press, free exercise of religion, and the right to assemble peacefully and petition the government
- **Second Amendment**: the right to bear arms
- **Third Amendment**: the right to refuse to quarter (house) soldiers
- **Fourth Amendment**: prohibits unreasonable searches and seizures and requires a warrant based on probable cause
- **Fifth Amendment**: protects due process, requires a grand jury indictment for certain felonies, protects against the government seizing property without compensation, protects against self-incrimination, and prohibits double jeopardy
- **Sixth Amendment**: the right to a fair and speedy criminal trial, the right to view criminal accusations, the right to present witnesses, and the right to counsel in criminal trials
- **Seventh Amendment**: the right to a trial by jury in civil cases
- **Eighth Amendment**: prohibits cruel and unusual punishment
- **Ninth Amendment**: establishes the existence of unnamed rights and grants them to citizens
- **Tenth Amendment**: reserves all non-specified powers to the states or people

The Structure and Functions of Different Levels of Government in the United States

The United States of America has three major branches in its federal government: the legislative branch, the executive branch, and the judicial branch. The legislative, executive, and judicial branches of

68

government all must adhere to the laws and regulations set forth by the United States Constitution, which was first ratified in 1789 and last amended in 1992. The United States Constitution is a living document that has a section known as the Bill of Rights. **The Bill of Rights** ensured that the **Constitution** remained a living document by setting the precedent for making changes, known as amendments. The Bill of Rights established the first ten amendments. There have since been 27 amendments made to the United States Constitution. The Bill of Rights also helped further establish the roles of the three branches of the federal government. Additionally, it constitutionalizes the separation of powers between the branches.

These branches function as follows:

Legislative Branch

The legislative branch is primarily responsible for creating laws, evaluating and accepting nominations for various positions in government, maintaining armies, and declaring war. The legislative branch is made up of Congress and various agencies that support Congress. In particular, Congress has a significant influence on how the United States handles foreign affairs. For example, all ambassadors nominated by the president of the United States must be approved by the Senate. In addition, any treaty that the president wishes to propose must be sent to the Senate for approval.

According to the Interstate Commerce Act of 1887, Congress has the ability to regulate commerce with a foreign nation, between states, and with Indian tribes. For example, if an American company wanted to do business with a foreign company and distribute their products in the United States, they would need to follow federal guidelines to do so. Interstate commerce refers to business between states, or the transfer and selling of products and services across state borders. For example, companies that utilize railroads to distribute their goods across state borders need to follow federal regulations on any restrictions that may be in place.

Congress regulates how the United States uses its resources to handle foreign and domestic affairs. They are responsible for analyzing the nation's current resources, like cash reserves and oil, and creating a budget. Every year, Congress must review and approve a budget for how much the government will spend for the next year. After this budget is passed through both the House and the Senate, it is sent to the president for approval. Large portions of this budget are dedicated to maintaining and improving the military, providing aid to other countries, and handling other foreign affairs. Therefore, Congress also has influence over how the president is able to make foreign policy decisions.

An example of their influence over foreign policy decisions is the exclusive ability of Congress to declare war. The Constitution is not specific on the process of declaring war. It is generally accepted that military force can be used to repel attacks against the United States, but actually initiating the war is a more controversial affair. While the president is commander in chief, they cannot initiate any hostilities without approval from Congress. Some presidents have participated in hostilities without congressional consent, however, which shows how modern-day presidents independently have a way to engage in military conflict. These situations allow the military to engage in conflict without an official declaration of war. This is an example of the evolution of the interpretations of the powers given to the president and Congress. Increased authority to engage in hostilities is being ceded to the president in recent times. The last official time the United States ever issued a declaration of war was against the Axis Powers in WWII. However, the United States has been involved in numerous foreign conflicts since then without an official declaration of war.

The president is able to make decisions on how foreign policy is enacted, but Congress provides them with the resources to do so. Congress has control over how money is spent on foreign affairs, and they have used this power numerous times to restrict action by the president. For example, one of President Barack Obama's campaign promises was shutting down Guantanamo Bay, the controversial military prison located on the coast of Cuba. Its primary function is to detain suspected terrorists. President Obama signed Executive Order 13492 the day that he assumed office. The primary purpose of this executive order was closing Guantanamo Bay and removing all of its current prisoners. Although President Obama signed this order, Congress voted to not give him any funds to actually move the prisoners to other locations. Since Congress has enormous control over how money is used, they play a significant role in determining foreign policy.

In addition to these responsibilities, Congress is also granted investigative powers. These investigations allow Congress to obtain information in order to make better decisions and understand the impact that certain events would have on the United States. As a part of this process, Congress is allowed to open investigations, gather evidence and witness testimony, and issue congressional subpoenas to compel witnesses to testify. An example of an investigation regarding foreign affairs is the United States House Select Committee on Benghazi. A select committee is temporarily created to investigate a specific event, while standing committees are permanent and regulate broader issues. This select committee was formed to obtain more information on the attacks on United States government facilities in Benghazi, Libya.

One of the most important standing committees in the United States government is the House Committee on Foreign Affairs. This body maintains jurisdiction over legislation regarding foreign affairs. They oversee the State Department, embassies, and diplomats. The United States Foreign Service, which is part of the State Department and executive branch of government, also falls under the oversight of Congress. The State Department and Congress work together to handle foreign affairs. The Senate Committee on Foreign Relations is a related body. Its main function is to analyze treaties that the president submits to the Senate for approval.

The United States Foreign Service was created by the Rogers Act of 1924. Its main purpose was to combine both the consular and diplomatic services of the United States into one coherent body. This made it easier to manage the various services offered while personnel were in other countries. They are led by a director general, a position created by Congress through the passing of the Foreign Service Act of 1946. After the passing of the Foreign Service Act of 1980, this position is now appointed by the president. This means that the president nominates a person for the role who is then confirmed by the Senate. The director general manages daily operations of the Foreign Service and also promotes others to the Senior Foreign Service. The Senior Foreign Service is made up of the top four ranks of the Foreign Service, and members serve important roles in diplomacy and ambassadorship.

The Foreign Service Act of 1980 further changed the structure of the United States Foreign Service. It added the ranks of the Senior Foreign Service, introduced danger pay for personnel working in dangerous or hostile environments, and created the Board of the Foreign Service. This board is made up of representatives from various government bodies and advises the secretary of state on all matters regarding the Foreign Service.

Members of the Foreign Service work all around the globe in various embassies and consulates. Their work within the United States is usually limited to around six years. However, after a maximum of ten years of domestic work, personnel must go abroad. Members must be prepared to have global availability. In order to support these members in foreign locations, the State Department maintains the Family Liaison Office. This resource provides support to Foreign Service personnel and their families and includes resources that help to address issues with working abroad for long periods of time, such as taking care of children and providing education and healthcare.

70

Congress consists of two distinct bodies, the Senate and the House of Representatives. The Senate is also referred to as the upper chamber of Congress, while the House of Representatives is the lower chamber of Congress. Each state has two senators that represent the entire state in government matters. Therefore, there are one hundred senators currently in the United States. Representatives represent their state's individual districts. The number of representatives that a state sends to Congress is proportionate to the size of their population. For example, larger states like California have more representatives than smaller states like Rhode Island. The House of Representatives is restricted to a maximum of 435 members by law. Together, there are a total of 535 members of Congress.

	House of Representatives	Senate
Membership	435	100
How Representation is Determined	Population of the state	Two Senators for each state
Length of Term	2 years	6 years

The requirements for being a senator or representative are different. In order to be eligible to be a senator, citizens must be at least thirty years old and have been citizens for at least nine years. Representatives must be at least twenty-five years old and have been citizens for at least seven years. Senators and representatives must also live in the state that they represent in government. Senators serve a six-year term, while representatives serve a two-year term.

The Senate and the House of Representatives differ in a few different ways. First, since the House is much larger than the Senate, the House usually tries to pass legislation quickly and keeps debate at a minimum. The Senate, however, can operate at a much slower pace. The Senate traditionally allows for nearly unlimited debate and can take their time to discuss issues. This unique tradition is known as the filibuster. The filibuster causes delays in voting, passing laws, and making decisions on important issues. The official way to end a filibuster is through a process known as "cloture." This process requires a two-thirds majority to end the filibuster.

Second, leadership between the two chambers differs. The House elects a speaker to control the calendar, or a schedule of when bills are debated and discussed. The speaker also influences what bills are discussed, presides over meetings, counts votes, appoints members to various committees, and inducts new members. The speaker is second in line for presidential succession, behind the vice president. The Senate is led by the majority leader and the minority leader. These leaders represent the interests of their political party. Both the Senate and House also have assistant leaders, known as whips. The whips gather members for votes, assist with meetings, and help keep order within the party. In addition to these leaders, the vice president of the United States is responsible for casting a vote when there is a tie in votes. Despite not being a senator, the vice president is considered to be the president of the Senate.

When the vice president is absent, the president pro tempore acts as the president of the Senate. They preside over Senate meetings and maintain order. They are also authorized to induct new members and sign new legislation. They are third in line for presidential succession. The president pro tempore is almost always a current member of the Senate, although this is not a specific requirement. They are generally the most senior senator in the majority party.

Executive Branch

The executive branch enforces the laws that the legislative branch creates. This branch is made up of the president, vice president, and the Cabinet. The president of the United States of America serves as its leader and is one of the most recognizable members of government. They represent the United States in foreign and domestic issues and serve as commander in chief of the United States Armed Forces. There are currently six branches in the United States military, including the Army, Air Force, Navy, Coast Guard, Space Force, and Marine Corps.

The president enforces laws with the help of the President's Cabinet, which consists of fifteen different cabinet positions that are focused on specific areas, such as defense, agriculture, energy, and more. These departments maintain daily operations of the federal government and are led by people who have been appointed by the president and are confirmed by the Senate. The president also has the authority to appoint numerous other government positions. These include heads of federal commissions like the Federal Reserve Board, ambassadors to different countries, and judges.

The vice president's main role is to be ready to succeed the president in case the president is unable to do their duty. This happens if the presidential office is left vacant through the death or incapacitation of the president. This is also true in other circumstances where the president is unable to do their duty. The vice president is also officially the president of the Senate, although the daily operations of the Senate usually fall to the president pro tempore. The vice president casts tiebreaking votes in the Senate and also presides over counting and receiving ballots for presidential elections.

Candidates for president must be at least thirty-five years old, a natural born citizen, and have lived in the country for at least fourteen years. Candidates for vice president must meet the same requirements. During presidential elections, voters indirectly vote for the next president through the Electoral College. The Electoral College is a process where voters place their ballots for their state's electors, who then vote for the next president. This is a mix between voting for the president through popular voting and through Congress.

Judicial Branch

The judicial branch is responsible for interpreting the law, settling disputes over the law, and determining whether laws are unconstitutional. The judicial branch consists of the Supreme Court, district courts, and circuit courts. There are ninety-four district courts and thirteen circuit courts. Each state has at least one district court, and more populous states have more available.

The Supreme Court is the highest authority within the federal judiciary system of the United States. Congress determines the number of judges on the Supreme Court. They currently consist of one chief justice and eight associate justices. When a spot on the Supreme Court opens, the president has the authority to nominate their choice of judge to the bench. These nominations are then confirmed by the Senate. Once judges are appointed to the Supreme Court, they have lifetime tenure. This means that justices serve the court until they resign, retire, die, or are impeached. Lifetime tenure is designed to encourage judges to remain apolitical and be free of influence from partisan pressure. This allows them to focus purely on justice and interpretation of the law.

The Constitution does not specify requirements for a Supreme Court justice. However, informal criteria created by the Department of Justice and Congress have been used for the nomination of justices. The chief justice, like other justices, is nominated by the president and confirmed by the Senate. The chief justice writes opinions, provides leadership to the other justices, and hears cases.

The Federal Government

The federal government is broken down into three separate branches, the legislative, executive, and judicial branches. These branches work together to regulate themselves and each other. Separation of

United States Government

powers refers to the ability for the three branches of government to limit each other's powers. This ensures that no one branch is more powerful than the others and can exert unequal influence.

This diagram illustrates the constitutional system as it pertains to the three branches of government:

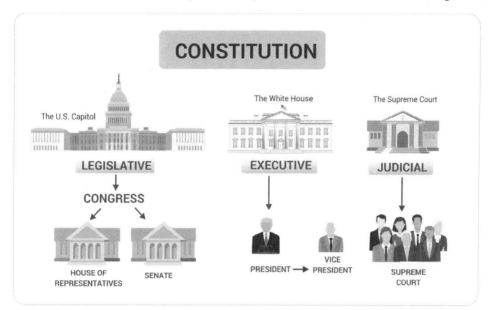

All three branches consequently keep an eye on one another through a process of **checks and balances**, ensuring that all power is separated and no branch gains too much authority over the citizens and government of the United States. The president has the power to appoint judges to the Supreme Court and veto laws made by Congress. Congress can overturn a presidential veto; it also controls the budget of the government. Additionally, Congress approves presidential court appointments and can remove judges if necessary. The Supreme Court can declare presidential acts and legislation as unconstitutional.

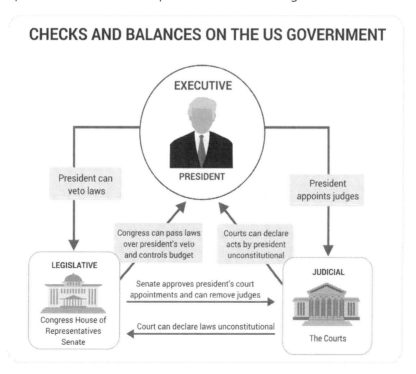

73

This content is provided exclusively for test preparation purposes and does not imply our support of any particular religious, political, or scientific point of view. Copyright © APEX Publishing. You have been licensed one copy of this document for personal use only. Any other reproduction or redistribution is strictly prohibited. All rights reserved.

Policy and Lawmaking

The process for a law to be created and ultimately drafted into law is very long. First, anyone in Congress who is interested in proposing a new law must create a written bill. This bill is like an early draft that outlines what the proposed law will entail. The bill must have a sponsor and gather support before it is presented to the various committees in the House. There, the bill is discussed and studied before being sent to the House floor for debate. The representatives will then vote, usually with either their voice (viva voce) or through recorded electronic means. If the bill passes with majority ruling, it will then go through the same steps in the Senate. If the bill once again reaches majority ruling, it is sent to the president for final approval. The president can sign the bill into law, veto or reject it, or do nothing. If the president does not do anything, this is referred to as a pocket veto. If Congress is not in session within ten days of the president not signing it, the bill is rejected and does not become law.

Government policies attempt to solve problems identified in society. They are a series of laws, rules, or regulations that help to address these issues. The first step to create a government policy is to identify an issue. Research needs to support creating a solution to the issue and explain why the issue is worth government intervention. This research gathers data and looks for potential fixes. Policy choices are created based on this study and offered to decision makers, who could be elected officials, senior bureaucrats, or other stakeholders.

Once a policy is decided on, it is time to actually implement the policy. While a policy may provide a general outline of what the problem is, it is usually the responsibility of other organizations to carry out the policy. For example, the landmark Brown v. Board of Education decision by the Supreme Court ruled that it was unconstitutional to racially segregate school children in schools. This reversed a previous decision made in 1896, Plessy v. Ferguson, which created the infamous "separate but equal" belief that upheld Jim Crow laws. Although the Supreme Court made the decision to desegregate schools, it was the responsibility of the many courts and school boards across the country to uphold this new government policy. After a policy has been implemented, extensive research is done to analyze its short-term and long-term costs and benefits.

State and Local Governments

Outside of the federal government, there are also state and local (municipal) governments in the United States. Under this federalist system, local governments, state governments, and the federal government share the responsibilities of governing the people. The state and federal governments share the most responsibilities. Both collect taxes, possess their own courts, and have their own systems of punishment. Yet their powers are also separate in some ways. State governments cannot maintain a military force or declare war like the federal government, and federal governments do not maintain total control over state public education.

These shared responsibilities become even more complex when local government is included. Local governments focus mostly on local services (such as emergency response units, utilities, and public libraries). However, some responsibilities, such as education, are shared by state and local boards. Local municipalities are also responsible for carrying out the functions necessary to ensure fidelity in the federal voting process. Lastly, all three types of governments join forces to maintain roads and carry out law enforcement initiatives.

Purposes and Characteristics of Various Global and Historical Governance Systems

The history of humanity has been marked by various government systems that have different purposes, functions, and characteristics. Below is a list of governance systems that should be reviewed and understood. This list is not comprehensive. Moreover, most real governments do not fall neatly into just one of these categories. Typically, most governments—historical and contemporary—draw from more than one governance category. For instance, the Soviet Union under Joseph Stalin was both communist and authoritarian. The United States can be considered a **democratic republic**, but it also has characteristics of **federalism**.

Authoritarian

Authoritarian governments allow the state—or a symbol of the state (such as a dictator)—to control every aspect of the citizens' lives. The Soviet Union was known for its authoritarian practices. It was also communist in character. It created intense systems of control that disempowered its citizens in the name of equality.

Communist

Cuba is a classic example of a **communist** government that still exists today. While communism is mainly an economic system, it is very much a political economy that tries to create equality by eliminating private property. Communism in theory, however, is different than communism in practice. In Cuba, much like in the Soviet Union, the Communist government helped pave the way to dictatorial authoritarianism. In Cuba, Fidel Castro was dictator for life from the 1950s until his death in the early 2010s. Since the Cold War (and even before that, around the age of the Bolshevik Revolution in Russia), the United States has been staunchly anti-communist in character.

Confederacy

There are two classic historical examples of confederacies. The first is the Iroquois Confederacy, a coalition of Native American tribes during the precolonial and colonial eras. The second is the Confederate States of America, which seceded from the Union during the Civil War era in American history. **Confederacies** limit the federal power of a central government. It is usually a coalition of states, provinces, or tribes. These states, provinces, and tribes maintain their sovereignty, only turning to federal support for unique, previously agreed-upon circumstances. Under the Articles of Confederation, the United States of America borrowed heavily from this model of governance.

Democracy (Pure/Popular)

Pure or **popular democracy** places full voting and governance powers in the hands of the people. Many national governments in Latin America followed this model of governance following revolutions in the 18th, 19th, and 20th centuries. Many early leaders in the United States of America thought this form of democracy represented chaos because it granted the masses too much power.

Democratic Republic

The United States government is traditionally known as a democratic republic. **Democratic republics** allow citizens to vote for representatives who, in turn, vote on their behalf. The electoral college is a classic example of a democratic republic: during the presidential election, citizens vote, but the electoral representatives ultimately cast the final vote for each state.

Dictatorship

When authoritarian governments place power into the hand of one leader, they are typically referred to as **dictatorships**. There are usually no constitutional checks and balances in this system of governance. Fidel Castro is a classic example of a dictator.

Monarchy

This form of government was popularized during antiquity and the Middle Ages. It places full ruling power in the hands of a monarch—a king or queen—who is usually believed to be divinely appointed. A good example of a traditional **monarchy** was England prior to the creation of parliament. With the inclusion of parliament and a constitution, modern-day England now has a constitutional monarchy; the king and queen are customary figureheads, while parliament and the constitution wield the most power. Breaking from England during colonial times, the United States has historically avoided this model.

Socialist

Drawing from Marxist theory, many **socialist** governments still exist today. They believe in an equitable distribution of goods, which is not the same as the abolition of private property or 100% equality in distribution of goods. Many countries in Europe have socialist tendencies. The United States has historically leaned toward capitalism and away from socialism. However, with the creation of the New Deal, the US became more socialistic in character (in limited fashion).

Theocracy

A religious organization, not humanity, is the supreme power. In a **theocracy**, people such as caliphs or priests become earthly symbols of religious prowess. ISIS is a recent example of a theocracy, which emphasizes the creation of an Islamic Republic. A historical example of a theocracy is Roman Catholic Spain. The United States has tried to separate church and state, making it anti-theocratic.

There are also three larger frameworks that might dictate the legislative nuances of the types of governments listed above: unitary systems, federal systems, and confederations. **Unitary systems** have concentrated power controlled by a centralized authority. Unitary systems emphasize national government over state government. **Federal systems** divide the power of the state and federal governments; they also place more power in the hands of the people via certain voting rights. **Confederations** emphasize decentralized power and concentrated authority, which takes hold when states have more power than the federal government.

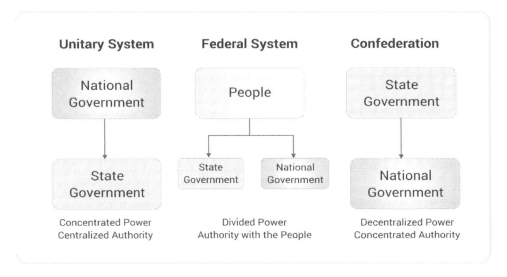

Practice Quiz

1. A filibuster can officially be ended by what procedure?
    a. Senate hold
    b. Presidential veto
    c. Vice president casting a tie-breaking vote
    d. Cloture

2. Which of the following Supreme Court decisions ruled that races could be "separate but equal?"
    a. *Dred Scott v. Sandford*
    b. *Plessy v. Ferguson*
    c. *Brown v. Board of Education*
    d. *Miranda v. Arizona*

3. After a president nominates a judge for the Supreme Court, who confirms the appointment?
    a. Senate
    b. State Department
    c. Justice Department
    d. Other members of the Supreme Court

4. What role does the United States Foreign Service play in foreign affairs?
    a. Creating investigative committees focused on foreign affairs
    b. Distributing resources to the president for foreign policy
    c. Providing personnel to staff American embassies and diplomatic missions
    d. Authorizing the president to declare war

5. What department was created in the aftermath of the September 11, 2001 attacks?
    a. Department of Energy
    b. Department of Homeland Security
    c. Department of Justice
    d. Department of State

See next page for answer explanations.

Answer Explanations

1. D: The filibuster is an extended delay in the Senate that prevents a vote from happening. The official way to end a filibuster is through a process known as "cloture." It requires three-fifths of the majority to end the filibuster. Choice *A* is an informal procedure that allows senators to prevent a debate from reaching the Senate floor. Choice *B* is an action that rejects bills but cannot be used to end the filibuster. Choice *C* is only necessary when the vice president needs to break a tie in the votes in the Senate.

2. B: The *Plessy v. Ferguson* decision by the Supreme Court is the origin of the phrase "separate but equal." It allowed segregation as long as facilities for each race were equal. In practice, this did not work, and this decision was deemed unconstitutional. Choice *A* ruled that Congress does not have the authority to prohibit slavery, and that Americans of African descent were not considered citizens and could not sue in federal court. Choice *C* overruled *Plessy v. Ferguson* and stated that the segregation of children in public schools was unconstitutional. Choice *D* ruled that all arrested individuals must be informed of certain rights that they retain during the arrest, and that they have access to counsel to defend them in court.

3. A: The Constitution grants the Senate the ability to confirm any appointments that the president makes, including judges to the Supreme Court. Choices *B*, *C*, and *D* do not play a role in confirming presidential appointments.

4. C: The United States Foreign Service supplies manpower to staff the many embassies around the world. They provide support for all personnel working in a foreign country. Choices *A*, *B*, and *D* are powers granted to Congress.

5. B: The Department of Homeland Security is one of the newest departments in the government. It was created in response to the September 11th attacks. Choice *A* was created in 1977. Choice *C* was created in 1870. Choice *D* was created in 1789 and is one of the oldest departments in government.

United States Society and Culture

European Exploration and Colonization

In what's commonly referred to as the "Age of Exploration," Europeans began exploring overseas to regions they'd never before seen. The Age of Exploration started in the early 15th century and lasted until the late 18th century, and in practice, it represents the earliest stage of globalization. Technological innovation greatly facilitated European exploration, like the **caravel**—a smaller and more maneuverable ship first used by the Portuguese to explore West Africa—and the *astrolabe* and *quadrant*, which increased navigators' accuracy.

European monarchies hired explorers primarily to expand trade routes, particularly to increase access to the Indian spice markets. There were other motivating factors, however, such as the desire to spread Christianity and pursue glory.

As exploration increased, European powers adopted the policies of mercantilism and colonialism. **Mercantilism** is an economic policy that prioritizes the wealth, trade, and accumulation of resources for the sole benefit of the nation. **Colonization** was an outgrowth of mercantilism that involved establishing control over foreign people and territories. Unsurprisingly, mercantilism and colonialism were a major source of conflict between native people, colonists, and colonizers.

In 1492, Christopher Columbus arrived in the Caribbean, though he initially, and mistakenly, believed he had landed in India. Over the next two centuries, European powers established several colonies in North America to extract the land's resources and prevent their rivals from doing the same. In 1565, Spain established the first European colony in North America at St. Augustine in present-day Florida. Along with building a South and Central American empire, Spain colonized Mexico and much of the present-day American Southwest, southeast, and heartland (Louisiana Territory). Sweden colonized the mid-Atlantic region of the present-day United States in 1638, but the Netherlands conquered these colonies in 1655. France colonized Canada, Hudson's Bay, Acadia (near present-day Maine), and Newfoundland. In 1717, France assumed control over the Louisiana Territory from Spain.

In 1607, England established her first colony at Jamestown. Six years later, Jamestown colonists imported the first slaves to North America. During the rest of the 17th century, British separatist Puritans (Pilgrims) arrived on the *Mayflower* in Cape Cod, Massachusetts. Great Britain conquered New Netherlands (New York) in 1674, effectively driving the Dutch out of North America.

England's North American holdings expanded into the Thirteen Colonies—Connecticut, Delaware, Georgia, Maryland, Massachusetts, New Hampshire, New Jersey, New York, North Carolina, Pennsylvania, Rhode Island, South Carolina, and Virginia. Some colonies were royal colonies, while others were chartered to business corporations or proprietary local governments. The chartered colonies generally allowed for more self-government, but the Crown withdrew the charters and placed all thirteen colonies under direct royal control by the second half of the 18th century.

The American Revolution

The aftermath of the French and Indian War (1756-1763) set the stage for a conflict between the American colonists and Great Britain. After defeating France and her Native American allies, England passed a series of controversial laws. First, the Proclamation of 1763 barred the colonists from settling west of the Appalachian Mountains in an effort to appease Native Americans. Second, the Quebec Act of 1774 granted protections to their recently acquired French-Canadian colonies. Third, England passed a series of taxes on the colonists to pay their war debt, including the Sugar Act (1764), Quartering Act (1765), Stamp Act (1765), Townshend Acts (1767), Tea Act (1773), and the Intolerable Acts (1774).

To the colonists, it appeared as if England was rewarding the combatants of the French and Indian War and punishing the colonists who fought for England. As a result, protests erupted, especially in New England. The most significant were those surrounding the Boston Massacre (1770) and the Boston Tea Party (1773). Colonists organized the First Continental Congress in 1774 to request the repeal of the Intolerable Acts and affirm their loyalty to the Crown. When King George III refused, the crisis escalated in April 1775 at the Battle of Lexington and Concord, the first armed conflict between British troops and colonial militias. A Second Continental Congress then met in Philadelphia, and the delegates issued Thomas Jefferson's Declaration of Independence on July 4, 1776. The Declaration of Independence declared that all people enjoyed basic rights, specifically the right to life, liberty, and the pursuit of happiness, and accused King George III of violating colonists' rights, which justified the American Revolution.

The Continental Army lost its first major offensive campaign in Quebec City in December 1775, but victories at Trenton and Saratoga boosted morale. The tides of war turned against England when the Americans and France signed the Treaty of Alliance in 1778. France sent resources and troops to support the Americans, and the Marquis de Lafayette served as a combat commander at the final decisive battle at Yorktown. On September 3, 1783, the Treaty of Paris secured American independence.

Founding of the United States

Enacted during the American Revolution, the **Articles of Confederation** was the original governing document of the United States. However, the Articles of Confederation was ineffective due to its weak central government. The government didn't include a president or judiciary branch, and Congress didn't have the power to tax or raise money for an army. The final straw was the Articles of Confederation's failure to handle the Shays' Rebellion (1786–1787). In May 1787, the Founding Fathers convened the **Constitutional Convention** in Philadelphia. George Washington served as the Convention's president, and James Madison wrote the draft that was the basis for the Constitution.

Slavery challenged the Constitutional Convention from the outset, foreshadowing the American Civil War. The South wanted slaves to count for representation, even though slaves couldn't vote, but not taxes, while the North advocated for the opposite. The **Three-Fifths Compromise** settled the issue by counting slaves as three-fifths of a person for taxation and representation. In addition, the delegates agreed to a compromise that allowed slave owners to capture escaped slaves in exchange for ending the international slave trade by 1808.

The delegates also debated representation in Congress. **The New Jersey Plan** proposed a single legislative body with one vote per state. In contrast, **the Virginia Plan** proposed two legislative bodies with representation decided by the states' populations. The delegates agreed to the Connecticut Compromise—two legislative bodies with one house based on population (House of Representatives) and the other granting each state two votes (Senate). Two other branches, the judiciary and executive, were also included in the final document, and a series of checks and balances divided power between all three branches. The Constitution also expressly addressed issues from the Articles of Confederation by providing for a significantly stronger central government.

Nine of the thirteen states needed to ratify the Constitution before it became law, and a heated debate over the Constitution spread throughout the nation. Those in favor of the Constitution, called the Federalists, produced and distributed the *Federalist Papers*, which James Madison, Alexander Hamilton, and John Jay wrote under the pseudonym "Publius." Thomas Jefferson and Patrick Henry led the Anti-Federalists and called for the inclusion of a bill of rights. The Constitution was ratified on June 21, 1778, and three years later, the Bill of Rights was added. The Bill of Rights is the first ten amendments to the Constitution ratified together in December 1791.

The Founding Fathers created a decentralized federal system to protect against tyranny. The Tenth Amendment is what enshrines the principle of **federalism**—the separation of power between federal, state, and local government. In general, the federal government can limit or prohibit the states from enacting certain policies, and state governments exercise exclusive control over local government.

Growth and Expansion of the United States

Shortly after gaining independence, the United States rapidly expanded based on **Manifest Destiny**—the belief that Americans hold special virtues, America has a duty to spread those virtues westward, and success is a certainty.

In 1803, President Thomas Jefferson purchased the Louisiana territory from France. **The Louisiana Purchase** included 828,000 square miles of land west of the Mississippi River. Unsure of what he had purchased, Jefferson organized several expeditions to explore the new territory, including the famous **Lewis and Clark Expedition**. To consolidate the eastern seaboard under American control, President James Monroe purchased New Spain (present-day Florida) in the *Adams-Onís Treaty* of 1819.

Conflict with Native Americans was constant and brutal. Great Britain allied with Native American tribes in the present-day Midwest, using them as a buffer to protect her Canadian colonies. Britain's support for Native American raids on American colonies ignited tensions and led to the War of 1812. Two years later, Great Britain and the United States signed the Treaty of Ghent, ending the war with a neutral resolution, and British support for the Native Americans evaporated. The Supreme Court's decision in *Worcester v. Georgia* (1832) later established the concept of tribal sovereignty; however, President Andrew Jackson refused to enforce the Court's decision. Consequently, Americans continued to colonize Native American land at will. President Jackson also passed the first of several Indian Removal Acts, forcing native tribes westward on the Trail of Tears.

Tensions on the American-Mexican border worsened after President John Tyler annexed Texas in 1845. That same year, James K. Polk succeeded Tyler after winning the election of 1844 on a platform of manifest destiny. President Polk ordered General Zachary Taylor to march his army into the disputed territory, which ignited the *Mexican-American War*. The United States dominated the conflict and annexed the present-day American Southwest and California through the 1848 Treaty of Guadalupe Hidalgo. Polk also settled the Oregon Country dispute with Britain, establishing the British-American boundary at the 49th parallel.

The United States purchased Alaska from Russia in 1867, and Hawaii was annexed in 1898 to complete what would become the fifty states.

The migration of settlers into these new territories was facilitated by technological innovation and legislation. Steamships allowed the settlers to navigate the nation's many winding rivers, and railroads exponentially increased the speed of travel and transportation of supplies to build settlements. Canals were also important for connecting the eastern seaboard to the Midwest. Thus, the fastest growing settlements were typically located near a major body of water or a railroad. Starting in 1862, Congress incentivized Americans to travel westward and populate the territories with a series of Homestead acts, which gave away public lands, called "homesteads," for free. In total, the United States gave away 270 million acres of public land to support the country's expansion.

Civil War

Congress repeatedly attempted to compromise on slavery, especially as to whether it would be expanded into new territories. The first such attempt was the **Missouri Compromise of 1820**, which included three parts. First, Missouri was admitted as a slave state. Second, Maine was admitted as a free state to maintain the balance between free and slave states. Third, slavery was prohibited north of the 36°30' parallel in new territories, but the Supreme Court overturned this in *Dred Scott v. Sandford* (1837).

The **Compromise of 1850** admitted California as a free state, allowed popular sovereignty to determine if Utah and New Mexico would be slave states, banned slavery in Washington D.C., and enforced a harsh **Fugitive Slave Law**. The **Kansas-Nebraska Act** *of 1854* started a mini civil war, as slave owners and abolitionists rushed into the new territories. Slavery eventually caused the collapse of the Whigs, the dominant political party of the early and middle 19th century. The Northern Whigs created the anti-slavery Republican Party.

Republican Abraham Lincoln won the election of 1860. Before his inauguration, seven Southern states seceded from the United States and established the **Confederate States of America** to protect slavery. On April 12, 1861, the first shots of the **Civil War** were fired by Confederate artillery at Fort Sumter, South

Carolina. On January 1, 1863, after the particularly bloody Battle of Antietam, President Lincoln issued the **Emancipation Proclamation**, freeing the Confederacy's 3 million slaves; however, slavery continued in Union-controlled states and territories.

Later that year, the Battle of Gettysburg gave the **Union Army** a decisive victory, turning back the Confederacy's advances into the North. President Lincoln's famous **Gettysburg Address** called for the preservation of the Union and equality for all citizens. After a series of Union victories, Confederate General Robert E. Lee surrendered at Appomattox Court House and ended the Civil War in April 1865. Less than one week after Lee's surrender, John Wilkes Booth assassinated President Lincoln during a play at Ford's Theater.

Vice President Andrew Johnson assumed the presidency and battled the Radical Republicans in Congress over the Reconstruction Amendments. Federal troops were deployed across the South to enforce the new amendments, but Reconstruction concluded in 1877. Immediately after the troops withdrew, the Southern stated enacted Jim Crow laws to rollback African Americans' right to vote and enforce segregationist policies.

Industrial Revolution

The First Industrial Revolution exploded in the United States during the War of 1812, as more American industrialists adopted British textile innovations. New manufacturing firms utilized the assembly line to increase production speed and accuracy. Each worker completed one individualized task on the assembly line, and the team of workers collectively produced the goods. New England manufacturers adopted the Waltham-Lowell labor and production system to maximize the use of new technologies such as the spinning jenny, spinning mule, and water frame. Eli Whitney's cotton gin was similarly revolutionary for the cotton industry.

The Second Industrial Revolution began after the Civil War and lasted until World War I. Technology again drove the economic changes, particularly in factory machinery and steel production. This era transformed the United States from an agricultural and textile economy into an industrial powerhouse. The invention of the telegraph and innovations in transportation like railways, canals, and steamboats further connected the economy.

Industrialization drove urbanization, as most new jobs were in booming city centers. To accommodate new arrivals from rural areas, cities had to adopt urban planning strategies to create a sewer system and facilitate the supply of gas and water. Economic opportunity also attracted waves of immigrants to American cities. Before 1880, most immigrants were English and Irish, but from 1880 to 1920, more than 20 million immigrants came from Central, Eastern, and Southern Europe.

Despite the explosion in wealth creation, the Second Industrial Revolution caused crises in political corruption, working conditions, and wealth inequality. Political machines, like Tammany Hall in New York, consolidated political power in major American cities under a party boss who doled out special favors to his constituents. A lack of government regulation also created unsafe labor conditions. Most laborers worked twelve-hour shifts, with minimal breaks, six or seven days every week, and child labor was rampant. The long hours, dangerous machines, and young workers led to workplace accidents, and death rates soared. Wages were also low, and income inequality exploded, which is why the Second Industrial Revolution is often referred to as the "Gilded Age."

Labor began to organize in response to dangerous working conditions and meager pay. Between 1881 and 1905, labor unions organized 37,000 strikes across every major industry. Anarchists, populists, and socialists challenged the political establishment, demanding reform for the working poor. These movements led to the rise of the Progressive Era (the 1890s to the 1920s). Progressives passed the direct election of US Senators (17th Amendment), anti-corruption laws, anti-trust laws, women's suffrage, and the prohibition of alcohol.

Early American Foreign Policy

In the late 19th century, a public debate raged over the United States' international role. Part of the public wished to heed George Washington's famous farewell address in which he warned against intervening in foreign conflicts. Another faction supported military intervention to free colonies, as France had done for the United States. The final group called for following the European model of imperialism.

Issued in 1823, the **Monroe Doctrine** promised that the United States wouldn't meddle in existing European colonies, but it also vowed that the US would consider any future European intervention to be a hostile act. President Theodore Roosevelt would later strengthen the Monroe Doctrine during his State of the Union address in 1904, explicitly threatening unilateral military intervention in Latin America whenever it suited American interests.

In 1898, the American battleship *USS Maine* exploded in Havana Harbor, and President McKinley declared war on Spain. In less than five months, the United States had defeated Spain and assumed control over her first overseas colonies—Puerto Rico, Guam, and the Philippines.

The outbreak of **World War I** in 1914 presented a serious challenge to the United States. President Woodrow Wilson attempted to keep the nation neutral, but his hand was ultimately forced. In 1915, German U-boats (submarines) torpedoed a British passenger ship *RMS Lusitania* carrying American passengers, and two years later, Britain intercepted the Zimmerman Telegram, which showed that Germany was attempting to conspire with Mexico to invade the United States. President Wilson had run out of options, and the United States declared war on Germany and joined the Triple Entente (Britain, France, and Russia). More than 116,000 Americans lost their lives serving in World War I, but the conflict was a turning point in American history, marking the arrival of the United States as a global power.

In the interwar period, known as the Roaring Twenties, there was rampant stock market speculation. On "Black Tuesday," October 29, 1929, the stock market crashed, sending the global economy off a cliff into the Great Depression. Immediately after winning the 1932 presidential election, Franklin D. Roosevelt launched the New Deal to increase employment, stimulate demand, and increase regulation over capital. Much of the current social welfare state—Social Security, unemployment insurance, disability, labor laws, and housing and food subsidies—date back to the New Deal. President Lyndon B. Johnson later introduced a series of legislation modeled after the New Deal collectively referred to as the War on Poverty or the Great Society. His aim was to alleviate poverty by increasing access to education, health care, and housing.

After **World War II** broke out in Europe, the United States again tried to remain neutral, but on December 7, 1941, Japan bombed Pearl Harbor. In response, President Roosevelt declared war on Japan. Germany preemptively declared war on the United States, who did the same in return. On June 6, 1944, commonly referred to as "D-Day," American forces landed on the beaches of Normandy, France, and by May 1945, American and Soviet forces had conquered Germany. However, the Japanese continued to fight in the

Pacific theater. To avoid what would've been a costly invasion of Japan's mainland, the United States dropped nuclear bombs on Nagasaki and Hiroshima, ending World War II.

20th Century Developments and Transformations

The major themes of the 20th century are industrialization, imperialism, nationalism, global conflict, independence movements, technological advancement, and globalization.

The United States and Europe completed the transition from agrarian to industrial economies in the early 20th century, and by the end of the 20th century, nearly the entire world had at least started industrializing. **Industrialization** created global wealth, exponentially improving the global standard of living, but it also caused explosive population growth and environmental destruction. Over the 20th century, the global population increased from 1.6 billion people to 6 billion people. This unprecedented population growth has been driving rapid deforestation, as more land is cleared for agriculture and settlements. In addition, industrialization has polluted the Earth's atmosphere, land, and oceans. As a result, temperatures are increasing, sea levels are rising, and biodiversity is declining. The 21st century will face dire consequences, like mass migration and global instability, if these trends aren't reversed.

The 20th century opened with much of Asia and Africa divided into European colonies. **Nationalism** was on the rise and used to justify European **imperialism** and **militarism**. Nationalism, imperialism, and militarism also markedly increased in the United States and Japan. The overwhelming majority of present-day countries didn't achieve independence until after the World Wars or the Cold War.

Early 20th century nation-states were entangled in a complex web of military alliances, and when Serbian nationalists assassinated Archduke Franz Ferdinand of Austria (1914), those alliances triggered a global conflict, World War I. *Russia* joined the **Triple Entente alliance** with Great Britain and France, but in 1917, Vladimir Lenin's Bolsheviks (communists) led an armed insurrection against the Russian Tsar, Nicholas II. Following the Russian Revolution, the **Bolsheviks** won a victory against the European-backed counterrevolutionaries, paving the way for the creation of the **Union of Soviet Socialist Republics** (*USSR*).

The Treaty of Versailles ended World War I in June 1919, and it included several of American President Woodrow Wilson's **Fourteen Points**. Wilson was an advocate for countries' right to self-determination, and his Fourteen Points helped discredit colonialism and imperialism as legitimate foreign policy goals. Part I of the Treaty established Wilson's League of Nations, but Germany was prohibited from joining until 1926. The United States also refused to join, further undermining the League's legitimacy. The Treaty of Versailles also forced Germany to claim total responsibility for causing World War I and pay extensive reparations. This amounted to a national humiliation for Germany, fueling a reactionary right-wing movement that culminated in Adolf Hitler's rise to power in the 1930s.

The global women's rights movement gained support because of World War I. When the men left to fight overseas, women joined the workforce and contributed to the war effort. British Parliament granted women the right to vote in 1918, and Germany did the same in the following year. President Woodrow Wilson also reversed his previous position and declared his support for the 19th Amendment (1920), establishing women's suffrage in the United States.

The Great Depression occurred between the World Wars, lasting from 1929 until the late-1930s. A stock market crash triggered a depression in the United States that quickly spread around the world. The Great Depression put enormous stress on Western governments to alleviate poverty and lessen the appeal of communist revolution. Some governments, like the United States and Great Britain, increased their public investment to increase employments and social services. Other governments, like Germany and Italy, transitioned from militarized nationalism into outright far-right fascism.

Hitler's **Nazi Party** exploited global instability in his efforts to right the perceived injustices inflicted on Germany during World War I. First, Nazi Germany remilitarized the Rhineland and stopped paying reparations under the Treaty of Versailles. Second, Hitler enforced collective punishments on German Jews as retribution for their alleged disloyalty to the state, previewing what would become the Holocaust. Third, Hitler supported Italy's invasion of Ethiopia (1935), and German forces fought a proxy war to assist the fascist Francisco Franco during the Spanish Civil War (1936-1939). Fourth, Hitler annexed two territories in 1938—Austria and the Sudetenland in Czechoslovakia—under the pretext of protecting ethnic Germans. Much of Europe was horrified by these events, but the leadership mostly followed a policy of appeasement, hoping to avoid a second global conflict.

One year later, in September 1939, the Nazis invaded Poland to clear *lebensraum* (living space) for Germans. Two days later, France and Britain declared war on Germany, igniting World War II. Germany, Italy, and Japan formed the **Axis alliance**. Japan immediately conquered China and the Korean Peninsula, and Germany added the conquest of mainland Europe and North Africa. Germany also signed a nonaggression pact with Joseph Stalin's Soviet Union, but Hitler broke the pact and invaded the Soviet Union in June 1941. This decision was disastrous, as it forced the Nazis into an expensive and bloody war of attrition. Hitler also committed significant resources to the Holocaust—his plan to exterminate Jews, gypsies, homosexuals, Afro-Europeans, and disabled people.

The United States entered World War II in 1941, changing the tides of war. In 1942 alone, the US Navy defeated Japan at the Battle of Midway; the Allies routed Italy and Germany in North Africa; and the Soviet Union decisively defeated Germany at Stalingrad. Nazi Germany agreed to an unconditional surrender on May 8, 1945, and an American nuclear attack forced Japan to surrender in September 1945.

With most of Europe and Asia lying in ruins, the United States and the Soviet Union were the only global superpowers to survive World War II. The Soviet Union's resilience was remarkable, considering the intense suffering Soviets endured, but they did benefit from consolidating power in Eastern Europe under Soviet-controlled satellite governments. The two superpowers engaged in a series of proxy wars, but the threat of nuclear war ultimately deterred a direct conflict. However, there were several close calls, any of which would have likely ended life on Earth.

The Cuban Missile Crisis (1962) began after the failed American **Bay of Pigs** invasion angered Cuba and the Soviet Union. The Soviets also objected to American ballistic missiles in Turkey, and they responded by covertly sending ballistic missiles to Cuba. American generals urged President John F. Kennedy to preemptively launch a nuclear strike against the Soviet Union, but an agreement was reached at the last minute. The Soviets dismantled their Cuban missile system, and the United States publicly promised not to invade Cuba. In addition, the United States secretly promised to dismantle her Turkish missile system.

At the end of the Cold War, the United States was the world's only remaining superpower. Without formal military opposition, the United States has increasingly used trade as a foreign policy tool. Until the Trump presidency, every American presidential administration has advocated for free-trade policies, such as the **North American Free Trade Agreement** (*NAFTA*). The United States has even helped potential rivals join the international community to prevent large-scale conflict and achieve American goals. For example, the United States integrated China into the world economy by pushing through their membership in the **World Trade Organization**. American economists argue that free trade benefits everyone in the

86

increasingly globalized world. The rise and proliferation of Internet-based technologies has also contributed to the rapid development of a global marketplace.

The Digital Revolution has increased globalization through technological innovations like the internet and social media. Now, people anywhere in the world, no matter how far away, can communicate instantaneously. This has resulted in greater appreciation of people's different backgrounds and lived experiences, an economic boom in the computer-based economic sector, and lower costs for many businesses. However, the Digital Revolution has also threatened privacy, increased automation's threat on employment, and allowed nation-states to spread dissent in foreign countries. For better or worse, the internet has been the most disruptive technological innovation since Gutenberg's printing press (1439).

Cold War Era

The United States and Soviet Union emerged from World War II as the world's preeminent superpowers. The Americans and Soviets considered each other to be an existential threat, but the development of nuclear weapon technology forced the two superpowers to avoid a direct conflict, which is why this period is known as the **Cold War**.

American Cold War era foreign policy followed the **domino theory**—the idea that if one country turned communist, so would neighboring countries. The United States also created the **North Atlantic Treaty Organization** (NATO) in 1949 to protect against Soviet aggression in Europe.

On June 25, 1950, North Korea invaded South Korea, and the United States entered the war to protect its ally and to prevent communism spreading across Asia. When General MacArthur disobeyed President Truman and crossed the 38th parallel, China entered the war on the side of North Korea, and the war turned into a bloody stalemate. All three combatants signed the **Armistice Agreement** on July 27, 1953, though the war never officially ended. The Korean War's brutality left a lasting impression on North Korea, heavily influencing the dictatorship's approach to the United States.

In August 1964, Congress passed the Gulf of Tonkin Resolution. Although Congress didn't declare war, the Resolution authorized President Lyndon B. Johnson's use of military force in Vietnam. As in Korea, the United States feared that if North Vietnamese communists prevailed, communism would spread across Asia. The Vietnam War was largely a military success, but it was a disaster politically. The draft proved to be enormously unpopular, and President Richard Nixon's decision to invade Cambodia and bomb Laos further buried public opinion. Domestic protests forced the United States to withdraw in 1973.

The United States also regularly conducted covert operations, trained rebels, and funded political opposition through the **Central Intelligence Agency** (*CIA*) to overthrow democratically elected socialist governments.

Non-exhaustive list of successful Cold War interventions:

- Iran (1953)
- Guatemala (1954)
- Dominican Republic (1961)
- Brazil (1964)
- Congo (1965)
- Indonesia (1965)

- Ghana (1966)
- Guyana (1968)
- Chile (1973)

Socialist governments were often replaced with strongman dictators, and the transition frequently resulted in civil wars. The United States also directly armed morally dubious proxy forces. President Ronald Reagan covertly sold weapons to Nicaraguan death squads, the "Contras," funding it through weapon sales to Iran in violation of an American arms embargo. Similarly, during the Soviet-Afghan War (1979-1989), the Carter and Reagan administrations gave $3 billion of taxpayer money to the mujahedeen (Islamic extremists) who fought alongside Osama bin Laden.

Besides military conflict and interventions, the United States competed with the Soviet Union in the Space Race. In addition to national pride, both superpowers hoped to advance their spying and rocket capabilities. As such, they both invested heavily in technology, some of which was enormously beneficial for society, like increased computing power. To the great surprise of Americans, on October 4, 1957, the Soviet Union launched the world's first satellite, **Sputnik 1**, into orbit. Less than four years later, Soviet cosmonaut Yuri Gagarin became the first human to enter space. On July 20, 1969, the United States struck back by landing the first humans on the Moon during the Apollo 11 mission. The Soviet Union repeatedly failed to land a crew on the Moon. Besides technological and scientific advancements, the Space Race also played a role in *détente*—the easing of tensions between the Cold War rivals—after the Soviets and Americans launched the *Apollo-Soyuz Project* (1971), their first joint space mission.

For domestic politics, the Cold War era was tumultuous. Throughout the 1950s, US Senator Joseph McCarthy led a series of increasingly conspiratorial criminal investigations. McCarthyism exploited Americans' fear of the Soviet Union, commonly referred to as the "**Red Scare**." The public hearings mixed unsubstantiated rumors with total hysteria, and the accusations ruined thousands of lives.

The **Watergate scandal** was the most dramatic domestic political event during the Cold War era. Although Richard Nixon was a popular incumbent on track for a landslide victory over Democrat George McGovern in the 1972 presidential election, Richard Nixon ordered his cronies to burglarize and spy on the **Democratic National Committee** headquarters. Then Nixon attempted to use intelligence agencies to cover up his involvement. After a tape surfaced of Nixon ordering the coverup, the House of Representatives impeached Nixon, and he resigned before the Senate convicted him. On September 8, 1974, President Gerald Ford controversially pardoned Nixon. Besides Nixon, Andrew Johnson and Bill Clinton are the only presidents to be impeached, but no president has ever been convicted (removed from office) by the Senate.

Martin Luther King's civil disobedience is one of the most successful forms of nonviolent protest in world history, particularly his March on Washington in 1963, which concluded with King's famous "I Have a Dream" speech. King's leadership during the Civil Rights movement directly led to the **Civil Rights Act** of 1964 and Voting Rights Act of 1965. Despite these legislative victories, political assassinations, bombings, and riots were commonplace in the United States from the late 1960s to the 1970s.

Shocking the world, the **Berlin Wall** fell in 1989, and national revolutions swept out the Soviets' puppet government in Eastern Europe. By late 1991, the Soviet Union had collapsed. Considerable credit is attributed to President Ronald Reagan for escalating the arm's race, which the Soviets couldn't afford, while simultaneously holding talks with Soviet General Secretary Mikhail Gorbachev.

Post-Cold War Era

Following the collapse of the Soviet Union, the United States became an uncontested superpower. No country in the world could match its economic and military might until China's emergence as a world power in the 2010s.

September 11, 2001 was a traumatic day for the United States, as terrorists hijacked four commercial airliners and crashed three of them into the World Trade Center and Pentagon. Osama bin Laden, the Saudi-born leader of Al-Qaeda, plotted the attacks from his base in Afghanistan. President George W. Bush responded by launching the **War on Terror**, declaring the entire world as a battlefield. Less than one month after the attack, the United States invaded Afghanistan to dismantle Al-Qaeda's training camps, but Osama bin Laden evaded the American military for nearly a decade. American Special Forces killed bin Laden at his Pakistani compound during the Obama administration. The War in Afghanistan is the longest war in American history.

More controversially, Bush invaded Iraq in 2003 based on his administration's claims that Iraqi dictator Saddam Hussein collaborated with Al-Qaeda and was producing "weapons of mass destruction." Both were false assertions, and the Iraq War was a failure for the nation's reputation and security. Shortly after toppling and executing Saddam Hussein, Iraq erupted in a bloody, sectarian civil war. One faction in the Iraqi Civil War would later form the Islamic State and carve a caliphate out of Syria and Iraq.

Opposition to the Iraq War became so fierce that it helped two American presidents, Barack Obama and Donald Trump—who share little else in common politically—win the presidency. President Obama withdrew from Iraq in December 2007, but an American-led coalition returned in 2014 to fight the Islamic State. President Obama expanded the War on Terror, largely relying on drone strikes and Special Operations forces to hunt terror cells in more than a half-dozen countries. In addition, Obama administration officials lied to Congress about the scope of a secret domestic surveillance program, which Edward Snowden exposed, angering civil liberty activists.

The financial crisis of 2007-2008 was a pivotal moment in recent American history. Large investment banks created an artificial bubble in the mortgage sector, and when it burst, the American government bailed them out at taxpayers' expense to prevent the economy from collapsing. Both sides of the political spectrum erupted in anger, directly leading to the anarchist and socialist *Occupy Wall Street Movement* and partially contributing to the growth of the libertarian Tea Party.

Practice Quiz

1. One factor that contributed to the rise of consumer economics in the United States of America was:
   a. The market revolution
   b. The Mexican-American War
   c. The Enlightenment
   d. The stock market crash of 1929

2. What countries originally formed the Triple Entente in World War I?
   a. The United States, Britain, and Canada
   b. The United States, Britain, and France
   c. Britain, France, and Russia
   d. Austria-Hungary, Germany, and Italy

3. What did President Franklin Delano Roosevelt call his legislative agenda?
   a. The War on Poverty
   b. The New Deal
   c. The Great Society
   d. Social Security

4. How did Jim Crow laws impact the American South?
   a. African American slaves could vote for the first time in American history.
   b. The South diversified from a one-crop economy.
   c. The South industrialized, following the Northern example.
   d. The Southern states contravened the Reconstruction Amendments.

5. Abraham Lincoln delivered his "House Divided" speech to the Republican state convention on June 16, 1858. In the passage below, when Lincoln used the phrase "a house divided," what was he most likely referring to?

> A house divided against itself cannot stand. I believe this government cannot endure, permanently, half slave and half free. I do not expect the Union to be dissolved—I do not expect the house to fall—but I do expect it will cease to be divided. It will become all one thing or all the other. Either the opponents of slavery will arrest the further spread of it, and place it where the public mind shall rest in the belief that it is in the course of ultimate extinction; or its advocates will push it forward, till it shall become lawful in all the States, old as well as new—North as well as South.

   a. Political conflicts in the White House
   b. Tensions between North and South over slavery
   c. Dissolution of the Union
   d. Ideological differences in his family

See next page for answer explanations.

Answer Explanations

1. A: The answer is Choice *A*, the market revolution. The market revolution witnessed the United States transition from a mostly self-subsistence agrarian economy to an interdependent consumer economy. The Mexican-American War, Choice *B*, and the Enlightenment, Choice *A*, have no historical relation to the rise of consumerism. And the stock market crash of 1929 was actually the result of the excesses of consumer culture, Choice *D*.

2. C: Britain, France, and Russia formed the Triple Entente in World War I, so Choice *B* is the correct answer. Canada and the United States both joined the Triple Entente, but they were not original members. Austria-Hungary and Germany fought against the Triple Entente. Italy allied with Austria-Hungary and Germany before the war broke out, but the Italians held out and later joined the Triple Entente once it appeared they would be victorious.

3. B: Choice *B* is the correct answer. President Franklin Delano Roosevelt's legislative agenda was called the New Deal, and it created the modern-day welfare state—Social Security, unemployment insurance, disability, labor laws, and housing and food subsidies. The War on Poverty and Great Society were Lyndon B. Johnson's agenda, though they were influenced by the New Deal. Social Security was part of the New Deal, not Roosevelt's legislative agenda.

4. D: Immediately after the federal government withdrew troops from the South, ending Reconstruction, the Southern states enacted Jim Crow laws. These laws contravened the Reconstruction Amendments by preventing African Americans from voting and enforcing segregationist policies. Therefore, Choice *D* is the correct answer. African Americans voted for the first time during Reconstruction, but following the passage of Jim Crow laws, they couldn't vote until the 1960s Civil Rights Movement. The South didn't diversify from a one-crop economy (cotton) or industrialize until the 20th century. In addition, it wasn't related to Jim Crow. If anything, Jim Crow contributed to the continued focus on cotton as sharecropping replaced slavery.

5. B: The speech was made before the Civil War, which began in 1861; it captures the rising tension over slavery between the North and the South. Choices *A* and *D* are incorrect because Lincoln is not talking about an actual house. Instead, he is talking about a nation divided over slavery by using the metaphor of a house. Choice *C* is incorrect because the speech was given in 1858, before the secession of South Carolina and the dissolution of the Union in 1861.

World History and Geography

Analyzing Historical Sources and Recognizing Perspectives

Every scholar, educator, and student of history must be able to analyze historical sources. These sources are usually categorized into two main groups: primary sources and secondary sources. **Primary sources** are the texts or artefacts that are representative of a particular event, moment, or era in the past because they were written during (or directly after) that event, moment, or era. Primary sources really capture the past. They help convey the effects of every event, the might of every moment, and the essence of every era. Primary sources are what scholars, educators, and students of history use to create secondary sources. **Secondary sources** recount or analyze events that happened in the distant past rather than the proximal present. While an example of a primary source would be a personal diary, journal, or letter, an example of a secondary source would be a textbook, scholarly article, or monograph. Secondary sources weave together excerpts from primary sources, synthesizing these facts with historical theories. There are also tertiary sources that serve as compendia of information derived from secondary sources.

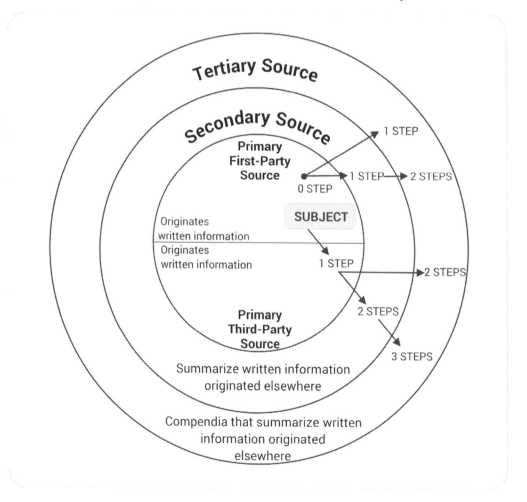

Regardless of whether the source is primary, secondary, or tertiary, it must be analyzed with a keen eye for unique perspectives. Some historians refer to this process as "deconstruction"—it is an analysis that breaks down the ideas constructed by a text or artefact. Deconstruction is essential for recognizing the biases embedded within every source. Every unique perspective in a text has its own set of biases, which are tied to the personal beliefs, preferences, blind spots, and values of the author. History centers on understanding every sources perspective and biases in order to make sense of what is fact and what is opinion. At times, the line separating fact and opinion becomes blurred, so scholars, educators, and students of history must try to assess the historical validity of a source. This means these stakeholders of historical analysis must infuse the old facts with new theories, breathing life into history by making unique inferences.

Throughout history, primary sources have naturally captured different personal perspectives. As soon as the ink hits the paper, reality becomes filtered through the biases of others. All history is an inevitable process of conscious selection. Authors of primary sources choose to tell about some details; they also choose to ignore others. All primary sources fail to capture the entire essence of history. They are entirely driven by point of view, or perspective. Sometimes these perspectives are shaped radically by ideals. History, in this sense, becomes a political platform. Below are two examples of primary sources that view desegregation from two radically different perspectives.

Governor George Wallace's Inaugural Address as Governor of Alabama: "Segregation Now, Segregation Forever" Speech (1963) "Today I have stood, where once Jefferson Davis stood, and took an oath to my people. It is very appropriate then that from this Cradle of the Confederacy, this very Heart of the Great Anglo-Saxon Southland, that today we sound the drum for freedom as have our generations of forebears before us done, time and time again through history. Let us rise to the call of freedom-loving blood that is in us and send our answer to the tyranny that clanks its chains upon the South. In the name of the greatest people that have ever trod this earth, I draw the line in the dust and toss the gauntlet before the feet of tyranny ... and I say ... segregation today ... segregation tomorrow ... segregation forever."	Dr. Martin Luther King, Jr.'s "Address at the Freedom Rally in Cobo Hall" (1963) "For Birmingham tells us something in glaring terms. It says first that the Negro is no longer willing to accept racial segregation in any of its dimensions. For we have come to see that segregation is not only sociologically untenable, it is not only politically unsound, it is morally wrong and sinful. Segregation is a cancer in the body politic, which must be removed before our democratic health can be realized. Segregation is wrong because it is nothing but a new form of slavery covered up with certain niceties of complexity. Segregation is wrong because it is a system of adultery perpetuated by an illicit intercourse between injustice and immorality. And in Birmingham, Alabama, and all over the South and all over the nation, we are simply saying that we will no longer sell our birthright of freedom for a mess of segregated pottage. In a real sense, we are through with segregation now, henceforth, and forevermore."

Notice how both men—Governor George Wallace and Dr. Martin Luther King, Jr.—are talking about the same topic (segregation) in the same year (1963), but they are viewing their historical context through two entirely different lenses, or perspectives. Governor Wallace is pro-segregation. Dr. King is anti-segregation. Two men, from two different cultures, with two different sets of biases, are analyzing the same historical context in two radically different ways.

Secondary sources function in the same manner. Scholars often take different stances about particular historical events or contacts. Below is a chart showing the ways in which different historians have analyzed the Great Depression.

Historian	Key Quotes	Summary of Perspective
FRIEDMAN AND SCHWARTZ	"The Depression, they claimed, was a result of a drastic contraction of the currency." "The Federal Reserve Board in Washington came to dominate monetary policy, with disastrous results."	The Depression was caused by a failure to control the supply of money. Federal Reserve was to blame for the Great Depression because of its monetary policy.
TEMIN	"The New Deal never ended the Depression because it did not spend enough."	The government did not intervene and spend enough money.
POWELL	"Even if [some events had happened differently], there would have been a Depression because of the severe monetary contraction."	The Depression was caused by monetary contraction.
BADGER	"Lack of demand was not offset in the early years of the Depression by any compensatory spending."	The US government did not spend enough money to stop the Depression.
KINDELBERGER	"The world economic system was unstable unless some country stabilized it."	The USA failed to take an economic lead in the world.
KENNEDY	"American banks were rotten."	American banks were unregulated and were to blame to for the Depression.

As this chart demonstrates, historians are inclined to take different stances on how they interpret history. Not every historian agrees about the root causes of the Great Depression. Each has their own perspective.

Different perspectives exist in history because history is a very human process. History is as diverse as human identities. So how can students of history figure out which perspective is right? This is a difficult question to answer. The "right" answer is the one that is the most objective. Objectivity is a fancy word for truthfulness—it is the quest to capture reality and convey that reality to others. Fenwick English (1992) once stated: "[One who strives for objectivity] is more interested in truthfulness than truth. The former is established by a continued pursuit never culminated." Like an asymptote on a mathematical graph, objectivity (truthfulness) is something you can get infinitesimally closer to, but it is something that may never be fully realized. Nevertheless, this reality should not stop students from searching for truthfulness. The "right" perspective is usually the one that is repeated most often by primary and secondary sources. Thus, students should continuously cross-reference relevant sources to get closer to historical objectivity.

Interconnections Among the Past, Present, and Future

Historical analysis is actually a reflection of both the past and present—it combines old primary sources with new secondary perspectives. Additionally, many scholars, educators, and students of history

94

introduce future implications into their research—they try to predict how historical themes, past and present, may play out in the future. The art and craft of historical analysis thus rests at the praxis of the past, present, and future. This is often overlooked by students. They believe history is something that is dead. But history is very much alive. It shapes the past, informs the present, and paves a path to the future.

In this sense, history has its own agency. It cannot fully be sequestered to the past because, as a sociological phenomenon, it impacts the present and future. In any given moment in time, we can be studying history (past), living it (present), and making it (future). This is a very difficult concept to understand, but the course of history has its own momentum. It is an inescapable force that moves both with, against, and without humanity. Below are a few anecdotes that illustrate different interconnections that can exist between the past, present, and future.

Example of how the PAST influences the PRESENT:

> Every year, Americans join together to memorialize D-Day on June 6. D-Day is a past moment. It occurred on June 6, 1944. It is the moment Allied forces—led by the Americans—landed on the beaches of Normandy and began marching eastward to defeat the Germans. It is a past moment that continues to have present-day effects.

This is an example of the past influencing the present because it is a historical moment that has contemporary memorials.

Example of how the PRESENT influences the PAST:

> Noticing the heartache brought on by the Great Recession (2007-2009), a young scholar writes an article in 2009 that compares the Great Recession to the Great Depression. The article changes the way historians understand the Great Depression, adding to the canon of historical reflections on the topic.

This is an example of how present moments can illuminate the past.

Example of how the PAST and PRESENT influence the FUTURE:

> Protesters decide to topple a Confederate statue on a college campus, breaking it into pieces; the damage is irreparable, and the crowd decides to erect a new statue of an African American leader.

This is a present event that destroys the past (a statue memorializing the Confederacy), which inevitably changes the future (both physically and philosophically).

Example how the FUTURE might connect to the PRESENT:

> Barring any imminent demise of humanity or its cognitive functions, our current moment in history will likely be reviewed by future historians. Since we have moved to a digital age, future historians may have to be skilled computer forensics experts who can unearth the past digital interactions of humanity.

This is a future scenario that will likely be shaped by present interactions.

Additionally, in history classrooms, **causation** and **correlation** are key to understanding the relationships (or lack of relationships) between the past, present, and future. Causation is more easily understood than correlation. For instance, events cause certain changes that have an effect on present actions, which, in turn, affect visions of the future and the future itself. But causation need not be linear or progressive when it comes to history; it is not always a timeline like in the textbooks. Future prospects can cause us to re-envision past occurrences, which, in turn, affect the way we view the present. However, most phenomena in history are not causally related—there is no direct line of cause and effect. Since history is chock full of mysteries and silences, it typically seems like a giant blob of ideas and actions. The events, people, and values that exist within this amorphous blob of details usually have loose connections that are called correlations. We know that these events, people, and values may be correlated in some way, but not directly or causally.

Notable Classical Civilizations in World History

Classical civilizations developed many innovations that contributed to our postmodern world—metal tools and weapons, written languages, calendars, representative government, professional militaries, urban planning, and large-scale farming, among others. These innovations allowed classical civilizations to conquer huge territories and establish historic empires. Examples of classical civilizations include Egypt, Greece, Persia, China, and Rome.

Ancient Egypt
Ancient Egypt's first ruling dynasty was established in the 32nd century B.C., and over the next three thousand years, Egyptian innovations were adopted by many other classical civilizations. In addition, Egypt was conquered and controlled by three of those civilizations—Greece, Persia, and Rome.

Developed out of necessity to limit the Nile River's annual flooding, Egyptian irrigation techniques changed the world. Where floods once washed away crops and settlements, Egyptian irrigation left a rich delta that could grow enough food to support an empire. To govern their empire, the Egyptians independently developed a writing system (hieroglyphs) and created a professional bureaucracy of clerks and writers (scribes). Egypt also signed the earliest formal peace treaty during a war with the Hittites. Egyptian pharaohs built enormous burial structures, such as the Great Pyramid. The demand for these massive public works incentivized the invention of new quarrying, surveying, and construction techniques.

Greece
Greek city-states, such as Sparta and Athens, started to develop in the 8th century B.C. Some of the city-states united to fend off the Persian Empire, and in 4th century B.C., Alexander the Great conquered a then-unprecedented empire that included Greece, Egypt, Persia, Syria, Mesopotamia, central Asia, and northern India. Alexander the Great's empire marks the start of the Hellenistic period, which lasted until the Roman Republic conquered the eastern Mediterranean and turned Greece into a Roman province.

Greek political systems and philosophy have had a major influence on Western civilization. The Greek city-states invented the principle of self-government and *demokratia* (direct democracy). Although Greece is considered the birthplace of democracy, the city-states were slave societies, and only the wealthy elite could participate politically. Still, Greece served as a model for Rome and early modern Europe on how to govern, collect taxes, and militarize.

The three most famous Greek scholars are **Socrates**, **Plato**, and **Aristotle**. All three are considered the fathers of Western philosophy, and their work continues to be studied in classrooms across the world. Plato's *Republic* and *Laws* are foundational texts in the field of political philosophy, and Aristotle's work in the physical sciences and logic were the basis for European scholarship throughout the Middle Ages. In addition to philosophy, Aristarchus was the first person to theorize that the Earth revolved around the

96

Sun; Archimedes discovered pi (π); and Euclid's *Elements* is a collection of mathematical definitions, theorems, and proofs that went unchallenged until the 19th century.

Persia

Cyrus the Great founded the first Persian Empire, the Achaemenid Empire, in the 6th century B.C., effectively turning a group of nomadic shepherds into one of the largest empires in history. His successor, Darius I, further expanded the empire from Eastern Europe to Central and South Asia. Alexander the Great overthrew Darius III and conquered the Persian Empire in 330 B.C.

The Persian Empire was multicultural, consisting of multiple civilizations with varying religions, languages, and ethnicities. Persian rulers took a "carrot or stick" approach to diplomacy. If a civilization willingly joined the Empire and paid taxes, they would receive some degree of self-government and enjoy better economic relations. If the civilization resisted, they were invaded and enslaved.

The Persian Empire was organized under a federal system, much like the American model of government. Persian rulers functioned as the central government, and they appointed satraps (governors) and records-keepers to every region. The satraps allowed for limited local self-government, depending on the region's relationship with the Persian Empire. In exercising control over their vast empire, Persians developed innovative roadway and postal systems that the Romans later expanded upon.

China

Ancient China was ruled under successive dynasties, beginning with the Xia dynasty (21st century B.C.) and ending with the Qing dynasty (1911). The dynasties legitimized their power through the Mandate of Heaven—the belief that a higher power selected the ruler. The Mandate of Heaven contributed to the concept of legitimization in political philosophy.

The Han dynasty (206 B.C.—220 A.D.) was a golden era for Chinese trade, technological innovation, and scientific advancement. Han rulers opened the Silk Road, a series of trade routes connecting China with the rest of the Asian continent and Roman territory. The Silk Road linked the Far East and West for the first time. To facilitate this multicultural trade, Han rulers issued one of the world's first uniform currencies. Han Chinese technological innovations included papermaking, wheelbarrows, steering rudders, mapmaking (grids and raised-relief), and the seismometer (measure earthquakes). In science and math, Han scholars discovered herbal remedies, square roots, cube roots, the Pythagorean theorem, negative numbers, and advanced pi (π) calculations.

Rome

The city of **Rome** was founded in the 8th century B.C. and initially ruled under a monarchical government. Rome transitioned into a republic in the latter half of the 6th century B.C. In the 1st century B.C., a series of civil wars destabilized the Roman Republic, which culminated with Gaius Julius Caesar seizing absolute power. Caesar's victory caused Rome's transition from a republic to an empire. The Roman Empire would become the largest in history. Political corruption, religious conflict, economic challenges, and repeated invasions by German tribes led to the empire splitting into Western and Eastern halves in 395 A.D. The Eastern half, known as the Byzantine Empire, outlasted the Western Empire, surviving until 1453.

Rome is often referred to as the birthplace of Western civilization, and its influence on world history cannot be overstated. James Madison used the Roman Republic's separation of powers as a model for the United States Constitution. Rome spread Greek philosophy and culture across its many territories, including advancements in architecture and urban planning. Roman law influenced the development of many legal practices, like trials by juries, contracts, wills, corporations, and civil rights. All Romantic languages evolved from Latin—French, Italian, Spanish, and Portuguese. Roman numerals are still commonly used. Rome adopted and mastered Persian theories related to bureaucracy, civil engineering, "carrot and stick" diplomacy, and multiculturalism. To build their large infrastructure projects, the Romans invented a superior form of concrete. The largest religion in the world, Christianity, also started in a Roman province (Judea), spread across the empire, and eventually became Rome's state-sanctioned religion.

Geography

Physical and Human Geography

A **physical system** refers to a region's landmass, environment, climate, and weather. **Human systems** are a group of people participating in a joint enterprise. Human systems adapt to and manipulate the physical system, and in doing so, they change the physical system. The extraction of resources is why physical systems change.

Human systems require the consumption of natural resources—air, fossil fuels, iron, land, minerals, sunlight, water, wind, wood, etc. Some resources are renewable, such as oxygen, fresh water, and solar energy, while others are finite. Nonrenewable resources, like fossil fuels, take millions of years to form; once they're depleted, they're gone. The variety and availability of resources plays an integral role in the human system's development, and the fight over resources also changes human systems when there's conflict.

The interaction between human and physical systems is most evident in economic development, particularly agriculture. Some regions are entirely barren, while others are rich in natural resources. Where a human system is located within that range will have an important, if not decisive, impact on its future. For example, an advanced human system has never developed in the Sahara Desert due to the lack of water and arable land. As such, the human system adapted to the harsh physical system by embracing a nomadic lifestyle. In contrast, nearly all ancient empires were located on or near a large river delta. The nutrient-rich soil enabled agriculture, and the resulting food production supported a large population. With a larger population, human systems based on agriculture could diversify their economies with the excess labor, form governments, and raise armies to conquer more land. All of this would be impossible in the Sahara without implementing some future technological innovation to moderate the physical system.

The interaction between the Native Americans and Europeans resulted in the rapid decline of the Native American system and drastic changes to the physical system. The European system's large-scale production of crops and livestock sustained permanent settlements, which facilitated the establishment of a centralized system of government. In contrast, the Native Americans were nomadic, making it easier for Europeans to drive native tribes off their land. Old World diseases also overwhelmed the Native American population, reaching some of the western tribes even before the arrival of European colonists. In addition, the Europeans were armed with superior weaponry—steel and firearms. As a result, the European system devastated the Native American system. The indigenous population in California dropped from 150,000 to 15,000 between 1848 and 1900.

The American takeover dramatically altered the physical system. Agriculture, industrialization, and urbanization have caused a sharp decline in wilderness, which now accounts for less than 5 percent of total American land. Similarly, the United States outside of Alaska has lost 60% of its natural vegetation. As wilderness and habitats decline, so does biodiversity. In the United States, 539 native species are extinct or missing, and more than one-third of all species are at risk. These trends are mirrored across the world as more countries industrialize. Only 23 percent of the world's wilderness remains, and the rate of habitat destruction has markedly increased over the last few decades. If current trends continue, two-thirds of all wild animal species will be extinct by 2020.

Furthermore, the human system is causing climate change by increasing the amount of carbon dioxide and methane in the atmosphere. Deforestation, land use changes, and the burning of fossil fuels release carbon dioxide into the atmosphere. Landfills, livestock, and rice cultivation produce methane. These gases blanket the atmosphere, preventing heat from escaping into space. The scientific data is undeniable. Sixteen of the hottest seventeen years on record have occurred since 2001, and global ice is melting at an unprecedented pace. Consequently, rising temperatures have increased the rate of extreme weather events and ocean acidification.

Using Geographic Concepts to Analyze Spatial Phenomena and Discuss Economic, Political, and Social Factors

The study of geography should not be confined to lifeless maps of counties, states, nations, and continents. Though these maps are, indeed, foundational to the study of geography, **geography** is also tied to the economic, political, and social trends of humanity. These geographic concepts play out over time and space, signaling changes in not only the spatial environments, but also the spatial phenomena that fill these environments. There is a reason why many scholars, educators, and students have turned to a field known as human geography: the field of geography centers much on the interaction of humanity with the spatial and physical environments.

Geographic concepts such as **nation-states** and **borders** have stirred economic, political, and social turmoil; they have spawned revolutions and genocides. The Mexican-American War was largely a war over imaginary lines we call borders. The American Civil War was largely over a geographic phenomenon we call **regionalism**. Even the war over words of the most recent presidential election in the United States had a lot to do with the concept of a rural-urban-suburban trichotomy in geography.

Other geographic concepts include migration, standard of living, and cultural diffusion. **Migration** occurs when people move from one place to another for economic, political, social, or environmental reasons. **Standard of living** describes the wealth, comfort, necessities, and luxuries that are available to people in a specific geographic area. **Cultural diffusion** happens when a certain culture and its corresponding traits, beliefs, and activities spread to other nationalities and ethnicities.

Put simply, geography is yet another interdisciplinary field that continues to be a highly influential contributor and outgrowth to human existence.

Thus, there are some basic geographical concepts that everyone should know (beyond the highly specified aforementioned terms such as border and nation state). Most geography teachers focus on what are called the seven major geographical concepts:

Space: The environmental and human characteristics placed on the physical arrangement, area, or pattern of a location. Space is also about the significance, organization, and distribution of this physical arrangement, area, or pattern of a location. Space, much like place, can have a personal or collective significance. It can be experienced in different ways. People studying geography analyze the connections and organizations of space, especially as it relates to human civilizations and global interactions.

Place: Places are absolute locations on the Earth's surface that are critical components of human identity, security, and culture. Humanity has the ability to actually alter the physical characteristics of place. They can also alter the existential characteristics that infuse meaning into these absolute locations.

Interconnection: Interconnection refers to the connectedness of human, natural, and environmental processes, which help create physical and cultural changes that are byproducts of human civilization. Interconnection is about the interplay between human and environmental forces, which are both considered part of geography. The agricultural revolution is a great example of the ways in which the interconnectedness of the environment and humanity created vast changes through symbiotic structures.

Change: Change is, at its core, about the environmental and human evolutions and evolutions that play out over time. Change is the ways in which cultures and physical places/spaces transform throughout history.

Environment: Environment is more than just space or place—it is about the biological, atmospheric, geological, and chemical processes that influence human decisions in a particular place. The environment is about the ways in which humans interact with waterways, food sources, chemical compounds, geological features, and climate changes.

Scale: Scale exists on a spectrum from extremely microcosmic to extremely macrocosmic; it is about minute details and vast superstructural generalizations. Geographers must decide the relative scale of a particular event, action, or phenomenon; they must think about how minor or major the impact.

Sustainability: Sustainability has become a crucial component of geographic study because it focuses on the ability of humanity (and life in general) to sustain or continue in the midst of wide-reaching geographical chain reactions that have severe consequences (i.e., pollution → global warming → loss of habitat → loss of food sources and/or animal species) in terms of biological persistence.

Uses of Geography

History is the story of interaction and conflict between interests, movements, cultures, societies, nations and empires. **Geography** is the key to understanding history. World leaders always include geographic considerations in their decision-making. As such, understanding geography helps explain the past, interpret the present, and plan for the future. This is especially true for any armed conflict due to the strategic importance of higher ground, supply routes, defensible borders, etc. The field of studying political power through the lens of geography is called **geopolitics**.

The three theories of geopolitical power with the most historic, contemporary, and future significance are the Heartland Theory, Rimland Theory, and Organic Theory.

Published in 1904, Halford John MacKinder's **Heartland Theory** emphasizes the strategic importance of Eastern Europe, Russia, and Western China. These three regions form the "Heartland," occupying a central position on the "World Island"—Africa, Asia, and Europe. MacKinder considered the rest of the world to be mere islands floating around the World Island. This reflects the Heartland Theory's Eurocentrism approach. Due to their military power and geographical proximity to Eastern Europe, MacKinder correctly identified Germany and Russia as the greatest threats to global security in the early 20th century.

The Cold War also heavily featured the Heartland, as the Soviet Union controlled most of Eastern Europe and worked closely with China. As a result, American foreign policymakers' primary goal was to weaken the Soviets' dominance in the Heartland. American forces used covert operations to sow dissent and discord throughout the region. For example, the Central Intelligence Agency (CIA) covertly funded Radio Free Europe—an American government program that broadcast news across Eastern Europe. In addition, the United States courted China as an ally, which culminated in President Richard Nixon's state visit to China in February 1972. Following the Soviet Union's loss of the Heartland and subsequent dissolution, the United States encouraged Eastern Europe to join the North Atlantic Treaty Organization (NATO), an American-led military alliance.

Like the Heartland Theory, the **Rimland Theory** is Eurocentrism, prioritizing the Eurasian continent above all other regions. However, the Rimland Theory differs in its emphasis on the "Rimland" (Eurasian coasts). Accordingly, the European coast, Middle East, and Asiatic coasts have the most geopolitical value. The Rimland Theory's author, Nicholas John Spykman, believed these regions served as a buffer between land and sea power. The theory predates the widespread use of airplanes, which detracts from some of the coastal regions' importance. However, the United States remains a military superpower through naval superiority.

Rather than name a strategically important region, the **Organic Theory** argues that nation-states need to consolidate political power and acquire new geographic territory in order to sustain themselves. In this concept, the nation-state operates like a living organism, and new territory provides the resources it needs to survive. First published by German Friedrich Ratzel in 1897, the Organic Theory was often combined with Social Darwinism—the idea that Darwin's natural selection applies to humans—to justify imperialism and racism. Nazi Germany was one of the Organic Theory's most vocal advocates.

Empires and nation-states have historically pursued their self-interest by consolidating political power and acquiring foreign territory. Mercantilism, colonialism, and imperialism are all related to conquering territory, and they were common European policies for centuries. The Roman Empire is another illustrative example. Rome started as a single city-state, conquered the Italian Peninsula, and then seized most of Europe, North Africa, the Balkans, and Asia Minor. Once a territory was captured, the Romans enslaved large populations of people, collected taxes, and extracted resources from the land. Each conquest increased Rome's political power, and Rome collapsed partially due to its inability to conquer and hold new territory.

The Organic Theory also helps explain why nation-states resist fracturing into smaller, independent states. If acquiring territory is the nation-state's lifeblood, then losing territory is a direct harm. In addition to undermining the government's legitimacy, losing territory could decrease the labor pool, natural resources, and military strength. It also means sharing a new border with what could be a hostile neighbor. This was the case in the American Civil War. President Abraham Lincoln didn't initially deploy military force to free the slaves. In fact, several of the border slave states remained in the Union for the entire conflict. Instead, President Lincoln wanted to preserve the Union and prevent the loss of territory, economic power, military power, and natural resources. Lincoln's reasoning was consistent with the Organic approach to geopolitics.

The present-day United States is not a traditional empire. Past empires have conquered and directly ruled over their territories. The United States hasn't added a major piece of territory since the Spanish-American War. Nevertheless, the United States' leverage over many nation-states is impossible to overstate. The United States has acquired political power by wielding military force to coerce countries and money to make them willing partners. The United States outspends its rivals on its military by a significant margin every year, though some of the difference can be attributed to higher labor costs.

American foreign policy revolves around geopolitics. The United States maintains approximately 800 military bases in 70 different countries, and the bases surround every potential challenger to American hegemony. The US Navy operates nineteen aircraft carriers, while the rest of the world has nine altogether. Consequently, the United States can exercise control over five oceans, challenge any coastal region it desires, and send military planes anywhere in the world at a moment's notice.

Other than a genuine interest in combatting terrorism, the wars in Afghanistan and Iraq served American geopolitical interests in the Middle East, a region that holds most of the world's oil reserves. Some think the Iraq War was motivated by the goal of "stealing" Iraqi oil, but that theory goes too far. The United States was more interested in exercising American power vis-a-vis Iran, Iraq's geographical neighbor. The United States is allied with all of the Sunni Muslim oil-producing countries (Saudi Arabia, Qatar, United Arab Emirates, etc.), and they are Iran's geopolitical rivals. As a result, the United States is constantly trying to prevent Iranian influence from spreading outside its territorial borders, as has happened in Lebanon and Syria.

Like its impact on predicting and understanding armed conflict, geopolitics is important for understanding trade and foreign aid decisions. Human systems have emphasized trading with their geographic neighbors since the prehistoric era. In addition to generating wealth, trade improves diplomatic relations and avoids conflict. Depending on the measure, the United States is either the largest or second-largest (after China) economy in the world, and the US leads the global financial industry. Consequently, the United States can curry favor by promising greater economic cooperation and donates twice the amount of foreign aid as the next-largest donor.

Interpreting Maps

Contrary to popular perception, geography is not simply about the study and creation of maps (that is **cartography**). Nevertheless, geography is, without a doubt, a very visual field; it focuses on interpreting visual representations of environmental processes and human behaviors (and the interconnectedness between the two). These visual representations can range from simple maps to complex **geographic information systems** (*GIS*). In fact, the entire field is becoming more and more technological in the midst of the current digital revolution. Geographers no longer focus solely on two-dimensional, handcrafted maps. They now take advantage of both two-dimensional and three-dimensional mapmaking technologies. First launched in 1978, the **global positioning system** (*GPS*) has also revolutionized the field of geography. Think about how complicated and user-friendly maps have become as a result of GPS technologies. Systems like Google Maps, for instance, are a perfect example of the rapid changes brought about by new geographic technologies. In many ways, human beings are interacting with their environments more than ever with the advent of smartphone GPS capabilities. The whole landscape—thanks to virtual reality and augmented reality—has quite literally changed. We are studying geography on a daily basis without even knowing it!

Most maps—traditional or digital—use **legends** to help the audience navigate the meaning and content of the tool. Legends provide visual representations and explanations of the content on a map; they are key for conveying the unique features of every map. Each legend consists of a set of symbols and a short description of the information it conveys. Although the placement of the legend varies from map to map, they are normally found with the corner or margins of a map. Below is an example of a traditional map legend:

MAP LEGEND

— Main road
— Other road
—+ Railway
═ Department boundary
—- Municipality boundary
▓ Water
▒ Inner city
░ Populated area
▒ Industrial area
▓ Forest

Specific types of geographic maps and graphics include contour maps, population pyramids, and climographs. **Contour maps** use contour lines to show elevations and slopes of land surfaces and features. A **population pyramid**, also known as an age-sex pyramid, is a graphical representation of a populations' distribution based on age and sex. **Climographs** describe a location's climate by displaying climatic elements on a graph or chart.

Regardless of technological changes, one thing remains the same about geography: it is still a field heavily devoted to case studies. Like many other scholars in the humanities and social sciences, geographers spend a lot of their time creating and analyzing geographic case studies. These studies try to consolidate and analyze data about particular geographical interconnections. The seven major geographical concepts are key for developing and examining case studies. Geographers analyze maps, geographic technologies, and data through the lenses of these seven major geographical concepts. These lenses assist geographers with better understanding the ways in which human beings bring changes to their spaces, places, and environments. It is up to the geographer to decide the scale of these changes and whether they are conducive to overall human or environmental sustainability.

Case studies usually focus on a particular process, space, place, or environment. In most instances, using visual and technological tools, geographers will cross-analyze multiple case studies. For example, a geographer may compare four major metropolitan cities that have similar population sizes or demographics. Or geographers may compare the educational outcomes of certain minority groups across different spaces, places, or environments. Geographers may even study the sustainability practices of one rural village over the course of a decade. The options are endless, but these case studies are crucial to expanding the academic canon of geographic understanding.

Foreign Policy and World Geography

The United States of America's approach to foreign policy is constantly influenced by world geography and history. Events that happen all around the world have changed how America implements its foreign policy. The world is connected now more than ever, and the United States responds to these changes to protect its interests and ensure the safety of its allies.

One of the biggest influences on American foreign policy is the presence of rival major powers. Historically, this has been countries like the Soviet Union or China. Because of the presence of these major superpowers, the world can be divided based on their sphere of influence. The best example of this was at the height of the Cold War, when the United States and Soviet Union were deadlocked in an ideological battle of will. The ideas of democracy and communism clashed, and major events during the Cold War, like the establishment of the Berlin Wall or the Space Race, were caused by the ongoing conflict between these two superpowers.

World geography has played an even more critical role in the development of foreign policy. World geography can be described as the relationship between different peoples and places. It describes what happens to the various continents, regions, and oceans in the world. Ever since becoming a major superpower, the United States has played a major role in how the globe operates. For example, America's vast industrial capabilities demand a huge amount of resources. Resources like oil and raw materials are constantly being transported to the United States, which greatly affects areas where these resources are gathered.

Oil is one major resource that has been the cause of both great progress and great suffering in world geography. Wars have been fought over it, and some countries depend heavily on the wealth that oil

104

brings. For example, modern-day Russia and Saudi Arabia are some of the largest exporters of oil in the world, and they greatly profit from it. Obtaining these resources inevitably releases large amounts of pollution into the environment. Regardless, the United States works with different countries around the world to obtain these resources.

Regarding foreign policy, the United States has involved itself in several conflicts due to the need to protect its own interests and citizens. For example, many important decisions regarding immigration are based on whether or not the United States can provide for potential immigrants. In addition to this, some question if the United States has a responsibility to immigrants. This is seen in its relationship with Mexico and much of Central and South America, where many immigrants come from. The constant border clashes and tension raised on the southern border are reminders of America's involvement with foreign countries. In particular, preventing illegal acts such as human and drug smuggling remains a huge issue involving the border and border control.

Overall, the United States has a vested interest to maintain its strength through its relationship with nations around the world. Through the many agreements with foreign nations, the United States is able to exert global influence and affect how the world operates. Events in even faraway places eventually require American attention, due to America's continued status as a global superpower.

Practice Quiz

1. Which of the following is NOT listed as one of the seven major geographical concepts?
   a. Space
   b. History
   c. Place
   d. Change

2. Why do geographers traditionally use case studies?
   a. Lobby for environmental sustainability changes
   b. Program GPS systems
   c. Collect and analyze important geographical data
   d. Communicate important theories to cartographers

3. What country successfully launched the first satellite into orbit?
   a. Japan
   b. Soviet Union
   c. Germany
   d. United States

4. What is the Organic Theory's thesis?
   a. Naval and air power is more important than territorial control.
   b. Africa, Asia, and Europe form the World Island, which is the most important landmass for geopolitics.
   c. Countries need to acquire political power and territory to survive.
   d. Communism will grow organically unless there's early military intervention.

5. Which of the following maps is the most subjective?
   a. Climate maps
   b. Political maps
   c. Population density maps
   d. Topographic maps

See next page for answer explanations.

Answer Explanations

1. B: The answer is Choice *B*, history. Space, Choice *A*, place, Choice *C*, and change, Choice *D*, are all elements of the seven major geographical concepts. History influences all these major concepts, and it is an important part of geography, but it is not included on this traditional list.

2. C: The answer is Choice *C*, collect and analyze important geographical data. While it can be argued that these case studies can influence sustainability lobbying efforts, Choice *A*, GPS systems, Choice *B*, and communications with cartographers, Choice *D*, they have most traditionally been used as a platform for data collection and analysis.

3. B: On October 4, 1957, the Soviet Union launched the first satellite, Sputnik 1, into orbit; therefore, Choice *B* is the correct answer. The United States was shocked by the Soviets' achievement, and they redoubled their efforts, culminating in the Apollo 11 mission's Moon landing. The Japanese and German space exploration program weren't active until 1969, and they weren't major competitors to the American and Soviet programs.

4. C: The Organic Theory argues that nation-states need to consolidate political power and acquire new geographic territory in order to sustain themselves. Under this conception, the nation-state operates like a living organism, and new territories provide the resources it needs to survive. Thus, Choice *C* is the correct answer. The Rimland Theory emphasizes the importance of naval power and coastal land, and the World Island is part of the Heartland Theory. In the Cold War era, American foreign policymakers created the domino theory to justify military intervention for limiting the spread of communism.

5. B: Choice *B* is the correct answer. Political maps are the most subjective, because territorial boundaries are frequently contested or otherwise in dispute. For example, 19th century political maps differed on the boundaries between the competing European colonies, as well as what constituted Native American territory. In the present day, there's dispute over who owns Crimea. In contrast, climate, population density, and topographic maps are all based on objective data.

English Expression

Grammatical Relationships

Adjectives and Adverbs

Adjectives are descriptive words that modify nouns or pronouns. They may occur before or after the nouns or pronouns they modify in sentences. For example, in "This is a big house," *big* is an adjective modifying or describing the noun *house*. In "This house is big," the adjective is at the end of the sentence rather than preceding the noun it modifies.

A rule of punctuation that applies to adjectives is to separate a series of adjectives with commas. For example, "Their home was a large, rambling, old, white, two-story house." A comma should never separate the last adjective from the noun, though.

Whereas adjectives modify and describe nouns or pronouns, **adverbs** modify and describe adjectives, verbs, or other adverbs. Adverbs can be thought of as answers to questions in that they describe when, where, how, how often, how much, or to what extent.

Many (but not all) adjectives can be converted to adverbs by adding *–ly*. For example, in "She is a quick learner," *quick* is an adjective modifying *learner*. In "She learns quickly," *quickly* is an adverb modifying *learns*. One exception is *fast*. *Fast* is an adjective in "She is a fast learner." However, *–ly* is never added to the word *fast*; it retains the same form as an adverb in "She learns fast."

Noun-Noun Agreement

When multiple nouns are included in the same sentence and are related to one another in that sentence, they need to agree in number. This means that if one noun is singular, all other related nouns in the sentence must be singular as well. Similarly, if one noun is plural, the rest should follow in form and be plural as well. Consider the following sentence with an error in noun-noun agreement:

> Mary and Sharon both have jobs as a teacher.

Because the noun *jobs* is plural, the noun *teachers*, which is also plural, must be used in place of *teacher*, which is singular.

> Mary and Sharon both have jobs as teachers.

Pronoun-Antecedent Agreement

Pronouns within a sentence must refer specifically to one noun, known as the **antecedent.** Sometimes, if there are multiple nouns within a sentence, it may be difficult to ascertain which noun belongs to the pronoun. It's important that the pronouns always clearly reference the nouns in the sentence so as not to confuse the reader. Here's an example of an unclear pronoun reference:

> After Catherine cut Libby's hair, David bought her some lunch.

The pronoun in the examples above is *her*. The pronoun could either be referring to *Catherine* or *Libby*. Here are some ways to write the above sentence with a clear pronoun reference:

> After Catherine cut Libby's hair, David bought Libby some lunch.

> David bought Libby some lunch after Catherine cut Libby's hair.

108

But many times, the pronoun will clearly refer to its antecedent, like the following:

> After David cut Catherine's hair, he bought her some lunch.

Pronoun Case

There are three **pronoun cases**: subjective case, objective case, and possessive case. Pronouns as subjects are pronouns that replace the subject of the sentence, such as *I, you, he, she, it, we, they* and *who*. Pronouns as objects replace the object of the sentence, such as *me, you, him, her, it, us, them,* and *whom*. Pronouns that show possession are *mine, yours, hers, its, ours, theirs,* and *whose*. The following are examples of different pronoun cases:

- Subject pronoun: *She* ate the cake for her birthday. *I* saw the movie.
- Object pronoun: You gave *me* the card last weekend. She gave the picture to *him*.
- Possessive pronoun: That bracelet you found yesterday is *mine*. *His* name was Casey.

Intensive Pronoun Errors

An **intensive pronoun** ends in "self" or "selves" and adds emphasis to the sentence's subject or antecedent. Like reflexive pronouns, intensive pronouns include the singular pronouns *myself, yourself, himself, herself,* and *itself,* and the plural pronouns *ourselves, yourselves,* and *themselves*. However, intensive and reflexive pronouns differ in that removing a reflexive pronoun will cause the sentence to no longer make sense, whereas intensive pronouns can be removed because they only add emphasis; they are not mandatory. An example of a sentence with an intensive pronoun is the following:

> We want to hear the author herself read the story.

The intensive pronoun *herself* adds emphasis that the speakers want to specifically hear the author read the story, rather than anyone else.

The most common error in the use of intensive pronouns is choosing the wrong pronoun; for example, using the plural pronoun when the singular one is needed, or using a singular pronoun when a plural one is needed. Using the same example from above, an error in agreement occurs in the following sentence:

> We want to hear the author themselves read the story.

Author is singular and *themselves* is plural, so there is an error in number agreement.

Pronoun Number and Person Errors

Pronouns must agree in number and person. However, it is common, unfortunately, for writers to shift between persons or numbers when using pronouns. For example, a sentence might start with third person pronouns (*he, she, it, they,* etc.), but then switch to second person. Or, a sentence might start in second person and switch to first or third person. The following sentence contains a pronoun shift in person:

> If you drink more water, most people see improvements in their skin and body composition.

This example begins with second person (using the pronoun *you*), but switches to third person (*their*). Consistency in person is needed. Therefore, the sentence should be one of the following two options:

> If you drink more water, you will likely see improvements in your skin and body composition.

> If they drink more water, most people see improvements in their skin and body composition.

Inappropriate pronoun shifts also occur when writers switch from using singular pronouns to plural ones, or vice versa. Sometimes, sentences will have errors in pronoun number and person.

Everyone should keep a journal about their life because you will want to pass the stories of your life along.

These sentences are usually easier to spot because the errors are two-fold and more apparent.

Vague Pronouns

A **pronoun** replaces a noun in a sentence, which is called the **antecedent.** It should be clear which noun the pronoun is replacing. Vague pronouns are unclear, cause ambiguity and confusion, may refer to more than one antecedent, and disturb the meaning of the sentence. Consider the following example:

Tommy gave Greg a gift card, and he blushed.

In the above sentence, *he* is the pronoun, but it isn't readily apparent who *he* refers to. Did Tommy blush or did Greg blush? It's plausible that either person blushed. Instead, the name of the person, the antecedent, needs to be used instead:

Tommy gave Greg a gift card, and Greg blushed.

The pronoun *it* is often the culprit in cases of a vague pronoun. Consider the following:

Grandma dropped the glass frame on her hand and it broke.

Did the frame break or did grandma's hand break? The pronoun *it* should be replaced with the proper antecedent to clarify the intended meaning.

Other times, there is no clear antecedent, which also causes ambiguity and confusion:

Mom called the store, but they didn't answer the phone.

Why is *they?* The store cannot answer the phone. A person answers a phone. Therefore, this sentence is incorrect. Instead, it should be amended in some way, such as the following:

Mom called the store, but no employees answered the phone.

Subject-Verb Agreement

Lack of subject-verb agreement is a very common grammatical error. One of the most common instances is when people use a series of nouns as a compound subject with a singular instead of a plural verb. Here is an example:

Identifying the best books, locating the sellers with the lowest prices, and paying for them *is* difficult.

The sentence should say "*are* difficult." Additionally, when a sentence subject is compound, the verb is plural:

He and his cousins *were* at the reunion.

However, if the conjunction connecting two or more singular nouns or pronouns is "or" or "nor," the verb must be singular to agree:

> That pen or another one like it is in the desk drawer.

If a compound subject includes both a singular noun and a plural one, and they are connected by "or" or "nor," the verb must agree with the subject closest to the verb: "Sally or her sisters go jogging daily"; but "Her sisters or Sally goes jogging daily."

Singular subjects need singular verbs and plural subjects need plural verbs. A common source of agreement errors is not identifying the sentence subject correctly. For example, people often write sentences incorrectly like, "The group of students *were* complaining about the test." The subject is not the plural "students" but the singular "group." Therefore, the correct sentence should read, "The group of students *was* complaining about the test." The converse also applies, for example, in this incorrect sentence: "The facts in that complicated court case *is* open to question." The subject of the sentence is not the singular "case" but the plural "facts." Hence the sentence would correctly be written: "The facts in that complicated court case *are* open to question." New writers should not be misled by the distance between the subject and verb, especially when another noun with a different number intervenes as in these examples. The verb must agree with the subject, not the noun closest to it.

Inappropriate Shifts in Verb Tense

A **verb** is a word or phrase that expresses action, feeling, or state of being. Verbs explain what their subject is *doing*. Three different types of verbs used in a sentence are action verbs, linking verbs, and helping verbs.

Action verbs show a physical or mental action. Some examples of action verbs are *play, type, jump, write, examine, study, invent, develop,* and *taste.* The following example uses an action verb:

> Kat *imagines* that she is a mermaid in the ocean.

The verb *imagines* explains what Kat is doing: she is imagining being a mermaid.

Linking verbs connect the subject to the predicate without expressing an action. The following sentence shows an example of a linking verb:

> The mango *tastes* sweet.

The verb *tastes* is a linking verb. The mango doesn't *do* the tasting, but the word *taste* links the mango to its predicate, sweet. Most linking verbs can also be used as action verbs, such as *smell, taste, look, seem, grow,* and *sound.* Saying something *is* something else is also an example of a linking verb. For example, if we were to say, "Peaches is a dog," the verb *is* would be a linking verb in this sentence, since it links the subject to its predicate.

Helping verbs are verbs that help the main verb in a sentence. Examples of helping verbs are *be, am, is, was, have, has, do, did, can, could, may, might, should,* and *must,* among others. The following are examples of helping verbs:

>Jessica *is* planning a trip to Hawaii.

>Brenda *does* not like camping.

>Xavier *should* go to the dance tonight.

Notice that after each of these helping verbs is the main verb of the sentence: *planning, like,* and *go.* Helping verbs usually show an aspect of time.

Verb tense helps indicate when an action or a state existed occurred or existed.

Simple present tense is used to indicate that the action or state of being is currently happening or happens regularly:

>He *plays* guitar.

Present continuous tense is used to indicate that the action or state of being is in progress. It is formed by the proper to be + verb + *-ing.*

>Unfortunately, I can't go to the park right now. I *am fixing* my bicycle.

Past tense is used to indicate that the action or state of being occurred previously. It should be noted, however, that in conversational English, speakers frequently use a mix of present and past tense, or simply present tense when describing events in the past. With that said, it is important for writers (and speakers in formal situations) to be consistent and grammatically correct in their verb tenses to avoid confusing readers. Consider the following passage:

>I scored a goal in our soccer game last Saturday. At the start of the first half, Billy kicked me the ball. I run toward it and strike it directly toward the goal. It goes in and we won the game!

The passage above inappropriately switches from past tense—*scored, kicked*—to present tense—*run, strike, goes*—and then back to past tense—*won.* Instead, past tense should be carried throughout the passage:

>I *scored* a goal in our soccer game last Saturday. At the start of the first half, Billy *kicked* me the ball. I *ran* toward it and strike it directly toward the goal. It *went* in and we *won* the game!

Structural Relationships

The Placement of Phrases and Clauses Within a Sentence
Clauses contain a subject and a predicate, while **phrases** only contain a noun with no verb or a verb with no noun, and they do not have a predicate. Clauses can be independent or dependent. **Independent clauses** can stand on their own as simple sentences. For example:

>She collects stamps.

112

Dependent clauses need independent clauses to form a complete sentence; they cannot stand alone. For example:

> Although she collects stamps ...

Phrases can take on many forms including prepositional phrases, gerund phrases, noun phrases, infinitive phrases, verb phrases, etc. Regardless of the type, phrases cannot stand alone as complete sentence.

Phrases and clauses must be appropriately placed in a sentence such that it is clear to readers what they are modifying.

Consider the following misplaced prepositional phrase:

> At the bottom of the pile, Lila found her scarf.

In the above sentence, the phrase *at the bottom of the pile* is intended to modify the noun phrase *the scarf* by providing details about where the scarf was found. However, as written, the prepositional phrase is next to the subject, Lila, so it is modifying Lila. This is incorrect because presumably Lila herself wasn't at the bottom of a pile, her scarf was.

Misplaced and Dangling Modifiers

Modifiers are optional elements that can clarify or add details about a phrase or another element of a sentence. They are a dependent phrase and removing them usually does not change the grammatical correctness of the sentence; however, the meaning will be changed because, as their name implies, modifiers modify another element in the sentence. Consider the following:

> Nico loves sardines.

> Nico, who is three years old, loves sardines.

The first simple sentence is grammatically correct; however, we learn a lot more from the second sentence, which contains the modifier *who is three years old*. Sardines tend to be a food that young children don't like, so adding the modifier helps readers see why Nico loving sardines is noteworthy.

Beginning writers sometimes place modifiers incorrectly. Then, instead of enhancing comprehension and providing helpful description for the reader, the modifier causes more confusion. A **misplaced modifier** is located incorrectly in relation to the phrase or word it modifies. Consider the following sentence:

> Because it is salty, Nico loves fish.

The modifier in this sentence is "because they are salty," and the noun it is intended to modify is "fish." However, due to the erroneous placement of the modifier next to the subject, Nico, the sentence is actually saying that Nico is salty.

> Nico loves fish because it is salty.

The modifier is now adjacent to the appropriate noun, clarifying which of the two elements is salty.

Dangling modifiers are so named because they modify a phrase or word that is not clearly found in the sentence, making them rather unattached. They are not intended to modify the word or phrase they are placed next to. Consider the following:

> Walking home from school, the sky opened and Bruce got drenched.

The modifier here, "walking home from school," should modify who was walking (Bruce). Instead, the noun immediately after the modifier is "the sky"—but the sky was not walking home from school. Although not always the case, dangling modifiers are often found at the beginning of a sentence.

Coordinating and Subordinating Conjunctions

Conjunctions connect or coordinate words, phrases, clauses, or sentences together, typically as a way to demonstrate a relationship.

> Tony has a cat *and* a rabbit.

> Tony likes animals, *but* he is afraid of snakes.

Coordinating conjunctions join words or phrases that have equal rank or emphasis. There are seven coordinating conjunctions, all short words, that can be remembered by the mnemonic FANBOYS: *for, and, nor, but, or, yet, so*. They can join two words that are of the same part of speech (two verbs, two adjectives, two adverbs, or two nouns). They can also connect two phrases or two independent clauses.

Subordinating conjunctions help transition and connect two elements in the sentence, but in a way that diminishes the importance of the one it introduces, known as the dependent, or subordinate, clause. They include words like *because, since, unless, before, after, whereas, if*, and *while*.

Fragments and Run-Ons

Every sentence must have a subject and a verb to be complete. As mentioned, **sentence fragments** are caused by absent subjects, absent verbs, or dangling/uncompleted dependent clauses. An example of a fragment is "Raining all night long," because there is no subject present. "It was raining all night long" is one correction. Another example of a sentence fragment is the second part in "Many scientists think in unusual ways. Einstein, for instance." The second phrase is a fragment because it has no verb. One correction is "Many scientists, like Einstein, think in unusual ways." Finally, look for "cliffhanger" words like *if, when, because,* or *although* that introduce dependent clauses, which cannot stand alone without an independent clause. For example, to correct the sentence fragment "If you get home early," add an independent clause: "If you get home early, we can go dancing."

A **run-on sentence** combines two or more complete sentences without punctuating them correctly or separating them. For example, a run-on sentence caused by a lack of punctuation is the following:

> There are too many people here for the number of available seats however there is nobody around who has access to the room with additional chairs.

One correction is, "There is a malfunction in the computer system; however, there is nobody available right now who knows how to troubleshoot it." Another is, "There is a malfunction in the computer system. However, there is nobody available right now who knows how to troubleshoot it."

114

An example of a **comma splice** of two sentences is the following:

> Xavier decided to buy the chicken, he had enough money.

Replacing the comma with a period or a semicolon corrects this. Commas that try and separate two independent clauses without a contraction are considered comma splices.

Correlative Conjunctions

Correlative conjunctions are pairs of conjunctions that must both be used in the sentence, though in different spots, to make the sentence grammatically sound. They help relate one aspect of the sentence to another. Examples of correlative conjunctions pairs are *neither/nor, both/and, not/but, either/or, as/as, such/that* and *rather/than*. They tend to be more like coordinating conjunctions rather than subordinating conjunctions in that they typically connect two words or phrases of equal weight in the sentence.

Parallel Structure

As mentioned, **parallel structure** in a sentence matches the forms of sentence components. Any sentence containing more than one description or phrase should keep them consistent in wording and form. Readers can easily follow writers' ideas when they are written in parallel structure, making it an important element of correct sentence construction. For example, this sentence lacks parallelism: "Our coach is a skilled manager, a clever strategist, and works hard." The first two phrases are parallel, but the third is not. Correction: "Our coach is a skilled manager, a clever strategist, and a hard worker." Now all three phrases match in form. Here is another example:

> Fred intercepted the ball, escaped tacklers, and a touchdown was scored.

This is also non-parallel. Here is the sentence corrected:

> Fred intercepted the ball, escaped tacklers, and scored a touchdown.

Word Choice

Idiomatic Expressions

Idiomatic expressions are phrases or groups of words that have an established meaning when used together that is unrelated to the literal meanings of the individual words. For example, consider the following sentence that includes a common idiomatic phrase:

> I know Phil is coming to visit this weekend because I heard it straight from the horse's mouth.

The speaker of this sentence did not consult a horse nor hear anything uttered from a horse in relation to Phil's visit. Instead, "straight from the horse's mouth" is an idiom that means the information came directly from an original or reliable source. As in the sentence above, it often means whatever said should be taken as truth because it was spoken by the person to which it pertains (in this case, Phil). The phrase is derived from the fact that sellers of horses at auctions would sometimes try to lie about the age of the horse. However, the size and shape of a horse's teeth can provide a fairly accurate estimate of the horse's true age. Therefore, the truth regarding the horse's age essentially comes straight from their mouth. The idiomatic expression came to mean getting the truth in any situation.

Finding errors in idiomatic expressions can be difficult because it requires familiarity with the idiom. Because there are more than one thousand idioms in the English language, memorizing all of them is impractical. However, it is helpful to review the most common ones. There are many webpages dedicated to listing and explaining frequently used idioms.

Errors in the idiomatic expressions are typically one of two types. The idiomatic expression may be stated improperly, or it may be used in an incorrect context. In the first type of issue, the prepositions used are often incorrect. For example, it might say "straight in the horse's mouth" or "straight with the horse's mouth." In the second error type, the idiomatic expression is used improperly because the meaning it carries does not make sense in the context in which it appears. Consider the following:

> He was looking straight from the horse's mouth when he complained about the phone his father bought him.

Here, the writer has confused the idiom "straight from the horse's mouth" with "looking a gift horse in the mouth," which means to find fault in a gift or favor.

Either type of error can be difficult to detect and correct without prior knowledge of the idiomatic phrase. Practicing usage of idioms and studying their origins can help you remember their meanings and precise wordings, which will then help you identify and correct errors in their usage.

Frequently Confused Words

The English language can be confusing and it is common for students to make mistakes in word choice, meaning, or spelling. **Homophones** are words that sound the same in speech, but have different spellings and meanings. For example, *to, too,* and *two* all sound alike, but have three different spellings and meanings. Homophones with different spellings are also called **heterographs**. **Homographs** are words that are spelled identically, but have different meanings. If they also have different pronunciations, they are heteronyms. For instance, *tear* pronounced one way means a drop of liquid formed by the eye; pronounced another way, it means to rip. Homophones that are also homographs are **homonyms**. For example, *bark* can mean the outside of a tree or a dog's vocalization; both meanings have the same spelling. *Stalk* can mean a plant stem or to pursue and/or harass somebody; these are spelled and pronounced the same. *Rose* can mean a flower or the past tense of *rise*. Many non-linguists confuse things by using "homonym" to mean sets of words that are homophones but not homographs, and also those that are homographs but not homophones.

The word *row* can mean to use oars to propel a boat; a linear arrangement of objects or print; or an argument. It is pronounced the same with the first two meanings, but differently with the third. Because it is spelled identically regardless, all three meanings are homographs. However, the two meanings pronounced the same are homophones, whereas the one with the different pronunciation is a **heteronym**. By contrast, the word *read* means to peruse language, whereas the word *reed* refers to a marsh plant. Because these are pronounced the same way, they are homophones; because they are spelled differently, they are heterographs. Homonyms are both homophones and **homographs**— pronounced and spelled identically, but with different meanings. One distinction between homonyms is of those with separate, unrelated etymologies, called "true" homonyms (e.g., *skate* meaning a fish or *skate* meaning to glide over ice/water). Those with common origins are called **polysemes** or **polysemous homonyms** (e.g., the *mouth* of an animal/human or of a river).

There are some words that do not abide by the typical rules when turning them into their plural form, and it's common for students to struggle forming and using these irregular plurals. While many words in English can become plural by adding –s or –es to the end, there are some words that have irregular plural forms. One type includes words that are spelled the same whether they are singular or plural, such as

116

deer, fish, salmon, trout, sheep, moose, offspring, species, aircraft, etc. The spelling rule for making these words plural is simple: they do not change. Other irregular English plurals change form based on vowel shifts, linguistic mutations, or grammatical and spelling conventions from their languages of origin, like Latin or German. Some examples include *tooth* and *teeth*, *man* and *men*, *child* and *children*, and *person* and *people*.

Wrong Word Usage

One of the most common reasons that a writer chooses the wrong word for a given application is if the word has multiple meanings and spellings. Words that have different meanings and spellings but sound the same are called **homophones**. These can be confusing for English Language Learners (ELLs) and beginning students, but even native English-speaking adults can find them problematic unless informed by context. Whereas listeners must rely entirely on context to differentiate spoken homophone meanings, readers with good spelling knowledge have a distinct advantage since homophones are spelled differently. For instance, *their* means belonging to them; *there* indicates location; and *they're* is a contraction of *they are*; despite different meanings, they all sound the same. *Lacks* can be a plural noun or a present-tense, third-person singular verb; either way it refers to absence—*deficiencies* as a plural noun, and *is deficient in* as a verb. But *lax* is an adjective that means loose, slack, relaxed, uncontrolled, or negligent. These two spellings, derivations, and meanings are completely different. With speech, listeners cannot know spelling and must use context; but with print, readers with spelling knowledge can differentiate them with or without context.

One other issue that students may have is misspelling certain difficult words. Spelling errors not only negatively affect the polished feel of an essay, but they can result in confusion, particularly if the spelling mistake results in the formation of a different, unintended word. One source of spelling errors is not knowing whether to drop the final letter *e* from a word when its form is changed; some words retain the final *e* when another syllable is added while others lose it. For example, *true* becomes *truly*; *argue* becomes *arguing*; *come* becomes *coming*; *write* becomes *writing*; and *judge* becomes *judging*. In these examples, the final *e* is dropped before adding the ending. But *severe* becomes *severely*; *complete* becomes *completely*; *sincere* becomes *sincerely*; *argue* becomes *argued*; and *care* becomes *careful*. In these instances, the final *e* is retained before adding the ending. Note that some words, like argue in these examples, drops the final e when the –ing ending is added to indicate the participial form, but the regular past tense form keeps the e and adds a –d to make it argued.

Other commonly misspelled English words are those containing the vowel combinations *ei* and *ie*. Many people confuse these two. Some examples of words with the *ei* combination include:

> *ceiling, conceive, leisure, receive, weird, their, either, foreign, sovereign, neither, neighbors, seize, forfeit, counterfeit, height, weight, protein,* and *freight*

Words with *ie* include:

> *piece, believe, chief, field, friend, grief, relief, mischief, siege, niece, priest, fierce, pierce, achieve, retrieve, hygiene, science,* and *diesel*

A rule that also functions as a mnemonic device is "I before E except after C, or when sounded like A as in 'neighbor' or 'weigh'." However, it is obvious from the list above that many exceptions exist.

People often misspell certain words by confusing whether they have the vowel a, e, or i. For example, in the following correctly spelled words, the vowel in boldface is the one people typically get wrong by substituting one of the others for it:

cem**e**tery, quant**i**ties, ben**e**fit, priv**i**lege, unpleas**a**nt, sep**a**rate, independ**e**nt, excell**e**nt, cat**e**gories, indispens**a**ble, and irrelev**a**nt

Some words with final syllables that sound the same when spoken but are spelled differently include *unpleasant, independent, excellent,* and *irrelevant.* Another source of misspelling is whether or not to double consonants when adding suffixes. For example, double the last consonant before –ed and –ing endings in controlled, beginning, forgetting, admitted, occurred, referred, and hopping; but do not double before the suffix in *shining, poured, sweating, loving, hating, smiling,* and *hoping.*

One final example of common misspellings involves either the failure to include silent letters or the converse of adding extraneous letters. If a letter is not pronounced in speech, it is easy to leave it out in writing. For example, some people omit the silent *u* in *gu̲arantee,* overlook the first *r* in *su̲rprise,* leave out the *z* in *reali̲ze,* fail to double the *m* in *recom̲mend,* leave out the middle *i* from *aspi̲rin,* and exclude the *p* from *temp̲erature.* The converse error, adding extra letters, is common in words like *until* by adding a second *l* at the end; or by inserting a superfluous syllabic *a* or *e* in the middle of *athletic,* reproducing a common mispronunciation.

Redundancy

Redundancy, in terms of word choice, refers to repeating the same words or phrases or using different words to restate the same thing. Writers should strive to be concise in stating their points and backing them up with adequate and relevant examples. Wordiness detracts from the overall takeaways from an essay and redundancy can bore readers. State the point and move forward. It only makes sense to reword it and reiterate the point if it needs explicit emphasis.

An example of wordiness can be seen in the following sentence:

In spite of the fact that I stayed home from school today, I still feel sick.

In spite of the fact is wordy. The five-word phrase can be replaced by the single word *although:*

Although I stayed home from school today, I still feel sick.

The following sentence demonstrates redundancy:

We often shop there most days .

Instead, one of the following two options is preferable:

We often shop there.

We shop there most days.

Conventions of Standard English Spelling and Punctuation

Capitalization

The first word of any document, and of each new sentence, is capitalized. Proper nouns, like names and adjectives derived from proper nouns, should also be capitalized. Here are some examples:

- Grand Canyon
- Pacific Palisades
- Golden Gate Bridge
- Freudian slip
- Shakespearian, Spenserian, or Petrarchan sonnet
- Irish song

Some exceptions are adjectives, originally derived from proper nouns, which through time and usage are no longer capitalized, like *quixotic, herculean*, or *draconian*. Capitals draw attention to specific instances of people, places, and things. Some categories that should be capitalized include the following:

- brand names
- companies
- months
- governmental divisions or agencies
- historical eras
- major historical events
- holidays
- institutions
- famous buildings
- ships and other manmade constructions
- natural and manmade landmarks
- territories
- nicknames
- organizations
- planets
- nationalities
- tribes
- religions
- names of religious deities
- roads
- special occasions, like the Cannes Film Festival or the Olympic Games

Exceptions

Related to American government, capitalize the noun *Congress* but not the related adjective *congressional*. Capitalize the noun *US Constitution*, but not the related adjective *constitutional*. Many experts advise leaving the adjectives *federal* and *state* in lowercase, as in *federal regulations* or *state water board*, and only capitalizing these when they are parts of official titles or names, like *Federal Communications Commission* or *State Water Resources Control Board*. While the names of the other planets in the solar system are capitalized as names, *Earth* is more often capitalized only when being described specifically as a planet, like *Earth's orbit*, but lowercase otherwise since it is used not only as a proper noun but also to mean *land, ground, soil*, etc.

119

Names of animal species or breeds are not capitalized unless they include a proper noun. Then, only the proper noun is capitalized. Generally, *antelope*, *black bear*, and *yellow-bellied sapsucker* are not capitalized. However, *Bengal tiger*, *German shepherd*, *Australian shepherd*, *French poodle*, and *Russian blue cat* are capitalized.

Stars, moons, and suns are not capitalized, but planets specific names and the Sun and the Moon, when referring to the Earth's specific sun and moon, are capitalized as proper nouns. Medical conditions like tuberculosis or diabetes are lowercase; again, exceptions are proper nouns, like Epstein-Barr syndrome, Alzheimer's disease, and Down syndrome. Seasons and related terms like winter solstice or autumnal equinox are lowercase. Plants, including fruits and vegetables, like poinsettia, celery, or avocados, are not capitalized unless they include proper names, like Douglas fir, Jerusalem artichoke, Damson plums, or Golden Delicious apples.

Titles and Names

When official titles precede names, they should be capitalized, except when there is a comma between the title and name. But if a title follows or replaces a name, it should not be capitalized. For example, "the president" without a name is not capitalized, as in "The president addressed Congress." But with a name it is capitalized, like "President Biden addressed Congress." Or, "Chair of the Board Janet Yellen was appointed by President Obama." One exception is that some publishers and writers nevertheless capitalize President, Queen, Pope, etc., when these are not accompanied by names to show respect for these high offices. However, many writers in America object to this practice for violating democratic principles of equality. Occupations before full names are not capitalized, like owner Mark Cuban, director Martin Scorsese, or coach Roger McDowell.

Some universal rules for capitalization in composition titles include capitalizing the following:

- The first and last words of the title
- Forms of the verb *to be* and all other verbs
- Pronouns
- The word *not*

Universal rules for NOT capitalizing include the articles *the, a,* or *an;* the conjunctions *and, or,* or *nor,* and the preposition *to,* or *to* as part of the infinitive form of a verb. The exception to all of these is UNLESS any of them is the first or last word in the title, in which case they are capitalized. Other words are subject to differences of opinion and differences among various stylebooks or methods. These include *as, but, if,* and *or,* which some capitalize and others do not. Some authorities say no preposition should ever be capitalized; some say prepositions five or more letters long should be capitalized. The *Associated Press Stylebook* advises capitalizing prepositions longer than three letters (like *about, across,* or *with*).

Punctuation

Commas

Commas separate words or phrases in a series of three or more. The Oxford comma is the last comma in a series. Many people omit this last comma, but many times it causes confusion. Here is an example:

I love my sisters, the Queen of England and Madonna.

This example without the comma implies that the "Queen of England and Madonna" are the speaker's sisters. However, if the speaker was trying to say that they love their sisters, the Queen of England, as well as Madonna, there should be a comma after "Queen of England" to signify this.

Commas also separate two coordinate adjectives ("big, heavy dog") but not cumulative ones, which should be arranged in a particular order for them to make sense ("beautiful ancient ruins").

A comma ends the first of two independent clauses connected by conjunctions. Here is an example:

I ate a bowl of tomato soup, and I was hungry very shortly after.

Here are some brief rules for commas:

- Commas follow introductory words like however, furthermore, well, why, and actually, among others.
- Commas go between city and state: Houston, Texas.
- If using a comma between a surname and Jr. or Sr. or a degree like M.D., also follow the whole name with a comma: "Martin Luther King, Jr., wrote that."
- A comma follows a dependent clause beginning a sentence: "Although she was very small, ..."
- Nonessential modifying words/phrases/clauses are enclosed by commas: "Wendy, who is Peter's sister, closed the window."
- Commas introduce or interrupt direct quotations: "She said, 'I hate him.' 'Why,' I asked, 'do you hate him?'"

Semicolons

Semicolons are used to connect two independent clauses but should never be used in the place of a comma. They can replace periods between two closely connected sentences: "Call back tomorrow; it can wait until then." When writing items in a series and one or more of them contains internal commas, separate them with semicolons, like the following:

People came from Springfield, Illinois; Alamo, Tennessee; Moscow, Idaho; and other locations.

Apostrophes

One use of the **apostrophe** (') is followed by an *s* to indicate possession, like *Mrs. White's home* or *our neighbor's dog*. When using the *'s* after names or nouns that also end in the letter *s*, no single rule applies: some experts advise adding both the apostrophe and the *s*, like "the Jones's house," while others prefer using only the apostrophe and omitting the additional *s*, like "the Jones' house." The wisest expert advice is to pick one formula or the other and then apply it consistently. One way of using apostrophes this way is by using *'s* after common nouns ending with *s* but using just an apostrophe after proper nouns or names ending with *s*. One common error is to place the apostrophe before a name's final *s* instead of after it: "Ms. Hasting's book" is incorrect if the name is Ms. Hastings.

Plural nouns should not include apostrophes (e.g., "apostrophe's"). Exceptions are to clarify atypical plurals, like verbs used as nouns: "These are the do's and don'ts." Irregular plurals that do not end in *s* always take apostrophe-*s*, not *s*-apostrophe—a common error, as in "childrens' toys," which should be "children's toys." Compound nouns like mother-in-law, when they are singular and possessive, are followed by apostrophe-*s*, like "your mother-in-law's coat." When a compound noun is plural and possessive, the plural is formed before the apostrophe-*s*, like "your sisters-in-laws' coats." When two people named possess the same thing, use apostrophe-*s* after the second name only, like "Dennis and Pam's house."

Ellipses

Ellipses (…) signal omitted text when quoting. Some writers also use them to show a thought trailing off, but this should not be overused outside of dialogue. An example of an ellipsis would be if someone is quoting a phrase out of a professional source but wants to omit part of the phrase that isn't needed: "Dr. Skim's analysis of pollen inside the body is clearly a myth … that speaks to the environmental guilt of our society."

Hyphens

Here are some rules concerning **hyphens (-)**:

- Compound adjectives like state-of-the-art or off-campus are hyphenated.
- Original compound verbs and nouns are often hyphenated, like "throne-sat," "video-gamed," "no-meater."
- Adjectives ending in *–ly* are often hyphenated, like "family-owned" or "friendly-looking."
- "Five years old" is not hyphenated, but singular ages like "five-year-old" are.
- Hyphens can clarify. For example, in "stolen vehicle report," "stolen-vehicle report" clarifies that "stolen" modifies "vehicle," not "report."
- Compound numbers twenty-one through ninety-nine are spelled with hyphens.
- Prefixes before proper nouns/adjectives are hyphenated, like "mid-September" and "trans-Pacific."

Parentheses

Parentheses ( ) enclose information such as an aside or more clarifying information: "She ultimately replied (after deliberating for an hour) that she was undecided." They are also used to insert short, in-text definitions or acronyms: "His FBS (fasting blood sugar) was higher than normal." When parenthetical information ends the sentence, the period follows the parentheses: "We received new funds ($25,000)." Only put periods within parentheses if the whole sentence is inside them: "Look at this. (You'll be astonished.)" However, this can also be acceptable as a clause: "Look at this (you'll be astonished)." Although parentheses appear to be part of the sentence subject, they are not, and do not change subject-verb agreement: "Will (and his dog) was there."

Quotation Marks

Quotation marks (" ") are typically used when someone is quoting a direct word or phrase someone else writes or says. Additionally, quotation marks should be used for the titles of poems, short stories, songs, articles, chapters, and other shorter works. When quotations include punctuation, periods and commas should *always* be placed inside of the quotation marks.

When a quotation contains another quotation inside of it, the outer quotation should be enclosed in double quotation marks and the inner quotation should be enclosed in single quotation marks. For example: "Timmy was begging, 'Don't go! Don't leave!'" When using both double and single quotation marks, writers will find that many word-processing programs may automatically insert enough space between the single and double quotation marks to be visible for clearer reading. But if this is not the case, the writer should write/type them with enough space between to keep them from looking like three single quotation marks. Additionally, non-standard usages, terms used in an unusual fashion, and technical terms are often clarified by quotation marks. Here are some examples:

My "friend," Dr. Sims, has been micromanaging me again.

This way of extracting oil has been dubbed "fracking."

Contractions are formed by joining two words together, omitting one or more letters from one of the component words, and replacing the omitted letter(s) with an apostrophe. An obvious yet often forgotten rule for spelling contractions is to place the apostrophe where the letters were omitted. For example, didn't is a contraction of did not; therefore, the apostrophe replaces the "o" that is omitted from the "not." Another common error is confusing contractions with possessives because both include apostrophes (e.g., spelling the possessive *its* as "it's," which is a contraction of "it is"; spelling the possessive *their* as "they're," a contraction of "they are"; spelling the possessive *whose* as "who's," a contraction of "who is"; or spelling the possessive *your* as "you're," a contraction of "you are").

Practice Quiz

Type A: Sentence Selection
Directions: For each item in this section, select the one sentence that best meets the requirements of standard written English.

1. Select the sentence that best meets the requirements of standard written English.
    a. Given the high amount of turnover, it's vital to take care for employees.
    b. There was a heated argue between the veteran lawmaker and the police captain.
    c. Scientists predict over the ten years that annual rainfall in this region will dramatically decline.
    d. Disappointed, the star basketball player looked up and saw the score on the screen.

Type B: Sentence Correction
Directions: For each item in this section, select the one underlined word or phrase that needs to be changed to make the sentence correct, or indicate that none of the underlined parts are in error.

2. Lawmakers <u>recently approved</u> a spending plan that would include, <u>between other things</u>, funds for a new bridge that <u>would connect the</u> island to the mainland.
    a. NO ERROR
    b. recently approved
    c. between other things
    d. would connect the

Type C: Sentence Correction II
Directions: For the items in this section, select the one word or phrase that needs to be used in place of the underlined text to make the sentence correct, or indicate that the underlined text is not in error.

3. Brazil is a large, beautiful country in <u>south</u> America, and its inhabitants mainly speak Brazilian Portuguese.
    a. NO ERROR
    b. South
    c. southernly
    d. southwards

Type D: Paragraph Organization

Directions: For each item in this section, select the ordering of sentences that results in the clearest, most well-organized paragraph.

4.

(1) On January 28, 1986, millions of people watched in horror as the space shuttle *Challenger* disintegrated on live television.

(2) The *Challenger* explosion was caused by a faulty O-ring on the spacecraft that didn't seal properly due to the cold weather on launch day.

(3) However, NASA insisted the launch proceed as planned.

(4) Several people had raised concerns about the design of the O-rings before the disaster.

    a.   3, 4, 2, 1

    b.   1, 2, 4, 3

    c.   1, 3, 2, 4

    d.   3, 4, 1, 2

Type E: Paragraph Revision

Directions: This section consists of several sentences that compose a paragraph. Read the paragraph carefully, and then answer the question that follows it.

5. Electric vehicles are the road to the future, and I am excited to see the world becoming less dependent on fossil fuels. Studies have shown that the world is trending toward using clean, renewable energy. Some of the latest advancements have made batteries last longer, and vehicles are able to travel greater distances than before. We must make charging stations readily available and increase funding for research into developing more advanced and efficient electric vehicles. We are already seeing definitive improvements, and the future is looking brighter than ever.

Which of the following statements would the author of this paragraph most likely agree with?

    a.   Renewable energy will be unable to meet the needs of future drivers.

    b.   Fossil fuel technology is rapidly growing alongside electric vehicles.

    c.   Enough research has been done regarding improvements to electric vehicles and technology.

    d.   One day, people will not need to rely on fossil fuels to power their vehicles.

See next page for answer explanations.

Answer Explanations

1. D: Choice *A* uses the incorrect phrase *care for* instead of *care of.* Choice *B* uses the verb *argue* instead of the noun *argument.* Choice *C* is missing the word *next* before *ten years.*

2. C: Choice *C* needs to use *among* instead of *between* in this instance. *Between* is used to refer to two or more distinct objects.

3. B: Choice *B* capitalizes the *South* in South America because *South America* is a proper noun. Choices *C* and *D* do not correctly capitalize the proper noun.

4. B: Sentence 1 establishes when the *Challenger* disaster happened. Sentence 2 explains what caused the disaster. Sentence 4 builds upon the disaster by mentioning that several people were concerned with aspects of the launch. Sentence 3 describes NASA's reaction to the concerns and completes the paragraph.

5. D: Choice *D* matches the author's optimism about future improvements to electric vehicles and the fact that the world is starting to move away from fossil fuels. Choice *A* is incorrect because the author is optimistic about the future and strongly believes that future technology will become even more advanced. Choice *B* is incorrect because the passage does not discuss advancements in fossil fuels. Choice *C* is incorrect because the author is advocating for more research to improve electric vehicles.

Situational Judgment

Adaptability

While positioned abroad, the Foreign Service Officer (FSO) will likely be required to respond to a variety of complex situations. Some of these situations can be dangerous to the FSO or the Americans they are serving in that nation. Some examples are a political crisis, an environmental disaster, or even an escalation to the use of military force. Consequently, all prospective FSOs are tested on their judgment in moments of crisis.

One of the qualities sought in an FSO's capacity for judgment is adaptability. Although FSOs are extensively trained by the State Department during their career, it is likely they will encounter problems for which their training has not provided a direct course of action. The ability to think flexibly and respond swiftly to crises is an FSO's **adaptability.** Mastering adaptability requires creativity, good communication skills—to be aware of suggested alternative courses of action—and a willingness to take calculated risks.

The FSO's purpose is to protect American lives and the United States' foreign policy interest. Risks must be chosen carefully so that the FSO does not jeopardize their mission. Times of crisis make fulfillment of this purpose difficult. Risk is justified if it provides the best chance of fulfilling the FSO's duty.

Decision-Making and Judgment

Prospective FSOs are expected to possess rational judgment. Their decision-making process must be intentional, and they must be able to identify sound evidence and derive logical conclusions from data. Instinct or intuition may point the FSO's judgment in the right direction, but a reliance on unconscious mental faculties leads an FSO to be more likely to make ineffective decisions. The difference between intentional and unintentional decision-making is analogous to the difference between "That seems right" and "Here's the explanation why this is correct."

Two key principles of sound judgment for an FSO are reliability and validity. The FSO needs to be able to evaluate the source of information and determine if it is true. Decisions made on unreliable data are, in turn, not reliable decisions. Reliability can be determined by questioning the source of the information for further details and considering the information in the context of already confirmed data. The data then needs to be used to draw a valid conclusion. Valid conclusions are those that are logically connected to the data. To illustrate, the rate of infection with which a disease is spreading is a valid piece of data when considering closing an embassy for quarantine. In contrast, that rate of infection is not valid data for choosing a contractor for a new building project.

Operational Effectiveness

Each FSO is required to be efficient and effective at accomplishing the operational objectives of the Foreign Service. These objectives are defined by the US government's foreign policy goals and then implemented by the FSOs stationed in each nation. Naturally, this means it is difficult to make sweeping statements about what specific operations a prospective FSO needs to keep in mind.

Some basic qualities that a prospective FSO should cultivate to maximize their effectiveness as a diplomat include being efficient, organized, decisive, and communicative. The FSO is expected to react quickly to new information, be capable of analyzing that information, understand how it fits into the strategic objectives of their position, and then communicate their understanding concisely with team members. A

127

diplomat is most capable of being a useful member of their team through both individual prowess and their ability to coordinate with others.

Professional Standards

Due to the nature of the position, it is important for an FSO to be able to hold themselves to a rigorous professional standard. As an overseas diplomat, the FSO often will have limited oversight from other members of the Foreign Service. Consequently, personal integrity and accountability are important qualities for prospective officers.

For the FSO to hold themselves to the highest standard of professionalism entails presenting themselves in a confident, reliable, and competent manner. This includes objectives as simple as maintaining a well-groomed appearance—in cultural context of where the FSO operates—and being punctual to meetings with local dignitaries, to potentially challenging objectives, such as fulfilling complicated promises, completing tasks accurately and in a timely fashion, and demonstrating trustworthiness and discretion. An FSO must be prepared to act as a representative of the United States at all times.

Above other elements, the FSO must prove their integrity to citizens, officials, and leaders of the country in which they have been stationed. Demonstrating that the FSO is reliable both eases the officer's duties and increases trust in the foreign policy of the United States.

Team Building

Each FSO is but a single piece within a larger team. This team might be defined as widely as the entire US Foreign Service or as narrowly as the FSO's immediate handful of coworkers at a consulate. Commitment to the Foreign Service's mission, willingness to provide support to team members, and the ability to ask for assistance when needed are all important personality traits sought after from prospective FSOs. The FSO should be prepared to prioritize the team's needs above their own.

One difficult aspect of supporting a team is an FSO's awareness of their own needs. It's important to engage in self-care for the sake of the team. The FSO is responsible for monitoring their own mental, physical, and emotional energy so they can perform effectively in a high-stakes environment.

Rapport between team members often builds naturally in the process of working together. Nonetheless, it is important for the FSO to choose to intentionally engage in both formal and informal team building. This is especially important for team leaders. Close relationships within a team facilitate trust, confidence, and speedy work during crisis situations. The FSO should seek out opportunities to provide moral support and develop rapport with people they work with regularly in both formal and informal settings.

Workplace Perceptiveness

A significant portion of an FSO's duties requires aptitude to navigate complex social situations in the workplace. This is because the FSO's day-to-day work requires frequent conversations with individuals with significant responsibilities who are often under emotional stress. Therefore, it is important for the FSO to cultivate **workplace perceptiveness** for use with coworkers and colleagues who work in other agencies or for different nations.

Some elements of this capacity include **identifying emotions, understanding social hierarchies,** and **displaying cultural sensitivity.** Emotional identification requires paying close attention to an individual's facial expression, their voice's tone and volume, and their body language. By watching carefully, the FSO can gauge some measure of an individual's emotional response to the conversation and guide the situation accordingly to achieve the FSO's objectives. Awareness of social hierarchies is especially important in crisis because it helps the FSO understand who is responsible for making decisions. It's also important not to undermine a local colleague or a Foreign Service superior, because the associated embarrassment can close off options for negotiation. Finally, all of this must be considered within the context of cultural sensitivity. Each culture's social norms—their etiquette—varies. Although much of this will be taught to an FSO prior to their deployment overseas, it is nonetheless important for the FSO to keep a close watch on the social behavior of local colleagues. By following the lead of local advisors, officials, and business acquaintances, the FSO can reduce the likelihood of performing a faux pas.

Overall Synthesis

The situational judgment portion of the FSOT tests prospective FSOs on their response to a variety of workplace and/or crisis situations. Some situations may be quite plausible—even daily occurrences in diplomatic work—whereas others are rarer. By asking how the prospective FSO would choose to act under hypothetical high-stress situations, the Foreign Service seeks to understand the candidate's potential to be a professional and competent representative of the US government abroad.

The FSOT may present a complicated variety of hypothetical situations during this portion of the exam. It's important to remember that the best course of action in one situation may not be the best in a later question. However, the following general principles can help candidates navigate the situational judgment test successfully:

- **Safety First:** The physical safety of people involved in the situation almost always should be the FSO's highest priority. They should navigate situations involving danger or crises by finding the strategy that mitigates the harm done.
- **Citizens First:** As a member of the US government, the FSO has a responsibility to look after American interests over the interests of the host nation. In particular, this extends to prioritizing the well-being of American citizens over local citizens, if necessary.
- **Soonest First:** A time-sensitive task, problem, decision, etc., has higher priority than one that is not time-sensitive. For situations that involve multiple time-sensitive elements, such as varying deadlines on different projects, it's usually best to give the greatest importance to the task that is due soonest.

Fortunately, many of the qualities of character and judgment that are tested for on the situational judgment test are commonly valued qualities of professionals in many fields. Although the exam's situations may at times feel intimidating due to their diplomatic context, it's important to remember that they are testing values that are common in most workplaces and social settings.

Practice Quiz

Directions: For each question in this section, select the BEST and WORST response to each scenario.

1. A tsunami devastates your host country, destroying the homes of tens of thousands of people. You are a staff member at the consulate charged with finding temporary housing for American citizens whose homes were lost or made inaccessible after the disaster. How do you respond?
    a. Open the consulate's public buildings as temporary housing with cots, blankets, and emergency food supplies.
    b. Direct homeless citizens to follow the directions of the local officials, and provide support to the host nation's disaster relief efforts.
    c. Reach out to the consulate's staff for volunteers to temporarily shelter homeless Americans.
    d. Seek emergency funding to rent or purchase any available and safe buildings nearby for the purpose of temporary shelter.

2. Your team is tasked with monitoring an election in your host nation and providing an up-to-date analysis of the most likely outcome to officials in the United States. Which of the following is the most reliable source of data about the political climate?
    a. Personally conducting a poll of local citizens on the street
    b. Discrete conversations with local officials
    c. Publicly available polls produced by an international nongovernmental organization
    d. Local news publications about the election

3. During a presentation to your team, a diplomatic security expert claims that the increasing rate of violent crime in four of the host nation's major cities, including the capital, indicates an increased risk of political violence during the next six months. What connection best explains the validity of the expert's claim?
    a. Increased violent crime has a correlation with future unrest.
    b. Violent crime is associated with poverty, which is a possible economic cause for revolutionary activity.
    c. The data spread over multiple cities.
    d. Violence is a common tactic for political intimidation.

4. You are assigned three different tasks by your supervisor. None of the tasks are of critical importance, but at least one coworker is waiting on each task to be completed to move on with their next task. Task one is of high importance and will take a long time to complete. Task two and task three are both of medium importance. The second task will take a moderate amount of time to complete, and the third task will take a short amount of time to complete. In what order do you complete these tasks?
    a. Task one, task three, task two
    b. Task one, task two, task three
    c. Task three, task one, task two
    d. Ordinary duties first

5. You have two tasks due in two hours. One was assigned by your supervisor. The second is from a local official. It's not clear that you can complete both tasks before the deadline. Which course of action do you take?
   a. Work at both tasks and submit completed material by the deadline, regardless of its quality.
   b. Prioritize the supervisor's task, and apologize to the local official if the second task is incomplete.
   c. Prioritize the local official's task, and apologize to the supervisor if the second task is incomplete.
   d. Contact the supervisor for directions.

6. A local official invites you to a formal celebration. Recently, you received a traditional formal outfit from another dignitary. You have received no additional directions from the official about the celebration's dress code. What do you wear to the event?
   a. Formal wear from the United States, such as a suit or a gown
   b. The gifted outfit
   c. An American outfit appropriate for a local business luncheon
   d. A local outfit tailored for your use

7. A coworker in your team at the embassy asks you to reconsider a decision you've made for your portion of the team's operations. They express concern that you are valuing the relationship with local contacts too highly and that this reduces the chance of meeting the whole team's objectives. How do you respond?
   a. Listen to the coworker's concerns and reassure them of your competence to maintain appropriate professional boundaries.
   b. Suggest to the team leader that you be assigned to work with different local contacts for a few weeks to reestablish emotional distance.
   c. Encourage the coworker to focus on their own objectives because your performance is the team leader's concern.
   d. Begin cultivating alternative local contacts to reduce the frequency with which you rely on the inappropriately close relationship.

8. During a meeting with local officials, a senior fellow FSO makes a factually inaccurate claim. The attendees' body language appears to indicate that they are unaware. How do you react?
   a. Wait for a lull in the conversation, and then politely correct your senior.
   b. Write a note on a scrap of paper to check if another American official adjacent to you noticed as well.
   c. Reach out to the FSO by email after the meeting and ask about their statement.
   d. Ask the FSO during the meeting about the source of their information.

9. You present a business proposal to a local contractor. While reading the document, the contractor's eyebrows furrow, they bite their lower lip, and they don't look at you or their surroundings. What is the best assessment of the contractor's body language?
   a. Frustration
   b. Anger
   c. Concentration
   d. Hesitation

10. You're attending your consulate's leadership meeting to discuss possible objectives for the consulate's staff to work toward. Which of the following objectives has the highest priority?

    a. Improving the number of requests for visas to travel to the United States, which are processed each week

    b. Revising an evacuation plan to include recent building renovations

    c. Facilitating the host nation's officials' submission of developmental aid requests

    d. Smoothing over relations between US business interests and the local government

See next page for answer explanations.

Chapter Quiz Answer Explanations

1. BEST: A: This choice is best because it makes effective use of resources immediately available to the FSO. Repurposing auditoriums, dining halls, and other large spaces in the consulate gives effective relief and mitigates possible security risks entailed in using private spaces, such as offices or staff housing. **WORST: B:** It is the consulate's responsibility to provide immediate emergency relief to American citizens. Other options should be explored first.

2. BEST: C: In general, NGOs are a reliable source of information, and an international organization is less likely to have bias in the process of creating the poll. It's also likely to have a sample size large enough to be relevant to the nation's demographics. **WORST: A:** Asking strangers their opinion is an unreliable method of gathering data because it doesn't account for demographics, and the locals may not be willing to discuss politics with a foreigner.

3. BEST: A: Choice *A* is the most valid explanation because it is a true correlation between the data and a possible outcome, without relying on additional steps, such as in Choice *B*. **WORST: C:** The geographical element does not logically connect with what the violence may mean. Rather, it indicates that the violence—and other possible outcomes—is widespread.

4. BEST: C: Completing task three first is most efficient because it can be completed quickly. This allows another worker to continue their project. **WORST: D:** When assigned ad hoc tasks, it's generally more efficient to complete those tasks prior to routine duties, especially if a coworker is relying on that task's completion.

5. BEST: C: Prioritizing the local official's task is the best choice because it maintains the FSO's reliability, improving local opinion of the US Foreign Service. **WORST: A:** Submitting both tasks in a haphazard—and possibly incomplete—state fulfills neither the supervisor's needs nor the needs of the local official. Quality work is more valuable than punctual work.

6. BEST: A: As a representative of the United States, wearing formal American dress is most appropriate unless an American or local superior has requested otherwise. **WORST: D:** Acquiring a separate local outfit is incorrect because it could be seen as an attempt to appropriate the local culture and an insult to the dignitary who presented the gift.

7. BEST: B: A temporary reassignment is the best option here because close relationships with citizens of the host nation are important for diplomatic success. Taking a break to evaluate your boundaries allows the team to still use your relationship with the local contacts when you return to duty. **WORST: C:** It's important to listen when a teammate expresses concern, even if they do not hold a formal position of authority over you. Even if you disagree with the concern, dismissing their opinion hinders good rapport within the team.

8. BEST: D: Framing the question this way gives the senior FSO a chance to correct themselves or to demonstrate their competence by explaining the possibly erroneous information. It strikes a balance between not undermining a senior coworker and ensuring that accurate information is presented to partners from the local government. **WORST: A:** A direct correction may undermine the senior FSO's credibility in the eyes of the locals.

9. BEST: C: The contractor's focused attention combined with their oral fidgeting (the chewed lip) most likely indicates that they are concentrating on the proposal rather than expressing an emotional reaction. **WORST: D:** Hesitant body language typically involves more eye motion and detachment from the source of discomfort.

10. BEST: B: Choice *B* is best because an up-to-date evacuation plan for the consulate is necessary as part of emergency preparedness. **WORST: C:** Although developmental aid is an important facet of US foreign policy, it is less important than furthering American interests, Choice *D*, or increasing the consulate's workflow efficiency, Choice *A*.

FSOT Practice Test #1

Part One: Job Knowledge

1. What is the name of the point at which the supply and demand curves intersect?
   a. Inflation
   b. Shortage
   c. Market-clearing price
   d. Zero-sum game

2. You are reading your team's evaluations of their colleagues' performances over the last month. Bob writes a scathing review of Jim's work, while Jim gives a balanced review of everyone's work equally. You know Bob can be a bit abrasive with others on the team and have received complaints about his attitude towards others. You also haven't received any other complaints about Jim's work. What is the most likely reason for Bob's negative review of Jim?
   a. Bob is writing a scathing review of Jim in response to Jim's equally negative review of Bob.
   b. Bob is letting his opinions about Jim influence his review of Jim's work.
   c. Jim has been playing a prank on Bob to make him think his work performance has been dropping.
   d. Jim has been slacking and letting his work performance deteriorate.

3. Which diplomatic action is NOT an example of soft power?
   a. The use of a religious figure (for example, the Pope) and their endorsement in order to convince a sympathetic population to support a cause or nation
   b. The use of economic sanctions against another country (for example, restricting what goods could be sold and to whom) in order to convince the affected population to support a cause or nation
   c. The use of beloved or revered cultural artifacts and signifiers (for example, the importance and spread of Japanese anime around the world) in order to convince a sympathetic population to support a cause or nation
   d. The use of educational opportunities (for example, the recruitment of foreign students to elite American colleges and universities) in order to convince a specific population to support a cause or nation.

4. If you put the phrase "concrete worker" in quotation marks when performing a Google search, what are you asking the search engine to do to the query?
   a. Search for the exact phrase "concrete worker" with no partial matches.
   b. Exclude the phrase "concrete worker" from a search.
   c. Search for the phrase "concrete worker" and all variations of it, such as "a worker of concrete."
   d. Require that the phrase "concrete worker" appears only once in a document to show it as a search result.

5. How long do senators serve?
   a. Two years
   b. Six years
   c. Four years
   d. Eight years

6. Congress is made up of what?
   a. President and vice president
   b. Secretary of state and Speaker of the House
   c. Senate and House of Representatives
   d. Supreme Court and federal courts

7. The first ten amendments are also known as what?
   a. Bill of Rights
   b. Articles of Confederation
   c. Charters of Freedom
   d. Declaration of Independence

8. The belief that the United States needed to settle all of North America was referred to as what?
   a. Yellow journalism
   b. Emancipation Proclamation
   c. Manifest Destiny
   d. City upon a Hill

9. What event ended United States isolationism during WWII?
   a. D-Day
   b. Pearl Harbor Attack
   c. Treaty of Versailles
   d. Bombing of Hiroshima and Nagasaki

10. What United States president advocated for the creation of the League of Nations and was considered its lead architect?
   a. Gerald Ford
   b. Harry Truman
   c. John F. Kennedy
   d. Woodrow Wilson

11. The percentage of smokers above the age of 18 in 2000 was 23.2%. The percentage of smokers above the age of 18 in 2015 was 15.1%. Find the average rate of change in the percent of smokers above the age of 18 from 2000 to 2015.
   a. -0.54%
   b. -54%
   c. -5.4%
   d. 0.54%

12. You are beginning research on the economic history of the country you work in. Which of the following would be the best starting point for your research?
   a. The most recent economic policy law passed in this country
   b. An economic policy expert in this country
   c. Local news coverage of economic policy changes
   d. A database of economic policy changes made in this country

136

13. During the Space Race, who was the United States's main rival?
    a. China
    b. Soviet Union
    c. Cuba
    d. North Korea

14. On the first four tests this semester, a student received the following scores out of 100: 74, 76, 82, and 84. The student must earn at least what score on the fifth test to receive a B in the class? Assume that the final test is also out of 100 points and that to receive a B in the class, he must have at least an 80% average.
    a. 80
    b. 84
    c. 82
    d. 78

15. If a user wanted to create a header and footer for their document, where would they click in Microsoft Word?
    a. Page Layout
    b. View
    c. References
    d. Insert

16. When did immigration to the United States shift from Great Britain to southeastern Europe?
    a. Early 18th century
    b. Early 19th century
    c. Early 20th century
    d. Early 21st century

17. An official government printing of a new law is what type of source?
    a. Primary source
    b. Informal source
    c. Tertiary source
    d. Academic source

18. What was NOT included in the Missouri Compromise of 1820?
    a. Slavery was banned in Washington, D.C.
    b. Missouri was admitted as a slave state.
    c. Slavery was prohibited in future northern territories.
    d. Maine was admitted as a free state.

19. What is the purpose of the Electoral College?
    a. It is a group that is responsible for staffing embassies and diplomatic missions around the world.
    b. It is the primary method for choosing the president of the United States.
    c. It refers to the process that determines the maximum number of Supreme Court justices.
    d. It is a location where senators discuss the presidential election.

20. What does SQL stand for in a database?
    a. Structured Query Language
    b. Saved Question Lost
    c. Separated Quality Log
    d. Shifted Quotient List

21. Who or what determines the number of Representatives from each state?
    a. The president
    b. The year when they became a part of the United States
    c. Wealth and gross income
    d. Total population

22. Which of the following is a good alternative description of an authoritative management style?
    a. Micromanagement
    b. Consultative
    c. Improvement
    d. Family

23. What is the main difference between persuasive and paternalistic management?
    a. Persuasive management includes sharing the logic behind decisions to the team; paternalistic does not.
    b. Paternalistic management may micromanage the team members; persuasive does not.
    c. Paternalistic management leaves employees to their own devices during work hours; persuasive does not.
    d. Persuasive management allows employees to ask questions; paternalistic does not.

24. Which of the following is a major risk to avoid when using consultative management?
    a. Irritating employees with positive platitudes
    b. Unaddressed conflict between team members
    c. Favoring certain employees' contributions over others
    d. Employees feeling like they don't have equal opportunity to contribute

25. What was the primary cause of widespread urbanization in the United States?
    a. The First Industrial Revolution
    b. The Second Industrial Revolution
    c. The Great Migration
    d. Successive waves of immigration

26. Which metrics are the most important to measure for employee performance evaluations?
    a. Compatibility with the team and positive attitude
    b. Productivity and total amount of completed work
    c. Current work experience and willingness to learn
    d. Whichever ones fit the job description the best

27. In case the president is unable to fulfill their duties, who is third in the line of presidential succession?
    a. Vice president
    b. President pro tempore of the Senate
    c. Speaker of the House
    d. Secretary of state

28. Your boss is proposing ideas for how to proceed with the next project. You think option A is best, but he insists that option B is better, even though you think option B will cause problems for the team. What would be the best way to convince your boss to switch to option A?
   a. Point out to your boss the obvious reasons option B won't work and tell him he should consider option A instead.
   b. Say nothing and wait several weeks for the problems to manifest. Then tell your boss how option A would have fixed this.
   c. Ignore your boss's decision and work according to option A anyway.
   d. Politely explain your reasoning behind preferring option A and how it fixes problems in option B.

29. In a database, what is the purpose of a macro?
   a. It creates an output like a graph that users can view.
   b. It automates certain tasks.
   c. It saves the document as a CSV file.
   d. It creates a new document for users to edit.

30. Which tool can be used to specifically retrieve information in a database?
   a. Chrome
   b. Google Docs
   c. SQL
   d. Excel

31. John F. Kennedy's "We Choose to Go to the Moon" speech, a portion of which is shown below, was given in 1962. Considering that this speech was delivered during the Cold War, which nation is John F. Kennedy alluding to with the phrase "hostile flag of conquest"?

> Those who came before us made certain that this country rode the first waves of the industrial revolutions, the first waves of modern invention, and the first wave of nuclear power, and this generation does not intend to founder in the backwash of the coming age of space. We mean to be a part of it—we mean to lead it. For the eyes of the world now look into space, to the moon and to the planets beyond, and we have vowed that we shall not see it governed by a hostile flag of conquest, but by a banner of freedom and peace. We have vowed that we shall not see space filled with weapons of mass destruction, but with instruments of knowledge and understanding.

   a. Great Britain
   b. Nazi Germany
   c. Soviet Union
   d. Iraq

32. When it was founded, what was the Republican Party's primary issue?
   a. States' rights
   b. Tax cuts
   c. Manifest destiny
   d. Abolition of slavery

33. Which of the following was the first European colony established in North America?
    a. St. Augustine
    b. Roanoke
    c. Jamestown
    d. Hudson's Bay

34. Who serves as the president of the Senate?
    a. Speaker of the House
    b. Chief justice
    c. Vice president
    d. President

35. Your boss wants you to draft a report analyzing how a change in foreign policy may potentially affect public approval of your home country within the country you work. What type of source is your boss asking you to prepare?
    a. Primary source
    b. Tertiary source
    c. Secondary source
    d. Comprehensive source

36. Which economic relief package also had the secondary goal of stopping the spread of communism following WWII?
    a. New Deal
    b. American Rescue Plan
    c. Marshall Plan
    d. CARES Act

37. Which of the following is a power granted to the president of the United States?
    a. Confirming Supreme Court nominations
    b. Approving treaties with foreign countries
    c. Granting pardons
    d. Impeaching federal officials

38. You have been conducting a special round of performance evaluations to determine candidates for promotion to a leadership position. Which of the following team members would be the best fit for a leadership promotion?
    a. Mary, who has plenty of past leadership experience and occasional anger issues
    b. Bob, who makes petty jokes about others and generally views himself as superior
    c. Stacy, who does excellent work and keeps to herself unless she needs help
    d. Jim, who gets along well with other and is considerate of the team as a whole

140

39. In economics, what does *game theory* refer to?
   a. Game theory refers to the tendency of individuals in an economic system to spend their capital on economically frivolous but personally enjoyable endeavors like video games and sports.
   b. Game theory refers to the study of the economics surrounding gambling.
   c. Game theory refers to the idea that economic/financial systems can benefit from "gamification," whereby aspects of their goods or services are altered and adjusted to reward user interaction in the same way a video game does.
   d. Game theory refers to the study of the mathematical models representing various strategic interactions between rational individuals.

40. A new employee has just been hired and put on your team, and they need additional training to learn the job. What sort of program should you offer them?
   a. Mentorship program
   b. Tutorial program
   c. Rehabilitation program
   d. Captaincy program

41. Sales tax is an example of what kind of tax?
   a. Inheritance tax
   b. Progressive tax
   c. Proportional tax
   d. Regressive tax

42. In a country with a closed economy, national saving is equivalent to what?
   a. Imports
   b. Investments
   c. Exports
   d. Consumption

43. A document that has a horizontal orientation is referred to as what?
   a. Italicized
   b. Portrait
   c. Landscape
   d. Painted

44. Which of the following describes the steps to conducting research effectively in the right order?
   a. Start with secondary sources, use filters, and end with primary sources.
   b. Start with specific searches, use citations, and end with specific sources.
   c. Start with a wide-ranged search, use filters, and end with specific sources.
   d. Start with tertiary sources, use secondary sources, and end with primary sources.

45. An embargo against a foreign country serves what purpose?
   a. It introduces a tax on goods imported into a country.
   b. It is a form of economic aid to another country.
   c. It severely restricts trade and the transfer of goods with another country.
   d. It improves relationships between countries.

46. What does CSV stand for?
    a. Caps Shift Validation
    b. Control Save Verified
    c. Colon Spaced Value
    d. Comma Separated Values

47. Which of the following is NOT a place you should put citations for your sources?
    a. In the footnotes of a page or slide
    b. On the first page or slide at the beginning of a presentation
    c. At the end of the report or on the final slide
    d. Directly in the text after you quote the source

48. What factor is used to help calculate real GDP?
    a. Price floors
    b. Inflation
    c. Unemployment rate
    d. Rent prices

49. When the supply is more elastic than the demand, who bears most of the tax burden?
    a. Poor individuals
    b. Wealthy individuals
    c. Producers
    d. Buyers

50. A team member approaches you in private and asks for help with a small problem. You are happy to help, and they are relieved, telling you they were unsure if it was appropriate to ask their boss for help with this easy task. You have gotten the feeling for a while that other team members may be having similar struggles. What is the best way to approach this situation?
    a. During the lunch break, casually ask your employees if they need help with anything.
    b. Tell this team member they can suggest anyone come to you for help.
    c. Announce an open-door policy where anyone can come to you with a problem, and you will help.
    d. Approach specific employees you suspect may need help and offer assistance.

51. What is data redundancy?
    a. Data that is stored in multiple locations
    b. Data that is stored in only one place
    c. Data that cannot be retrieved successfully
    d. Data that is incorrect or inaccurate

52. An athlete records her times for a series of runs as 25, 18, 23, 28, 30, 22.5, 23, 33, and 20 minutes. What is the mode of the athlete's times?
    a. 16 minutes
    b. 20 minutes
    c. 23 minutes
    d. 33 minutes

53. In order to estimate deer population in a forest, biologists obtained a sample of deer in that forest and tagged each one of them. The sample had 300 deer in total. They returned a week later, harmlessly captured 400 deer, and found that 5 were tagged. Use this information to estimate how many total deer were in the forest.
    a. 24,000 deer
    b. 30,000 deer
    c. 40,000 deer
    d. 100,000 deer

54. What was the Zimmerman Telegram?
    a. A famous telegram from Germany to the United States describing the experiences of a Jewish German family during the Holocaust
    b. An intercepted communication from Germany to Mexico stating Germany's willingness to help Mexico invade the United States
    c. A telegram that announced Germany's invasion of the Sudetenland
    d. A new type of telegraph invented during the Second Industrial Revolution

55. If the demand for a certain good drops as people's income rises, what is this good called?
    a. Inferior good
    b. Luxury good
    c. Normal good
    d. Public good

56. What does the Heartland Theory state?
    a. Holding Eurasia's coastal areas would control all of the world's resources.
    b. Naval supremacy creates the most powerful countries and empires.
    c. Nations need to constantly seek resources to survive.
    d. Whoever controls eastern Europe would control most of the world.

57. Which of the following is NOT an autocratic management style?
    a. Authoritative
    b. Paternalistic
    c. Visionary
    d. Persuasive

58. What are the two economic goals contained in the dual mandate of the United States Federal Reserve?
    a. Low interest rates and low inflation
    b. High employment and price stability
    c. Price stability and high interest rates
    d. High inflation and high employment

59. Which term best describes the relationship between the Japanese attack on Pearl Harbor and the United States' entry into World War II?
    a. Correlation
    b. Causation
    c. Opposition
    d. Indirect connection

60. What event immediately signaled the end of the Cold War?
   a. Collapse of the Soviet Union
   b. Vietnam War
   c. Cuban Missile Crisis
   d. Korean War

Part Two: English Expression and Usage

Type A: Sentence Selection
Directions: For each item in this section, select the one sentence that best meets the requirements of standard written English.

1. Select the sentence that best meets the requirements of standard written English.
   a. The Financial District of New York City is home to many notable buildings, including the One World Trade Center.
   b. The Prime Minister was engaged in a disagreement with the President, of India.
   c. There are twelve federal reserve Banks, and they are located in different locations of the United States.
   d. The Attorney needed time to review all of the case information.

2. Select the sentence that best meets the requirements of standard written English.
   a. The senate introduced a bill for consideration.
   b. The library needed repairs; because of a snowstorm.
   c. The United Nations has the purpose of maintaining international harmony.
   d. The office ordered new clipboards notebooks pens and paper clips.

3. Select the sentence that best meets the requirements of standard written English.
   a. The three Police Officers tried their best to defuse the situation.
   b. While campaigning the politician needed to hire additional assistants.
   c. The International Committee of the Red Cross is considered an intergovernmental organization.
   d. I needed to get out and vote; but my workplace would not allow it.

4. Select the sentence that best meets the requirements of standard written English.
   a. The expert on foreign policy is secretary of state Mateo Jackson.
   b. The networking event was being held in Seattle, Washington.
   c. The investor's stocks were supposed to accrued interest.
   d. I forgot to bring my calculator for the exam, so my friend lended me his.

5. Select the sentence that best meets the requirements of standard written English.
   a. The US Congress passed a bill related to improving public education.
   b. The discussions between Australia and the United States were for Diplomatic matters.
   c. The war that broke out, was devastating for the country's citizens.
   d. The representative was sent to China since there was a meeting between foreign officers there, their goal was to discuss trade negotiations because inflation was negatively affecting both countries.

144

6. Select the sentence that best meets the requirements of standard written English.
   a. The House of representatives currently has 435 voting members.
   b. The national park service ensures that the United States' national parks are well maintained.
   c. The professor was invited by npr to discuss the current political climate.
   d. It was time for the United States to withdraw its troops from the war; they had been in Afghanistan for far too long.

7. Select the sentence that best meets the requirements of standard written English.
   a. The United States set a goal of strengthening its alliances; Japan was one of the major focuses for this campaign.
   b. The Louvre is located in Paris, France and receives up to 10.8 Million visitors per year.
   c. The Firefighters worked tirelessly to save the home from completely burning down.
   d. The committee was focused on allocating funds, to the new courthouse being built downtown.

8. Select the sentence that best meets the requirements of standard written English.
   a. He flown to Los Angeles for a business meeting.
   b. Her boss had a reputation of working his employees into the knight.
   c. Sarah and her mother wanted to opened a frozen yogurt shop.
   d. The animal shelter was holding an adoption event for senior cats.

9. Select the sentence that best meets the requirements of standard written English.
   a. Bella told her mother, "My professor said that there would be 'no exceptions' for late work."
   b. Have you heard of the euphemism "over the hill?"
   c. Because their son had poor grades his parents hired a tutor.
   d. The student's were excited to go outside for recess.

10. Select the sentence that best meets the requirements of standard written English.
    a. The janitor was responsible for many tasks such as locking the building and ensuring the metal detectors were functioning properly in order to keep the school safe both in the morning and afternoon.
    b. Trevor had been playing the cello since he was a young boy.
    c. The wolves chases deer throughout the forest.
    d. The homeowner told the movers to put his bedroom set over their.

11. Select the sentence that best meets the requirements of standard written English.
    a. Foot ball was Jared's favorite sport to watch on television.
    b. The basketball hit the backboard and did not going into the hoop.
    c. Men and women perform different styles of gymnastics in the olympics.
    d. Baseball uses the term *inning* to describe the portion of the game in which teams switch between playing offense and defense.

12. Select the sentence that best meets the requirements of standard written English.
    a. The Taj Mahal is an Islamic mausoleum located in Agra, India.
    b. The city of Philadelphia is home to the independence national historical park.
    c. The great wall of China is over 13,000 miles long.
    d. The hague is a city in the Netherlands and is located on the North Coast.

13. Select the sentence that best meets the requirements of standard written English.
   a. The submarine was used for gathering intelligence because the two country's were at war.
   b. Its important to eat a balanced diet and exercise regularly.
   c. Cassie's dog Bruno needed to go to doggy daycare on Wednesday's.
   d. The delivery driver ran over my neighbor's mailbox.

14. Select the sentence that best meets the requirements of standard written English.
   a. I spreaded jam on my toast for breakfast.
   b. Many people vacationed on the aisle because of the clear blue water and beautiful palm trees.
   c. Before big meetings, the CEO would tap into a more confident alter ego of himself.
   d. It was only 8 in the morning, and I all ready completed all of my chores.

15. Select the sentence that best meets the requirements of standard written English.
   a. The raisins on the counter is going to be used for oatmeal cookies.
   b. The raccoon crawled into the trash can and are eating table scraps.
   c. Neither the shoes nor the belt is in the closet.
   d. Every cat were given the rabies vaccine at the clinic.

16. Select the sentence that best meets the requirements of standard written English.
   a. To qualify for the job, he was required to pass a Mathematics exam.
   b. Prime Minister Justin Trudeau has held the position since 2015.
   c. She decided to ride her bicycle to work rather then taking the bus.
   d. The restaurant was closed every saturday.

17. Select the sentence that best meets the requirements of standard written English.
   a. The doctor left work earlier than usual because there were no appointments scheduled.
   b. To prevent illness, Carol washed her hands often.
   c. The carpet cleaners abandoned their job; because their cleaning equipment broke.
   d. Her lawyer said "I don't think you will win this case."

Type B: Sentence Correction
Directions: For each item in this section, select the one underlined word or phrase that needs to be changed to make the sentence correct, or indicate that none of the underlined parts are in error.

18. The world trade organization has the job of ensuring that global trade runs smoothly and without disturbance.
   a. NO ERROR
   b. world trade organization
   c. has the job
   d. and without disturbance

19. To host the Olympics is a prestigious honor for any country; it can boost tourism and the economy.
   a. NO ERROR
   b. the Olympics
   c. country; it
   d. tourism and the economy

146

20. The <u>Universal Declaration of Human Rights</u> is a <u>document; held by</u> the United Nations, focused on the <u>freedom of all humans.</u>
   a. NO ERROR
   b. Universal Declaration of Human Rights
   c. document; held by
   d. freedom of all humans

21. The federal government of <u>the US</u> has three <u>branches: executive,</u> <u>legislative, and</u> judicial.
   a. NO ERROR
   b. the US
   c. branches: executive,
   d. legislative, and

22. The <u>agent's arrived</u> at the location where the <u>politician's speech</u> would <u>be held</u>.
   a. NO ERROR
   b. agent's arrived
   c. politician's speech
   d. be held

23. <u>He asked</u> the TSA <u>agent "W</u>hat am I not allowed to bring into the <u>airport?"</u>
   a. NO ERROR
   b. He asked
   c. agent "What
   d. airport?"

24. The <u>journalist's story</u> had <u>an affect</u> on the outcome of <u>the November</u> election.
   a. NO ERROR
   b. journalist's story
   c. an affect
   d. the November

25. There are two <u>national cemeteries</u> run by the US <u>Army; the</u> larger of the two is located in <u>Arlington Virginia.</u>
   a. NO ERROR
   b. national cemeteries
   c. Army; the
   d. Arlington Virginia

26. The <u>postcard</u> <u>read, "Happy</u> Holidays from <u>the Smith's</u>" and featured a picture of the family dog.
   a. NO ERROR
   b. postcard
   c. read, "Happy
   d. the Smith's

27. I was upset to hear that <u>the queen</u> of <u>the United Kingdom</u> had passed <u>away?</u>
   a. NO ERROR
   b. the Queen
   c. the United Kingdom
   d. away?

28. The carnival mirror created an allusion; it made me look much taller than I actually am.
    a. NO ERROR
    b. The carnival
    c. allusion
    d. much taller

29. The nanny, who had worked for the family for six years, had to quit her job do to medical problems.
    a. NO ERROR
    b. nanny, who
    c. years, had
    d. do to

30. I help my local church last Friday because they set up a food drive for underprivileged families.
    a. NO ERROR
    b. help
    c. set up
    d. underprivileged

31. The United States postal service has an annual budget of over $200 million.
    a. NO ERROR
    b. United States
    c. postal service
    d. $200 million

32. The 2008 economic crisis caused people across the nation to lose their jobs homes and vehicles.
    a. NO ERROR
    b. The 2008
    c. caused people
    d. jobs homes and vehicles

33. Kathy looked at her in the mirror and thought, "Wow, I look really nice today!"
    a. NO ERROR
    b. at her
    c. thought, "Wow,
    d. today!"

34. The World Health Organization is monitoring a global outbreak of cholera, which can cause diarrhea and dehydration.
    a. NO ERROR
    b. World Health Organization
    c. cholera, which
    d. diarrhea and dehydration.

Type C: Sentence Correction II
Directions: For the items in this section, select the one word or phrase that needs to be used in place of the underlined text to make the sentence correct, or indicate that the underlined text is not in error.

35. Countries in the European Union must respect a diverse <u>variation</u> of laws and regulations, or else they risk suspension.
    a. NO ERROR
    b. variety
    c. vaccination
    d. vacancy

36. The United States' Second Amendment grants citizens the right to <u>bear</u> arms, although there are exceptions where someone may not be allowed to own any weapons.
    a. NO ERROR
    b. bare
    c. break
    d. better

37. Cuba and the United States began diplomatic relations at the Summit of the <u>Americas in 2015.</u>
    a. NO ERROR
    b. Americas, in 2015
    c. Americas; in 2015
    d. Americas – in 2015.

38. <u>Me and my grandmother</u> were travelling to France for Christmas.
    a. NO ERROR
    b. Myself and my grandmother
    c. Me plus my grandmother
    d. My grandmother and I

39. There are UN Forces in Africa whose mission is to maintain <u>piece</u> in the area.
    a. NO ERROR
    b. peace
    c. peak
    d. pacifism

40. The <u>whether</u> was gloomy, which was not ideal for a beach vacation.
    a. NO ERROR
    b. wether
    c. weather
    d. waver

41. Meredith was excited to tell her parents that she had been <u>excepted</u> into medical school.
    a. NO ERROR
    b. expected
    c. excluded
    d. accepted

42. Since the administration would not aid the employees, it was now every teacher for <u>themselves</u>.
    a. NO ERROR
    b. themself
    c. himself
    d. herself

43. The Panama Papers were financial <u>documents,</u> leaked to German journalist Bastian Obermayer.
    a. NO ERROR
    b. document,
    c. documents;
    d. documents

44. You need many items when you go fishing at the <u>lake; a</u> fishing rod, lures, reels, bait, and a bobber.
    a. NO ERROR
    b. lake, a
    c. lake: a
    d. lake. A

45. The city has decided that <u>their are</u> not enough bike lanes on the roads.
    a. NO ERROR
    b. there are
    c. they are
    d. they're

46. Alexander Graham Bell, <u>whose</u> best known for inventing the telephone, was from the United Kingdom.
    a. NO ERROR
    b. who is
    c. whoose
    d. whom is

47. The judge concluded that the sentence <u>are</u> too long for a misdemeanor crime.
    a. NO ERROR
    b. be
    c. is
    d. run

48. The story about the young boy saving his friend, <u>which</u> appeared on the news channel, inspired people in the community to donate to his college fund.
    a. NO ERROR
    b. who
    c. whom
    d. that

49. He contacted an attorney for legal <u>council</u> regarding an estate dispute.
    a. NO ERROR
    b. conciliation
    c. counsel
    d. conceal

50. She took a trip to the Van Gogh museum in Amsterdam, the Netherlands.
    a. NO ERROR
    b. van gogh museum in Amsterdam, the Netherlands
    c. Van Gogh Museum, in Amsterdam, the Netherlands
    d. Van Gogh Museum in Amsterdam, the Netherlands.

51. Abraham Lincoln once <u>said, "Whatever</u> you are, be a good one."
    a. NO ERROR
    b. said "Whatever
    c. said Whatever
    d. said, "whatever

Type D: Paragraph Organization
Directions: For each item in this section, select the ordering of sentences that results in the clearest, most well-organized paragraph.

52.
(1) To perform photosynthesis, the plant needs sunlight, carbon dioxide, and water.
(2) Those molecules are then used to create glucose, which the plant feeds on in order to stay alive.
(3) Photosynthesis is the process of plants creating their own food source.
(4) The plant takes energy from the sun in order to breakdown the molecules of the carbon dioxide and water.
    a. 4, 2, 3, 1
    b. 1, 2, 4, 3
    c. 2, 1, 4, 3
    d. 3, 1, 4, 2

53.
(1) The dispute was over state rights and slavery.
(2) The war finally ended in 1865 with the defeat of the Confederacy.
(3) One of the major events of the war was the Emancipation Proclamation, which freed all of the slaves held within rebellious states.
(4) The American Civil War began in 1861 and was a dispute between the Union and the Confederacy.
    a. 4, 1, 3, 2
    b. 1, 3, 4, 2
    c. 2, 1, 4, 3
    d. 3, 4, 1, 2

54.
(1) The Republic of Texas declared independence from Mexico in 1836.
(2) The annexation bill was signed by President John Tyler with the approval of most Texans.
(3) Tensions rose after the annexation, and the Mexican-American War broke out.
(4) However, it wasn't until 1845 that the Texas annexation into the United States would take place.
    a. 4, 1, 2, 3
    b. 3, 1, 2, 4
    c. 1, 2, 3, 4
    d. 1, 4, 2, 3

55.

(1) Although these are a few popular examples, individual countries may require a variety of different types.

(2) A travel visa is used to allow a foreigner to remain within or leave a country.

(3) There are different types of visas based on the foreigner's purpose within the country they are travelling to.

(4) Some examples are the short-stay visa, the immigrant visa, and the official visa.

    a.   2, 3, 4, 1

    b.   1, 3, 4, 2

    c.   4, 2, 1, 3

    d.   3, 1, 2, 4

56.

(1) It was created in 1923, in an effort to separate Turkey from the Ottoman Empire.

(2) These principles include republicanism, populism, nationalism, laicism, statism, and reformism.

(3) Kemalism is the official ideology of the Republic of Turkey.

(4) The ideology consists of six different principles.

    a.   2, 1, 4, 3

    b.   3, 2, 4, 1

    c.   3, 1, 4, 2

    d.   2, 4, 3, 1

57.

(1) Geopolitics refers to the way that the Earth's geography influences politics.

(2) Thus, geopolitical scientists would study the ongoing issues involved to determine the causes, such as if a mainland wants control of an island in order to lay claim territorial claims on the waters between them.

(3) One example of a modern geopolitical issue relating to these subcategories would be a mainland wanting control over a nearby island.

(4) Land and water are both subcategories within the geographical space studied by geopolitics.

    a.   1, 4, 3, 2

    b.   3, 2, 1, 4

    c.   4, 2, 1, 3

    d.   2, 3, 1, 4

58.

(1) The letters D.C. stand for the name of that district, the District of Columbia.

(2) Washington D.C. is the capital of the United States.

(3) Instead, the nation's capital is part of a district.

(4) Unlike most cities in the United States, Washington D.C. is not part of a state.

    a.   4, 2, 1, 3

    b.   2, 4, 3, 1

    c.   1, 4, 3, 2

    d.   2, 1, 4, 3

Type E: Paragraph Revision

Directions: This section consists of several sentences that compose a paragraph. Read the paragraph carefully, and then answer the question that follows it.

152

59. In politics, when multiple heads of government come together to address an international matter, this event is called a summit meeting. Leaders from various countries meet to discuss policies, mutual problems, and strategic solutions. Summit meetings, or summits, are particularly important during times of war or global tension. They may make use of media coverage in order to keep citizens informed about what discussions are taking place. They also have high levels of security in order to protect the high-profile attendees.

Which of the following additions would best strengthen the content of the above paragraph?

    a. A history of where the word *summit* came from
    b. A breakdown of what a summit schedule may look like
    c. Examples of notable summits and what they accomplished
    d. A mention of when the next upcoming summit is

60. Zoology is a branch of biology that focuses on the animal kingdom. Zoology covers such topics as evolution, classification, behavior, and physiology. These topics may focus on individual animals or a population as a whole, or they may extend to the environment the animal lives in.

What is the main purpose of the paragraph above?

    a. To introduce readers to important zoologists
    b. To convince readers to join the field of zoology
    c. To report on modern events happening in zoology
    d. To educate readers about what zoology is

61. Modern basketball was invented by James Naismith in 1891. The original purpose of the game was to give athletes a way to stay fit in the cold months when football was not in season. Each team had nine players, and the players were required to follow 13 different rules. Instead of the hoops and nets that are used today, the players threw a ball into a fruit basket that was attached to a balcony. After 45 years, the sport was recognized by the Olympics and slowly began to evolve into the game we know today.

What is the main purpose of the paragraph above?

    a. To give a brief history of basketball
    b. To provide a biography about James Naismith
    c. To track how basketball has changed over time
    d. To explain how basketball improves the body

62. To make your own candles at home, you need a few materials: wax, fragrance oil, a wick, and a container to use as a mold. It is best to use soy wax. To begin, you must measure out the wax and melt it in a double boiler for 15 minutes. While the wax is melting, attach your wick to the container of your choice. When the wax has melted, it is time to add a few drops of fragrance oil. Then pour the melted wax into the container. Let the wax harden for a few hours before trimming the wick. Your candle is complete!

Which of the following additions would best strengthen the instructive paragraph above?

    a. A cost breakdown of each ingredient
    b. The amounts of each ingredient you need
    c. A brief history about candle making
    d. A description of different scents you can use

63. Many hospitals in the United States are understaffed. Understaffing leads to doctors and nurses being overworked. When they are forced to perform on little sleep, it is more common to see mistakes. More focus should be placed on improving the work conditions for healthcare professionals. Without the proper support, this problem will only continue to worsen.
Which of the following additions would best strengthen this paragraph?
   a.   A personal anecdote from a janitor
   b.   A list of major New York hospitals that are understaffed
   c.   Some examples of the mistakes that could be made by overworked healthcare professionals
   d.   A breakdown of medical school tuition costs

64. Mahatma Gandhi was a revolutionary from India. He campaigned for freedom by using nonviolent protest, which eventually led India to gain independence from British rule. His teachings have become famous around the world, especially in civil rights protests. He was assassinated in 1948 by a Hindu nationalist.
Which sentence would function best between Sentence 3 and Sentence 4?
   a.   However, some people did not agree with Gandhi's political beliefs.
   b.   Gandhi was born in October 1869.
   c.   He was a lawyer but struggled to open a successful law firm in India.
   d.   He was killed by gunshot wounds.

65. The California Gold Rush began in 1848. The news that gold had been found in California spread across the United States. The western portion of the US became overrun with prospectors looking to make a fortune. It is estimated that the gold extracted was worth billions of dollars. The economy was thriving during this time. However, the prosperity came at the cost of the lives of Native Americans. Their population took a steep downturn due to disease and genocide.
Which of the following statements is true based on the above paragraph?
   a.   The gold rush did not increase the population of California.
   b.   The gold rush helped the United States gain its independence from British rule.
   c.   There was not much gold for prospectors who traveled to the area.
   d.   The gold rush negatively impacted the lives of Native Americans.

Part Three: Situational Judgment

Directions: For each question in this section, select the BEST and WORST response to each scenario.

1. Your office receives a call from an American citizen living in your host country. They are speaking quickly, and their voice sounds panicked. The citizen reports that their renewal request for their work visa has been denied. As they talk, the citizen begins to catastrophize, enumerating this denial's negative impacts. How do you respond?
   a.   Reassure the caller that your office will reach out to the host nation's State Department and negotiate seeking approval.
   b.   Ask the caller to take a few deep breaths and then provide more information about the work visa.
   c.   Process the life change with the caller to help them cope with their anxiety over the rejected visa.
   d.   Transfer the caller to a more knowledgeable staff member.

2. You receive notice that you will be transferred to a new post in a different country in one week. You are already familiar with the official language(s) of the host nation. How do you adjust to the new post?
   a. Traverse the host city on foot, and use public transportation to become familiar with the local culture.
   b. Read your predecessor's documentation to learn about typical conflicts they handled in this position.
   c. Practice learning the faces and names of all personnel at the office, consulate, or embassy.
   d. Study the State Department's briefing materials about foreign policy goals while operating in the host nation.

3. There is a change in your host nation's immigrant worker laws. You need to learn the new rules as quickly as possible for your position in a consulate helping American citizens navigate employment in the host nation. How do you learn these new rules?
   a. Request the legal text from an appropriate authority of the host nation and read the text of the new law.
   b. Reach out to American coworkers in the Foreign Service with legal expertise for a comprehensive breakdown.
   c. Use news or political media targeting a lay audience to understand the changes in policy and law.
   d. Direct a staff member under your supervision to research the new rules and present a briefing for your department.

4. You have two reports due and are unsure if you'll be able to complete both on time. They are both considered urgent. The reports concern a recent industrial accident that caused 131 casualties and 7 deaths. There were no American casualties in the accident. One report is for a senior official in the State Department summarizing potential dangers to US interests. The second is to an official in the host nation developing new safety protocols to prevent future accidents. How do you choose which report to prioritize?
   a. Prioritize the American official's report because you're not a participant in the host nation's regulatory process.
   b. Prioritize the American official's report to avoid delays in American disaster relief being delivered to your host nation.
   c. Prioritize the local official's report to protect American citizens currently working in the same industry as the recent accident.
   d. Prioritize the local official's report to make it clear that the US government is concerned for the well-being of foreign partners.

5. One of the staff members in your team at the embassy has been posted to a new assignment on short notice. As the team's leader, how do you redistribute that person's work until a new staff member arrives?
   a. Take the bulk of their duties on yourself.
   b. Distribute their duties evenly between all members of the team, including yourself.
   c. Add any leadership tasks to your workload and distribute other tasks evenly.
   d. Query for volunteers among your team to take on particular duties, and then distribute the rest evenly.

6. The head of security at a consulate decides to increase the intensity of security checkpoints at consulate entrances. Which of the following is a reasonable explanation for this decision?
  a. The host nation's leaders have expressed frustration with American foreign policy decisions.
  b. The consulate has received credible terroristic threats from a known local extremist political faction.
  c. An employee was recently mugged while off-site.
  d. Several staff members expressed feeling insecure due to local unrest.

7. A seismologist demonstrates a pattern of increased tectonic activity off the host nation's coastline over the last six months. They claim that the risk of a disaster, such as a tsunami, has increased. One of your coworkers suggests that an evacuation plan should be developed to prepare for this emergency. Is this a valid conclusion from the geologist's data?
  a. Yes, because the geologist is a subject matter expert.
  b. Yes, because emergency preparedness is important.
  c. Yes, because the increased risk of danger requires a response.
  d. No, because the data require more predictive information about the risk before a decision can be made.

8. The Foreign Service in Washington reaches out to your intelligence-gathering team because they've received a tip about insurgent activity in the host nation's capital. Their informant reports that materials necessary for creating explosives have been transported to a warehouse in the city. Which of the following statements best indicates that this tip is unreliable?
  a. Your team's background checks on the warehouse employees did not find insurgent connections.
  b. The Foreign Service is either unwilling or unable to provide details about their source.
  c. The pattern of deliveries to that warehouse has not deviated from the norm.
  d. A review of security footage did not find any after-hours or covert deliveries.
  e. Your team's local informants have not heard about a possible attack in the near future.

9. After reviewing data collected by an intelligence-gathering team about regional insurgent activity, an analyst concludes that a terrorist attack targeting one of the host nation's governmental buildings is very likely to happen in the next month. Which of the following statements describes information that makes the analyst's conclusion a valid inference?
  a. Four different individuals provided a tip during the last seven days about an imminent attack.
  b. The report indicates a 25 percent increase in the number of known insurgents traveling through the capital area.
  c. The local government announced a mandatory curfew for all citizens two weeks ago.
  d. A mining facility reported a missing shipment of controlled explosives.
  e. The frequency with which insurgent leaders published threats targeting the nation's government doubled over a period of two months.

10. You need to provide a yearly update about the host nation's disease control program to an elected representative who does not have the relevant academic training. What is the best communication tool for this task?
  a. Schedule a thirty-minute teleconference to brief the representative.
  b. Summarize the information in the body of an email with a full report attached.
  c. Reach out to the representative's staff and provide the information to a qualified subordinate.
  d. Send the report to the representative's chief of staff and let that individual judge the best way to proceed.

156

11. You field an emergency phone call from an American citizen in your host nation reporting that one of their family members has been arrested. The police are not permitting communication with the arrested person, even by legal counsel. Which of the following do you report this situation to first?
   a. The ambassador
   b. Your supervisor
   c. The embassy's legal expert
   d. The State Department's Operations Center

12. A senior official assigns your team an additional task for the month. As team leader, it is your job to decide which team member will focus on the senior official's project. Which of the following is the most efficient choice?
   a. A subject matter expert
   b. The team member with the fewest tasks
   c. You, so the official knows you're taking it seriously
   d. The team member with the best record for on-time task completion

13. You need to coordinate a search and rescue operation with local authorities to find a missing American citizen. From past experience, you know the local leader in question is proficient in written English but struggles with spoken English. You are familiar in passing with the province's most common dialect. What is the best way to coordinate the operation with this leader?
   a. Establish plans using written communication, such as email, in preference to face-to-face contact.
   b. Hire a translator to support the local leader during meetings.
   c. Hire a translator to support you during meetings.
   d. Coordinate so that additional FSOs are present during meetings for language support.

14. Your supervisor assigns an extra report to your list of tasks this week. In addition, you have an analysis that is due this week to a different department, and an intelligence summary for a senior official in Washington that is due early next week. Which of the following tasks do you prioritize when organizing your workflow for the week?
   a. The report for Washington because of the official's seniority
   b. Your usual workload to avoid asking your teammates to cover it
   c. The other department's analysis so they can make early use of the data
   d. The new report so your diligence impresses the supervisor

15. You are stationed in a country where the local culture values flexibility in schedules over punctual timekeeping. There is a business meeting scheduled at a cafe at 1:00 pm. How do you plan to attend this meeting?
   a. Arrive at 1:00 pm, order a drink, and wait for the other attendees if necessary.
   b. Arrive at 1:00 pm and bring a laptop to productively continue other work until other attendees arrive.
   c. Arrive at 1:00 pm and use a smartphone or pocket-sized notebook to make productive use of empty time, as needed.
   d. Wrap up in-progress tasks at the office and aim to arrive before 1:30 pm.

16. You have a meeting with an FSO stationed in another city and are going to be more than an hour late because of a delay in the country's public transport system. What is an appropriate course of action?
    a.   Apologize for arriving tardy to the meeting site.
    b.   Call the FSO to report the delay and offer to reschedule.
    c.   Text, email, or use another method of digital communication to report tardiness to the FSO.
    d.   Seek out another method of transportation, such as a taxi or renting a car, to minimize or eliminate the delay.

17. Two of your staff have fallen ill, and without their labor, the project your team is working on for the State Department will not be delivered on time. What is your most important responsibility as the team's leader?
    a.   Seek out additional resources to complete the project on time.
    b.   Inform your point of contact that the project will be late due to your team's recent illness.
    c.   Take on the ill team members' labor yourself.
    d.   Inform your point of contact that the project has fallen behind and that you will devise solutions for the State Department to implement until the project is delivered.

18. One of your coworkers is falling behind on their contribution to a team project and asks you for assistance to catch back up. How do you respond?
    a.   Provide assistance within context of your expertise while at the office.
    b.   Provide any assistance requested while at the office.
    c.   Provide any assistance requested, including working outside the office.
    d.   Do not provide assistance, because you are not qualified to complete their portion of the team's project.

19. While working at the embassy, you notice that a coworker outside your own team is consistently working longer hours than the rest of their team. Your team receives weekly reports from them as part of ordinary operations, and you've noticed that the quality of these reports is decreasing. The individual often looks harried and tired. Do you act on these observations?
    a.   Yes, by reaching out to the individual's superior and discretely expressing concern about their workload.
    b.   Yes, by asking if they need temporary assistance completing their weekly reports.
    c.   No, because it's more professional to avoid interference with another team's operations.
    d.   No, because it's more appropriate to spend mental and emotional energy on your own workload.

20. Your team has been assigned a new member, who is also new to diplomatic work in your host nation. How do you help them integrate into your team?
    a.   Speak with your team leader and volunteer to formally be assigned as their mentor.
    b.   Ensure that they're invited to participate in social functions associated with work.
    c.   Double-check their work, and speak with the new teammate if it isn't up to standard.
    d.   Informally mentor them in the workplace by providing contextual information, directing them to learning resources, and describing routine procedures.

21. During a team meeting, one of your coworkers amicably declines a suggestion of getting together after work because they're going out with some locals they've befriended. You reflect that this coworker has lately spent more nonwork time with local friends than with Foreign Service colleagues. How do you respond?
   a. Do nothing. A coworker's personal life is their own to do as they see fit.
   b. Privately ask your team leader if the coworker's friendship is appropriate in the context of diplomatic work.
   c. Ask what your coworker's plans are, out of curiosity.
   d. Suggest that the two groups socialize together.

22. Your team at the local consulate has been assigned a new leader who was previously stationed somewhere else in your host nation. As one of their employees, how can you facilitate the transition in leadership so that the team's operations are not disrupted?
   a. Prepare a short document for the new leader describing the team's weekly operations.
   b. Offer to walk the new leader through your list of trainings for new staff members.
   c. Pick out a simple welcome gift with your teammates to give to the new leader.
   d. Unilaterally support the new leader's methods and decisions, even if they depart from prior practices.
   e. Use questions to encourage both coworkers and the new leader to explain their decision-making processes during team meetings.

23. Your team's leader goes on sick leave with little warning while your team is trying to meet an important deadline. How do you work with your team to respond to the leader's absence?
   a. Look to the most senior team member for guidance.
   b. Suggest a team meeting to figure out how to portion out the leader's tasks.
   c. Propose that the team determines who has authority as an interim leader.
   d. Ask the next person up the hierarchy to designate an interim leader.
   e. Advocate proceeding without someone taking the leader's role until the team has further information about the absent leader's health.

24. During your first week in a new host nation, you're invited to a dinner with both American and local officials to welcome you to the country. You've received basic education on dining etiquette but still aren't entirely confident about how to proceed. Which lead do you follow at the dinner?
   a. The nearest citizen of the host nation
   b. Your immediate superior
   c. A non-American translator who works with your embassy
   d. Relying on what you've been taught and watching attendees' reactions to identify mistakes

25. While in a conversation with a local contact, they look down at the ground, and then up at the ceiling, before breathing in deeply and sharing a piece of information. What is the contact's probable emotional association with this information?
   a. Sorrow
   b. Fear
   c. Shame
   d. Anxiety

26. You're teleconferencing with a group of policymakers about your host nation's economic policies. Several attendees have questions. Which of the following individuals do you prioritize when it comes to relaying information?
    a. A senator who is on the Joint Economic Committee
    b. A senior official from Germany
    c. A congressperson who is on the Foreign Affairs Committee
    d. A senior member of the Treasury

27. You have been directed to inform a local leader of the American government's refusal of financial support to the host nation's military. How do you control your expression and physical actions to present appropriate body language for this situation?
    a. Maintain eye contact and a soft voice, and use conciliatory hand gestures.
    b. Maintain eye contact, and speak firmly and clearly, with few physical gestures.
    c. Maintain eye contact, cross arms, and choose against intentionally controlling tone of voice.
    d. Avoid eye contact, relax shoulders and arms, and stand in a neutral position.

28. The alarm for dangerous weather starts ringing in your office. How do you respond?
    a. Follow procedure and head to an emergency shelter.
    b. Go through your floor and ensure no one is left behind.
    c. Search online to confirm the weather conditions.
    d. Message a coworker to check if a weather drill was scheduled for today.

Test #1 Answer Explanations

Part One: Job Knowledge

1. C: The market-clearing price reflects the price at which the demand perfectly equals the supply. Choice *A* indicates an overall increase in the price of all goods and a decrease in purchasing power. Choice *B* is a condition where the demand is greater than the supply. Choice *D* is an economic theory that states that one group cannot gain benefits without another group experiencing loss.

2. B: Given what you know about Bob and Jim in this scenario, the most likely reason for Bob's negative review of Jim is that Bob is letting his subjective personal feelings about Jim affect his review of Jim's work. Employees should do their best to be objective and ignore personal feelings when performing evaluations of each other. Choice *A* is incorrect because Jim has written a fair and balanced review of everyone and has not tried to single out Bob's work. Choice *C* is incorrect because there's been no indication that Jim has tried to intentionally trick Bob somehow. Choice *D* is incorrect because no other evaluations of Jim's performance have been negative.

3. B: Choice *B* is correct because it is an example of hard power, not soft power. In diplomatic parlance, direct actions taken by a state to influence another state can generally be sorted into two categories. *Soft power* refers to actions taken by a state that induce voluntary action. *Hard power* actions are generally those that force a certain group or population into a certain course of action. Choices *A, C,* and *D* are therefore incorrect because they all involve a voluntary action on behalf of the recipient population to accept those attempts. Choice *B*, on the other hand, is an example of hard power since economic sanctions directly impact a population's ability to exist normally and forces them into action.

4. A: When performing a Google search, if a phrase is surrounded by quotation marks, the search engine will interpret that to mean that it should look for exact matches for that phrase and exclude partial matches. A minus sign is required to exclude terms, so Choice *B* is incorrect. Variations of a phrase in quotation marks are ignored, so Choice *C* is incorrect. There isn't a method to specify the number of times the quoted parameter appears in a search result, so Choice *D* is incorrect.

5. B: Senators serve six-year terms. Choice *A* is the term for a representative. Choices *C* and *D* are not the terms that senators serve. Senators may choose to run for reelection after their six-year term is finished.

6. C: Congress is part of the legislative branch, which creates laws. The Senate and the House of Representatives together are referred to as Congress. Choice *A* makes up part of the executive branch. Choice *B* lists two individuals in different branches of government. The secretary of state is part of the executive branch, while the Speaker of the House is a member of Congress. Choice *D* makes up the judicial branch.

7. A: The Bill of Rights outlines the most fundamental rights that citizens of the United States have, including freedom of speech, religion, assembly, and more. Choice *B* is the first constitution written by the newly created United States after they declared independence. Choice *C* is the name given to three documents that played an important part in the founding of the United States. These documents are the Constitution, the Bill of Rights, and the Declaration of Independence. Choice *D* is a document that outlined the Thirteen Colonies' desire to gain independence from Great Britain.

Test #1 Answer Explanations

8. C: Manifest Destiny greatly shaped American perception about its special role in spreading its ideals across the continent and expanding its territory. Choice *A* is journalism based on exaggerating and sensationalizing the news. Choice *B* was a declaration by Abraham Lincoln to formally free all slaves in Confederate states. Choice *D* is a popular saying about American exceptionalism and emphasizes the moral character of America.

9. B: The Japanese attack on Pearl Harbor resulted in the United States formally entering WWII on the Allied side and ending its isolationist policies. Choice *A* was an Allied invasion of Normandy occurring after the United States had already entered the war. Choice *C* was a treaty signed in 1918 and involved WWI, not WWII. Choice *D* marked the end of WWII and occurred four years after Pearl Harbor.

10. D: Woodrow Wilson famously proposed a series of fourteen points to promote world peace and end WWI. He advocated for an international peacemaking organization, leading to the creation of the League of Nations. Choices *A, B,* and *C* were not majorly involved in creating the League of Nations.

11. A: The formula for the rate of change is the same as slope: change in y over change in x. The y-value in this case is the percentage of smokers and the x-value is the year. The change in percentage of smokers from 2000 to 2015 was 8.1%. The change in x was $2000 - 2015 = -15$. Therefore,

$$\frac{8.1\%}{-15} = -0.54\%$$

The percentage of smokers decreased 0.54% each year.

12. D: Tertiary sources make great starting points for more focused research, so in this situation, the best choice is starting with a database that covers the history of economic policy changes.

13. B: The Space Race was a competition between the United States and the Soviet Union to establish the successful exploration of space. It was one of the major events of the Cold War. Choices *A, C,* and *D* were not heavily involved in the Space Race with the United States.

14. B: Let x be equal to the fifth test score. Therefore, in order to receive, at minimum, a B in the class, the student must have:

$$\frac{74 + 76 + 82 + 84 + x}{5} = 80$$

Therefore:

$$\frac{316 + x}{5} = 80$$

Solving for x gives $316 + x = 400$, or $x = 84$. Therefore, he must receive at least an 84 out of 100 on the fifth test to receive a B in the course.

15. D: Headers and footers can be added by looking in the "Insert" tab. Choice *A* changes the orientation and margins of the text. Choice *B* changes how the page appears on the screen, such as showing a single page or two pages at once. Choice *C* is mainly used to add citations and notes in the document.

162

This content is provided exclusively for test preparation purposes and does not imply our support of any particular religious, political, or scientific point of view. Copyright © APEX Publishing. You have been licensed one copy of this document for personal use only. Any other reproduction or redistribution is strictly prohibited. All rights reserved.

16. C: American immigrants' homeland first changed dramatically in the early 20th century. The American colonists were mostly British, and immigration until the late 19th century was mostly confined to the British Isles. In the late 19th century and early 20th century, immigrants arrived from southeastern Europe en masse. This placed considerable strain on American society, as the current residents were Protestant, and the new immigrants were Catholic and Jewish.

17. A: An official printing of a new law is a primary source since it is a direct source of information. It isn't informal or academic, so Choices *B* and *D* are incorrect. A tertiary source in this case would be a database of relevant laws instead of the direct text of a law, so Choice *C* is incorrect.

18. A: The question is asking what was NOT included in the Missouri Compromise of 1820. The Missouri Compromise had three parts: Maine was admitted as a free state; Missouri was admitted as a slave state; and slavery was prohibited in new territories north of the 36°30' parallel. The only answer that doesn't name a part of the Missouri Compromise is Choice *D*, so it must be correct. The Compromise of 1850 banned slavery in Washington, D.C.

19. B: The Electoral College chooses the next president indirectly. Voters select electors who choose the next president. The electors' vote typically matches the state's popular vote. Presidents must receive 270 out of a possible 538 votes to become president. Choice *A* is the main purpose of the United States Foreign Service. Choice *C* is incorrect because the Constitution, not the Electoral College, determines the number of Supreme Court justices. Choice *D* is incorrect because the Electoral College is a method of voting, not a physical location.

20. A: SQL stands for Structured Query Language. SQL is used in combination with databases to retrieve information. Choices *B, C,* and *D* are not what SQL stands for.

21. D: The Constitution states that the number of representatives from a state depends on its total population. Larger states will have more representatives. Choices *A, B,* and *C* are not relevant factors for determining the number of state representatives.

22. A: Authoritative management can also be described as micromanagement, focused on every detail of team members' work and guiding them every step of the way. Consultative is a term more indicative of democratic management, so Choice *B* is incorrect. Improvement is more representative of transformational management, so Choice *C* is incorrect. Family is an alternate descriptor for paternalistic management, so Choice *D* is incorrect.

23. D: Both persuasive and paternalistic managers will explain the reasons for their decisions to their team members; this makes Choice *A* incorrect. However, persuasive managers will entertain questions from the team members to provide the opportunity to explain those reasons, whereas paternalistic managers will not give that opportunity, making Choice *D* correct. Both management styles involve micromanaging employees to some degree and constant supervision, so Choices *B* and *C* are both incorrect.

24. C: Consultative management focuses on gathering input directly from each team member, so a major risk is favoring certain team members' input more strongly than others. All team members should be equally considered. Irritating employees with platitudes is a risk of paternalistic management, so Choice *A* is incorrect. Unaddressed conflict is a risk of laissez-faire management styles, so Choice *B* is incorrect. Consultative management tries to address all employees equally and directly, so a risk of employees feeling that they aren't being given equal opportunity should be very unlikely, making Choice *D* incorrect.

25. B: The United States first industrialized during the First Industrial Revolution to replace the decline in British imports caused by the War of 1812. However, this development was limited to towns in the Northeast. Urbanization didn't occur until after the Civil War, and it was caused by the Second Industrial Revolution's technological innovations, like steel production, railways, and more sophisticated factory machinery. The Great Migration and successive waves of immigration increased the pace of urbanization, supplying labor to the urban boom. Yet, urbanization wouldn't have occurred without the Second Industrial Revolution transforming America from an agricultural to industrial economy.

26. D: Many of these metrics are important, but it is most important to consider the job position you are reviewing. Productivity may be more or less important than attitude, depending on the main roles of the job. Since any of these metrics could be more or less important than the others, Choices *A*, *B*, and *C* are all incorrect.

27. B: The third in line in the presidential line of succession is the president pro tempore of the Senate. Choice *A* is first in line. Choice *C* is second in line. Choice *D* is fourth in line.

28. D: In this situation, it's important to be firm and assertive but not aggressive towards a superior. By calmly explaining your reasoning for supporting option A and why it addresses problems from option B, you may come across as more assertive and knowledgeable without trying to upstage or talk down to a superior. Choice *A* is incorrect because the tone is too aggressive and likely won't be received well. Choice *B* is incorrect because it's too passive-aggressive; it allows the problems to manifest before doing anything to address them. Choice *C* is incorrect because completely ignoring your boss is both rude and disruptive to team cohesion.

29. B: Macros are useful tools that automate repetitive tasks. Choices *A*, *C*, and *D* are possible applications for a macro but are not what the term itself refers to.

30. C: SQL is a tool primarily used to filter and retrieve data from a database. Choice *A* is a web browser for accessing the internet. Choice *B* is a word-processing software. Choice *D* is a spreadsheet software.

31. C: The United States and the Soviet Union were the two superpowers of the Cold War, racing to go to the moon. Choice *A* is incorrect because the United States was an ally of Great Britain at this time. Choice *B* is incorrect because Nazi Germany had already fallen by 1962. Choice *D* is incorrect because tensions between Iraq and the United States did not begin until Desert Storm of the 1990s.

32. D: Northern Whigs and Free Soil Democrats created the Republican Party to advocate for the abolition of slavery, so Choice *D* is the correct answer. Abraham Lincoln was the first Republican to be elected president. The Republicans exposed the Southern theory of states' rights, and their pro-business agenda didn't develop until after the Civil War. Manifest destiny also wasn't the Republicans primary issue; it was slavery.

33. A: Spanish explorers established St. Augustine in 1565. All other colonies were founded at least a decade later. Sir Walter Raleigh founded Roanoke in 1585, making it the first British colony, but it was abandoned in 1590. Established in 1607, Jamestown was the first successful British colony. The British explorer Henry Hudson explored Hudson's Bay in the 1610s, and the French established trading outposts in the area during the 1670s. Thus, Choice *A* is the correct answer.

34. C: The vice president is also the president of the Senate. However, most of the daily operations of the Senate usually fall to the president pro tempore of the Senate. Choice *A* is the leader of the House of

164

Representatives. Choice *B* leads the Supreme Court and is also the head of the judicial branch. Choice *D* is the head of the executive branch.

35. C: A report providing analysis or commentary on something is a secondary source. A primary source would be a direct description of the foreign policy changes, so Choice *A* is incorrect. A tertiary source would be an explorable database of foreign policy changes, so Choice *B* is incorrect. *Comprehensive source* is a false term, so Choice *D* is incorrect.

36. C: The Marshall Plan provided economic relief to war-torn Europe after WWII. One of its objectives was to decrease the influence of communism by increasing positive relations between the United States and Europe. Choice *A* was a series of economic reforms in the 1930s by President Franklin Roosevelt to provide relief to Americans affected by the Great Depression. Choice *B* was signed by President Joe Biden to increase the economic recovery of the nation following the COVID-19 pandemic. Choice *D* was signed by President Donald Trump at the height of the COVID-19 pandemic to stimulate the economy.

37. C: The Constitution grants the president the ability to grant pardons to individuals who have committed a federal crime. Choice *A* is incorrect because the Senate confirms Supreme Court nominations, while the president is the one who selects them. Choice *B* is a power granted to Congress. Choice *D* is one of the powers of the House of Representatives.

38. D: Of these four candidates, Jim is the best choice for a leadership promotion based on the evaluations. With a level head and considerate nature, he is a good match for a leadership position on the team. Mary has plenty of experience, but her anger issues could cause trouble when problems within the team come up, so Choice *A* is incorrect. Bob's behavior towards his team members will likely cause frustration and conflict among the people he's supervising, so Choice *B* is incorrect. Stacy is a promising choice, but if she doesn't socialize much with the team, then it will be difficult to gauge how well she will be able to convey information to them as a leader, so Choice *C* is incorrect.

39. D: Choice *D* is correct because game theory is the study of mathematical models designed to represent strategic interactions between what are called "rational actors"—people acting in the service of their own interests. Game theory has major implications for understanding why and how people spend money and make financial decisions. Choice *A* is incorrect because game theory does not focus only on frivolous choices, although some rational actors may choose to spend their money frivolously. Choice *B* is incorrect because game theory does not focus on gambling. Choice *C* is incorrect because game theory is not concerned with gamification.

40. A: Putting this new employee in a mentorship program with a more experienced team member is one way to help bring the new employee up to speed on the team's jobs and type of work. *Tutorial programs* and *captaincy programs* are false terms, so Choices *B* and *D* are incorrect. A rehabilitation program is for helping people recover from health problems and is unrelated, so Choice *C* is incorrect.

41. D: Sales tax is an example of a regressive tax, which affects low-income individuals more heavily than wealthier individuals. Choice *A* refers to the taxes someone pays when they receive assets from a deceased person. Choice *B* is a tax that affects wealthier individuals more heavily than low-income individuals. Choice *C* is a tax that affects people based on a proportion of their income.

42. B: A closed economy is one in which there are no imports or exports. National savings is the total sum of a country's private and public savings. Since there is no exchange of goods, national savings will be equivalent to investments. Choices *A* and *C* are incorrect because there are no imports or exports in a closed economy. Choice *D* uses current resources to satisfy the country's needs, which is the opposite of investment.

43. C: Landscape orientation is horizontal, or on its side. Choice *B* is vertical orientation of the page. Choices *A* and *D* are not terms used to describe page orientation.

44. C: An effective process of conducting research is to start with wide searches, use filters and tools to narrow your search, and then end with exploring specific sources. Choice *A* starts too specific with secondary sources, so it is incorrect. Choice *B* starts specific and says to use citations instead of filters or tools, so it is incorrect. Choice *D* starts and ends correctly, but doesn't specify to use filters or tools, so it is incorrect.

45. C: An embargo is similar to a sanction but more severe. It is a total ban on trade with another country, usually used as a punishment. Choice *A* is a tariff. Choices *B* and *D* are incorrect because an embargo is not a form of economic aid and severely reduces trade within a country, decreasing relations and punishing the recipient of an embargo.

46. D: CSV stands for Comma Separated Values. Choices *A, B,* and *C* are not what CSV stands for.

47. B: Putting a list of your sources at the very beginning of your presentation or report is a poor choice because it can be awkward or confusing for many readers or listeners. Citing a source in the footnotes, immediately after a quotation, or at the end of the report or presentation are all preferred methods, so Choices *A, C,* and *D* are all incorrect.

48. B: Real GDP is adjusted for inflation and is considered more accurate than the nominal GDP. Choices *A, C,* and *D* are not used to calculate real GDP.

49. D: Elasticity measures to what degree buyers and producers will change their supply or demand in response to price changes in a good. When the supply is more elastic than the demand, buyers will be responsible for more of the tax. Choice *C* is responsible for more of the tax when demand is more elastic than the supply. Choices *A* and *B* are incorrect because the tax burden will fall on buyers in general, not specifically the wealthy or poor.

50. C: The best approach in this situation is to openly announce that you're willing to help anyone with any problem, without singling anyone out or trying to force your assistance on your team. Casually asking during the lunch break may seem to your team like you're trying to supervise or micromanage them rather than assist them, so Choice *A* is incorrect. Telling the employee you just helped to spread the word could be awkward and may not be as successful as announcing it yourself, so Choice *B* is incorrect. Singling out employees you suspect may need help could be uncomfortable for them, and they may turn you down out of fear or anxiety, so Choice *D* is incorrect.

51. A: The same data that is stored in multiple locations can cause issues when transferring the data to other software. Databases help to reduce data redundancy and organize the data in an easy-to-understand format. Choices *B, C, and D* do not correctly describe data redundancy.

52. C: The mode is the time from the data set that occurs most often. The number 23 occurs twice in the data set, while all others occur only once, so the mode is 23 minutes.

53. A: A proportion should be used to solve this problem. The ratio of tagged to total deer in each instance is set equal to one another, and the unknown quantity is a variable x. The proportion is:

$$\frac{300}{x} = \frac{5}{400}$$

Cross-multiplying gives $120,000 = 5x$, and dividing through by 5 results in 24,000.

54. B: Choice *B* is the correct answer. The Zimmerman Telegram was a message from Germany to Mexico that stated Germany's willingness to help Mexico invade America. Great Britain intercepted the Zimmerman Telegram and delivered it to the American government, hoping it would persuade the United States to join the Triple Entente. Germany didn't invade the Sudetenland until World War II, and the Zimmerman Telegram wasn't a type of telegram or related to the Holocaust.

55. A: An inferior good will decrease in demand as people's income rises. Examples include certain canned or frozen foods because people could choose to purchase more expensive, healthier options as their incomes increase. Choice *B* is a good that is sold at a premium and is not necessary. Choice *C* is a good that increases in demand as income increases. Choice *D* is a good that is provided to everyone and is usually free of charge.

56. D: The Heartland Theory placed strategic importance on eastern Europe and emphasized that controlling this area, also known as the Heartland, would lead to world dominance. Choice *A* is the Rimland Theory, which emphasizes areas outside of the Heartland. Choice *B* is a belief by Alfred Thayer Mahan, who believed that a nation's strength was linked to its naval power. Choice *C* is the Organic Theory.

57. C: Visionary management is a laissez-faire management style, not autocratic. Authoritative, paternalistic, and persuasive are all autocratic management styles, so Choices *A*, *B*, and *D* are all incorrect.

58. B: Choice *B* is correct because high employment and price stability are the goals of the Federal Reserve, the central banking system of the United States. Created in the early twentieth century, the Federal Reserve is primarily concerned with preventing and alleviating financial crises in the United States.

59. B: The Japanese attack on Pearl Harbor and the United States' entry into World War II have a cause-and-effect relationship. Choice *A* is incorrect because the relationship is causation, not correlation. Choice *C* is incorrect because these two events are causally related rather than in opposition to one another. Choice *D* is incorrect because this particular cause-and-effect relationship is direct.

60. A: The collapse of the Soviet Union in 1991 was the immediate end of the decades-long Cold War. Choice *B*, *C*, and *D* were events that happened at the height of the Cold War, not at its end.

Part Two: English Expression and Usage

1. A: Choice *A* correctly capitalizes the district, city, and specific building mentioned. These are all proper nouns and should always be capitalized. It also correctly uses a comma to separate the independent and dependent clauses. Choice *B* is incorrect for two reasons: first because it adds an improper comma after *President*, and second because *prime minister* and *president* do not need to be capitalized unless they directly precede someone's name, as in: "President Jane Sanchez." Choice *C* is incorrect because *Federal*

Reserve should be capitalized since it is a proper noun and a government institution. Choice *D* is incorrect because *attorney* should not be capitalized since it is not being used as a formal title.

2. C: Choice *C* correctly capitalizes *United Nations* due to its being a governmental organization. Choice *A* incorrectly leaves *Senate* uncapitalized. It is an official body of government and should always be capitalized. Choice *B* is incorrect because a semicolon is used to connect an independent clause and a dependent clause. Choice *D* is incorrect because it does not use proper punctuation; this sentence requires commas between all listed items.

3. C: Choice *C* is correct because it correctly capitalizes the name of the specific organization, and it also uses correct punctuation. Choice *A* incorrectly capitalizes *police officers*, which is not a formal title and does not require capitalization. Choice *B* is incorrect because it does not use a comma after the introductory phrase *While campaigning*. Introductory phrases should be followed by a comma. Choice *D* is incorrect because it uses a semicolon to separate an independent clause from a dependent clause. A semicolon should only connect two related independent clauses.

4. B: Choice *B* is the correct answer. It correctly capitalizes the city and state. It also uses correct punctuation. Choice *A* does not correctly capitalize *Secretary of State*, which in this case is being used as Mateo Jackson's formal title. (The sentence "The expert is the secretary of state" would also be correct.) Choice *C* is incorrect because the verb should be in the present tense, not the past tense. The correct verb form in this sentence is *accrue*, not *accrued*. Choice *D* uses the incorrect conjugation of the verb *lend*. It should be *lent*, not *lended*.

5. A: Choice *A* correctly capitalizes *US Congress* and uses correct punctuation. It contains no errors. Choice *B* incorrectly capitalizes the adjective *diplomatic*. The noun form, *diplomat*, should only be capitalized if it is being used as a formal title for a specific person. Choice *C* incorrectly uses a comma. There is no need to separate those two parts of the sentence. Choice *D* is a run-on sentence since it contains too many clause; each half of the sentence cause an independent clause and a dependent clause. For clarity, the independent clauses should be separated into separate sentences: "The representative was sent to China since there was a meeting between foreign officers there. Their goal was to discuss trade negotiations because inflation was negatively affecting both countries."

6. D: Choice *D* uses correct punctuation. The semicolon is correctly separating two related independent clauses. Choice *A* does not correctly capitalize *House of Representatives*, which is a formal legislative part of the government. Choice *B* does not correctly capitalize the *National Park Service*, which is a government agency and should be capitalized as such. Choice *C* does not correctly capitalize *NPR*, which is a specific news organization and an acronym. It should be capitalized for both of those reasons.

7. A: Choice *A* is correct for two reasons. It correctly capitalizes the names of the countries mentioned, and it uses a semicolon to join two independent clauses. Choice *B* incorrectly capitalizes *million*, which is not a proper noun and should not be capitalized. Choice *C* is incorrect because *firefighters* should not be capitalized. It is not being used as a formal title for any specific person. Choice *D* is incorrect because it places a comma where there should be none.

8. D: Choice *D* uses correct verb tense and subject-verb agreement. Choice *A* is incorrect because the sentence should use the past tense, *flew*, not the past participle, *flown*. Choice *B* is incorrect because it should read *night* instead of *knight*. The words are homophones, which means that they sound the same but are spelled differently and have completely different meanings. Choice *C* is incorrect because it should use the infinitive, which is *to open*, not *to opened*.

168

9. A: Choice *A* correctly uses a comma to introduce a line of dialogue. It also uses the correct form of double quotation marks for the professor's words; double quotation marks are standard in American English. There are no errors in the sentence. Choice *B* is incorrect because it places the question mark inside the quotation marks, even though the question is not a part of the quotation. Choice *C* is incorrect because it does not include a comma after the introductory dependent clause. Choice *D* is incorrect because it incorrectly uses an apostrophe in the word *students* to denote possession when there is none.

10. B: Choice *B* is correct because it uses correct punctuation and grammar. It has correct subject-verb agreement, and it does not contain any errors. Choice *A* is incorrect because it has too many phrases, and it does not use any commas to correctly separate these phrases. Choice *C* is incorrect because it does not have correct subject-verb agreement; the noun *wolves* is plural while the verb *chases* is singular. Choice *D* is incorrect because it uses the wrong word, *their*. It should use the word *there* to indicate a location.

11. D: Choice *D* is the correct answer because the sentence does not contain any errors. The punctuation and grammar function well. Choice *A* is incorrect because *football* should not be separated into two words. Choice *B* is incorrect because *going* is in the wrong tense; the verb should be *go*. Choice *C* is incorrect because *Olympics* should be capitalized since it is a proper noun.

12. A: Choice *A* is correct because it correctly capitalizes all the proper nouns in the sentence. This includes the capitalization of a major religion, a notable landmark, a city, and a country. Choice *B* is incorrect because it neglects to capitalize the proper noun that is the name of the park. Choice *C* is incorrect because the name of the international landmark is a proper noun, the Great Wall of China. Choice *D* is incorrect because it does not properly capitalize the name of the city, which is a proper noun.

13. D: Choice *D* is correct because it does not contain any errors. It correctly adds an apostrophe to denote the neighbor's possession of the mailbox. Choice *A* is incorrect because it adds an unnecessary apostrophe to form the word *country's* when the correct word is *countries*. Choice *B* is incorrect because there is should be an apostrophe in the word *it's* when it is a contraction of *it is*. Choice *C* is incorrect because it adds an apostrophe to the word *Wednesdays*, when there should be none because it is plural, not possessive.

14. C: Choice *C* is the correct answer because it correctly uses a comma after the introductory phrase. Additionally, it uses the correct spelling of the word *alter*, rather than *altar* which has a different meaning. Choice *A* is incorrect because *spreaded* is an incorrect conjugation. *Spread* is an irregular verb and is not conjugated with -ed in the past tense. Choice *B* is incorrect because the sentence uses the homophone *aisle*, although the sentence is talking about an *isle*, which is another word for island. Choice *D* is incorrect because the sentence should use the word *already*, which means that something has occurred before a specific time. The two words *all ready* describes a state of preparedness, which does not apply for this sentence.

15. C: Choice *C* is correct because it has subject-verb agreement. In a sentence that uses either/or or neither/nor, the verb must agree with the noun (which is the subject) closest to it. In this case the closest noun is the singular *belt*, and the verb is correctly written as the singular verb *is*. The other choices are incorrect because they do not have subject-verb agreement. Choice *A* has the subject *raisins*, which would require a plural verb. The sentence incorrectly uses *is* instead of *are*. Choice *B* is incorrect because the singular subject *raccoon* does not match the plural verb *are*. Choice *D* is incorrect because the singular subject *cat* does not match the plural verb *were*.

16. B: Choice *B* is correct because it correctly capitalizes the formal title and name of the person mentioned. Choice *A* is incorrect because academic subjects do not need to be capitalized. Choice *C* is incorrect because it uses *then* when the correct word choice would be *than*. *Then* is used to refer to time, and *than* is used to compare things (the bike and bus in this case). Choice *D* is incorrect because Saturday is a day of the week and should be capitalized.

17. B: Choice *B* is correct because it has correct grammar, spelling, and punctuation. The comma is used appropriately after the introductory dependent clause. Choice *A* is incorrect because there is an unnecessary comma before the dependent clause. Choice *C* is incorrect because the semicolon is placed incorrectly before the word *because*. Choice *D* is incorrect because there is no comma before the line of dialogue and after the word *said*.

18. B: Choice *B* is correct because *World Trade Organization* is a proper noun and should be capitalized as such. The other underlined phrases are correct within the context of the original sentence. They follow the conventions of standard English. Choice *A* is incorrect since Choice *B* is an error in the sentence.

19. A: Choice *A* is correct because there is no error in the original sentence. *Olympics* is correctly capitalized; therefore, Choice *B* is incorrect. Choice *C* is incorrect because *country; it* is not an error; the semicolon correctly joins two independent clauses that are related. Choice *D* is not an error since it follows the standard conventions of English.

20. C: Choice *C* is correct because it correctly identifies the error in the sentence. A semicolon should only be used to join independent clauses. In this case, the second portion of this sentence is not an independent clause; it is a relative clause. Choice *A* is incorrect because there is an error in the sentence. Choice *B* is incorrect because Universal Declaration of Human Rights is correctly capitalized as a proper noun and is not an error. Choice *D* is incorrect because the phrase *freedom of all humans* contains no error.

21. A: Choice *A* is correct because there is no error in the sentence. It uses proper punctuation and has a clear structure. The colon is accurately used for a list placed at the end of a clause. Choice *B* is incorrect because *US* is correctly abbreviated and is therefore not an error. Choice *C* is incorrect because the colon is properly used. Choice *D* is incorrect because there is no problem with the comma placement in this section.

22. B: Choice *B* is the correct answer because it contains an apostrophe error. An apostrophe in this manner would typically be used to show possession. The sentence should have the plural form of *agents*, rather than the possessive form. Choice *A* is incorrect because there is an error in the sentence. Choice *C* is incorrect because the politician has possession over the speech they are giving; thus, the apostrophe is being correctly used. Choice *D* is an incorrect answer because the words be *held* correctly follow *would*.

23. C: Choice *C* is correct because it contains the error in the sentence. There should be a comma after the word *agent*. A comma should be used when introducing a direct quote. Choice *A* is incorrect because there is an error in the sentence. Choice *B* is incorrect because there is no error with the first two words of the sentence. There is no problem with the verb or the tense being used. Choice *D* is incorrect because the question mark is correctly placed inside the quotation marks.

24. C: Choice *C* is correct because the phrases uses the homophone *affect* incorrectly. The correct word would be *effect*. Choice *A* is incorrect because there is an error in the sentence. Choice *B* is incorrect because the phrase uses the apostrophe correctly to denote possession. Choice *D* is incorrect because the month is capitalized appropriately.

170

25. D: Choice *D* is the correct answer because there is an error in the underlined portion. There should be a comma between the city and the state. Choice *A* is incorrect because of the aforementioned error. Choice *B* is incorrect because there is no error in the phrase *national cemeteries*. Choice *C* is incorrect because the semicolon is being used appropriately. It is joining two independent clauses that are related.

26. D: Choice *D* is the correct answer because there is an error in the underlined portion. An apostrophe should only be used to show possession. Since the sentence is referring to the family members in the plural, there should be no apostrophe. Choice *A* is incorrect because there is an error in the sentence. Choice *B* is incorrect because *postcard* is written appropriately. Choice *C* is incorrect because the sentence is correctly using a comma before a quote, quotation marks, and appropriate capitalization.

27. D: Choice *D* is the correct answer because the punctuation being used is not appropriate for the sentence context. The sentence is not asking a question. It is a statement, so a period would be the correct punctuation. Choice *A* is incorrect because there is an error with the punctuation. Choice *B* is incorrect because *queen* is being used generically and does not need to be capitalized. Choice *C* is incorrect because the name of the country is being capitalized correctly.

28. C: Choice *C* is correct because it is the answer that features an error in the sentence. The sentence uses the word *allusion*, which means an indirect reference to something. The sentence should use the homonym *illusion*, which means a false perception of something. The context of the sentence fits with that definition. Choice *A* is incorrect because there is an error in the sentence. Choices *B* and *D* do not contain any type of error and are thus incorrect.

29. D: Choice *D* is the correct answer because *do* should actually be spelled as *due*. *Do* means to perform while *due* in this context means to be the result of. That matches the context better and corrects the homonym error. Choice *A* is incorrect because there is an error in the sentence. Choices *B* and *C* do not contain errors and are thus incorrect answers.

30. B: Choice *B* is the correct answer because it contains a verb tense error. The sentence states that the help occurred in the past. Therefore, the verb should be in the past tense: *helped*. Choice *A* is not correct because of the tense error that is present. Choice *C* is not correct because *set up* is correctly separated into two words. *Setup* or *set-up* would have been incorrect. Choice *D* is incorrect because it is an appropriate word choice, and it is spelled correctly.

31. C: Choice *C* is the correct answer because the words *postal service* are part of the formal name of a government agency and should be capitalized as such. The correct form would be *United States Postal Service*. Choice *A* is incorrect because there is a capitalization error in this sentence. Choice *B* is incorrect because *United States* is correctly capitalized. Choice *D* is not correct because the dollar amount is written correctly with a dollar sign.

32. D: Choice *D* is the correct answer because there are missing commas. There should be commas to separate the nouns in the list. Choice *A* is incorrect because of the punctuation errors. Choice *B* is incorrect because the first word of the sentence is properly capitalized, and the year is written correctly. Choice *C* is incorrect because the term *caused people* is appropriately used, and it is spelled correctly.

33. B: Choice *B* is the correct answer because the subject is looking at her own reflection. The word should be the reflexive pronoun *herself*, not *her*. Choice *A* is incorrect because there is an error in the sentence. Choice *C* is incorrect because there is no error in the transition into a quote. Choice *D* is incorrect since there is no error with the punctuation at the end of the sentence.

34. A: Choice *A* is the correct answer because there is no error in the sentence. The name of the organization is capitalized correctly, so it cannot be Choice *B*. Choices *C* and *D* are incorrect because they do not contain any errors.

35. B: Choice *B* is the best possible correction for the original sentence. *Variety* refers to a great number of things. The context word *diverse* clues us into this being the correct word choice. *Variation* refers to a change from something already established, which is not relevant in this context. Choice *C* and *D* do not fit with the context and are incorrect.

36. A: Choice *A* is the correct answer since there is no error with the original underlined word. It uses the correct form of *bear*. In this context, *bear* means to carry. *Bare*, which is Choice *B*, refers to being uncovered. That does not work in this context and is incorrect. Choices *C* and *D* are not relevant to the context of the original sentence and are not correct.

37. A: Choice *A* is the correct answer since there is no error with the original underlined section. There does not need to be any punctuation between the underlined words. Choice *B* is incorrect because a comma would be needed only if two independent clauses were being joined by a conjunction. This is not the case. Choice *C* is incorrect because a semicolon is used to join related independent clauses, which is not the case. Choice *D* is incorrect because, although an em dash is highly versatile, it is incorrect for this sentence.

38. D: Choice *D* is the correct phrasing for the original sentence. Using *me* is incorrect in this sentence. Whenever the person speaking is doing the action, the correct phrasing is to say *I*. Choice *D* is the only option that uses *I* instead of some form of *me* or *myself*. Choices *B* and *C* are incorrect for this reason. Choice *A* is incorrect because there is an error in the original underlined portion.

39. B: Choice *B* is the correct answer because it fixes the homophone error with the right word. *Piece* refers to a portion of something. *Peace* refers to a lack of disturbance, which is the word that fits best with the context of the original sentence. Choice *A* is incorrect because there is a word choice error. Choice *C* is incorrect because the word *peak* does not fit in the context of the original sentence. Choice *D* may seem to fit the context of the original sentence. However, *pacifism* is a political stance; its adherents are against war. UN forces are typically sent to maintain a lack of disturbance—*peace*—not to enforce one political view, *pacifism*.

40. C: Choice *C* is the correct answer because it fixes the homophone error with the right word. *Whether* is a word used to indicate choice between alternatives. *Weather* is the correct word for this context, as it refers to the conditions of the atmosphere. This is relevant to the enjoyment of a beach vacation. Choice *A* is incorrect since there is an error. Choice *B* is incorrect because *wether* is a type of ram. Choice *D* is incorrect because *waver* is an unrelated word that means to shake.

41. D: Choice *D* is the correct answer because it fixes the homophone error with the right word. *Excepted* would mean to be left out of a group. For the context of this sentence, *accepted* is the better word choice. It means to be received as adequate, which is the judgement that medical schools give out for admissions. Choice *A* is incorrect since there is a word choice error. Choice *B* is incorrect because *expected* means that something is anticipated as likely to happen. Choice *C* is incorrect because *excluded* means to be left out of something, similar to the original word error. This does not work with the context of the sentence.

42. B: Choice *B* is the correct answer because it fixes the singular/plural pronoun mistake in the original sentence. The subject of the sentence is *teacher*, and it is singular. Therefore, the next pronoun which refers to the same subject, should agree in number. *Themselves* is incorrect because it is plural. The

172

correct answer would be to make it the singular form of *themself. Himself* and *Herself* are incorrect because the original subject is not gender specific.

43. D: Choice *D* is the correct answer because it corrects the punctuation error. There does not need to be a comma in this place, and Choice *D* successfully eliminates it. Choice *A* is not correct because there is an unnecessary comma. Choice *B* is not correct because it makes the word *document* singular, and Panama Papers is a plural noun. Choice *C* is not correct because there is no need for a semicolon in this place since it would not be joining two independent clauses.

44. C: Choice *C* is the answer choice that corrects the punctuation error in the original sentence. Colons are used before lists, such as the one seen in this sentence. Colons and semicolons cannot be used interchangeably; therefore, the original sentence's semicolon must be replaced by a colon. This is why Choice *C* is the best answer. Choice *A* is incorrect because there is a punctuation error. Choice *B* is incorrect because a comma should not be used before an extensive list. Choice *D* is not correct because the new second sentence would be a sentence fragment.

45. B: Choice *B* is correct because it corrects the homophone error. This sentence uses the wrong word, *their. They're, there*, and *there are* homophones; that means they all sound the same but have different meanings and different spellings. The sentence uses *their*, which is a possessive pronoun. *There* is the more appropriate word choice because it is an adverb referring to the existence or location of something. Choice *A* is incorrect because there is an error in the sentence. Choice *C* is incorrect because in the context of *bike lines on the roads*, the phrase *there are* is the most logical answer. Choice *D, they're*, is the contraction of *they are* and is incorrect for the same reason as Choice *C.*

46. B: Choice *B* is the answer that corrects the error in the original sentence. *Whose* is used to denote possession. This does not work in the context of this sentence. The phrasing of *who is* works better for the sentence's purpose. Choice *A* is incorrect because there is an error in the sentence. Choice *C* is not correct because it misspells *whose.* Choice *D* is not correct because *whom* is the object of a verb, which is not the case in this sentence.

47. D: Choice *D* is the answer that corrects the subject-verb agreement error. *Are* is a plural present verb which means that it is incorrect for this sentence. Choice *D* is correct because *is* is a singular verb and meets the criteria for subject-verb agreement. Choice *A* is incorrect because there is an error present. Choice *B* is incorrect because *be* is improper grammar since it is a present subjunctive and does not work with the sentence. Choice *C* is incorrect because *run* is a plural verb, and the sentence requires a singular verb.

48. A: Choice *A* is the correct answer because *which* is correctly used in this sentence. *Which* is used to introduce nonrestrictive clauses. In this case, it is not imperative to know that the story was on the news in order to understand that it inspired people. Choice *B* is incorrect because *which* is referring to the story and not a person, so it would not be appropriate to use *who.* Choice *C* is incorrect for the same reason as Choice *B.* Choice *D* is incorrect because *that* is used for restrictive clauses and that does not apply in this case.

49. C: Choice *C* is correct because *counsel* is the best word for the context of the sentence. *Counsel* refers to advice or guidance, which is something that an attorney would provide in this situation. Choice *A* is incorrect because *council* refers to a committee of people and does not fit this sentence. Choice *B* is incorrect because *conciliation* means to stop someone from being angry. This does not apply to the context of this sentence. Choice *D* is incorrect because *conceal* means to hide, which has no relation to the sentence.

50. D: Choice *D* is the correct answer because it corrects the capitalization error in the original sentence. The museum's name is a proper noun, so the entirety of the name should be capitalized. Choice *D* does this correctly without changing the punctuation. Choice *A* is incorrect because there is a capitalization error present. Choice *B* is incorrect because the proper noun should be capitalized. Choice *C* is incorrect because it adds an unnecessary comma between the name of the museum and the city.

51. A: Choice *A* is correct because there is no error in the original sentence. It properly introduces the quote with a comma and double quotation marks. Choice *B* is incorrect because there needs to be a comma to introduce the quote. Choice *C* is incorrect because the quotation marks are missing. Choice *D* is incorrect because the first word in the quote should be capitalized.

52. D: Choice *D* is correct because the order of 3, 1, 4, 2 creates the best flowing paragraph. Sentence 3 introduces the topic being discussed with a simple definition. Sentence 1 describes the necessary materials for that process. Sentence 4 explains the action taking place. Sentence 2 describes the end result. The sentences in this order make the most logical sense since they follow a linear structure.

53. A: Choice *A* is the sentence order that creates the most logical paragraph. Sentence 4 introduces the topic being discussed. Sentence 1 further elaborates on the first sentence. Sentence 3 mentions a major part of the war, which happened in the middle of the timeline. Sentence 4 describes the end of the war. This is the most logical sequence of events and creates a well-organized paragraph.

54. D: Choice *D* is correct because the order of 1, 4, 2, 3 creates the best flowing paragraph. Sentence 1 introduces the topic being discussed. Sentence 4 uses a transition word with *however* to signal the discrepancy between the independence and the annexation. It naturally flows after Sentence 1 for this reason. Sentence 2 goes more into depth about how the annexation came about, so it most naturally comes after the first mention of annexation, which is in Sentence 4. Sentence 3 fits best as the last sentence because it talks about what happened after the annexation. This order makes the paragraph read linearly and clearly.

55. A: Choice *A* is correct because the order of 2, 3, 4, 1 creates the most logical paragraph. Sentence 2 comes first because it introduces the topic of visas. Sentence 3 is the most logical follow-up to this because it is elaborating on the topic, and it is also the first mention of different types of visas. Sentence 4 elaborates on some examples of visas, which flows logically from the previous sentence. Sentence 1 comes after 4 because it uses the transition word *although*, which is referring to the examples mentioned in the previous sentence. This order creates the most logical paragraph.

56. C: Choice *C* is correct because it creates a paragraph that flows smoothly. Sentence 3 comes first because it introduces the topic being discussed. In the next sentence, sentence 1, the word *it* is a direct reference to the topic, *Kemalism*, which is mentioned in Sentence 3. Sentence 4 comes next because it introduces a more in-depth fact about the ideology of Kemalism. Lastly, Sentence 2 expands on the in-depth fact that was mentioned in the previous sentence. This is the best order of sentences since every line builds on the previous one in a way that makes logical sense.

57. A: Choice *A* is the best option for creating a clear, well-structured paragraph. Sentence 1 introduces the topic and is the best choice for the first sentence. Sentence 4 flows the best as the next sentence since it expands on what the focus of the subject is. Sentence 3 should come after because it provides an example. Sentence 2 expands on this example and only works well after Sentence 3. This order creates a logical and well-structured paragraph that is easy to understand.

58. B: Choice *B* is the best order for creating a well-structured paragraph. Sentence 2 is the best option for the beginning of the paragraph. It is introducing the topic, which is Washington, D.C. Sentence 4 fits best as the next sentence because it tells what is unique about the city. Sentence 3 elaborates on sentence 4, explaining where the city is located. Sentence 1 follows logically because it explains the name of the district. This order presents the clearest and most organized paragraph possible.

59. C: Choice *C* is the best addition to the original paragraph. The original paragraph gives a general breakdown of what a political summit is. In order to help readers understand the purpose of a summit, it would be useful to include a historical example. Choice *A* would not be useful since this paragraph does not aim to explain the linguistic history of the word. Choice *B* would not be useful because it is too specific to a single meeting. Choice *D* is also too specific to be relevant enough for inclusion.

60. D: Choice *D* is correct because it best describes the purpose of this paragraph. This paragraph gives introductory information about zoology. It does not go into depth about the subject. Choice *A* is incorrect since the paragraph never mentions specific zoologists. Choice *B* is incorrect because the paragraph is not persuasive in any way. Choice *C* is incorrect because the paragraph never mentions any current events happening in zoology.

61. A: Choice *A* is correct because it best describes the purpose of the paragraph. The paragraph describes the history of basketball. It discusses how basketball became popular and briefly mentions that it has changed over time. The best description for this is to say that the paragraph is telling readers about the history of basketball. Choice *B* is incorrect because James Naismith is only mentioned as the inventor. There are no additional facts provided about him. Choice *C* is incorrect because although the paragraph says that basketball has changed over time, it does not go into specifics about that. Choice *D* is incorrect because there is no description about what basketball does to the human body.

62. B: Choice *B* is the best addition to the paragraph. This paragraph tells readers how to make their own candle at home. It breaks down each ingredient and the steps needed. However, it does not mention the specific amounts of ingredients needed. This is important information for instructions. Without this information, the reader will get stuck on one of the first steps (measuring out the wax). Choice *A* would be difficult to include because the prices of ingredients are always fluctuating and are dependent on the brand. Choice *C* would not be helpful to readers since this is meant to be a how-to paragraph. Choice *D* is not needed since the reader will see what fragrance scents are available when they are buying the ingredients.

63. C: Choice *C* is correct because it would be a strong addition to this paragraph. It would add emotional effect by mentioning how this problem hurts sick or injured patients. Choice *A* would not be a good addition because an overworked janitor may not be in a position to really harm patients, and even if they are, the paragraph is about doctors and nurses. Choice *B* would not be a good addition because the focus of the paragraph is on the United States, not just New York. Choice *D* would not be a good addition because although the cost of medical school may inhibit people from choosing a medical career, it does not directly relate to the current working conditions for healthcare professionals.

64. A: Choice *A* is a strong transition sentence between Sentence 3 and Sentence 4. It relates to both sentences. It explains that Gandhi was not universally liked, which Sentence 3 may suggest. It also addresses why Gandhi was killed, which Sentence 4 mentions. Choice *B* is not a strong transition sentence because the information is unrelated to the sentence that comes before and after it. It would fit better at the beginning of the paragraph, where general information is provided. The same goes for Choice *C*, which is unrelated to Sentence 3 and 4. Choice *D* is information that should come after Sentence 4, so it would not work in the placement called for in the question.

65. D: Choice *D* is the only statement that can be verified as true based on the information provided in the paragraph. The gold rush led to the deaths of many Native Americans; therefore, it is true to say that they were negatively impacted. Choice *A* is incorrect because the paragraph states that there was a large influx of people to California. Choice *B* is incorrect because British rule is not mentioned in the paragraph. Additionally, the gold rush happened well after the US gained its independence, although that is not explicitly stated in the paragraph. Choice *C* is incorrect because the paragraph states that there was enough gold to be valued at billions of dollars.

Part Three: Situational Judgment

1. BEST: B: By providing immediate directions to the caller, the FSO has the best chance of helping them calm down. Acquiring further information helps the FSO make an informed decision about what to do next. **WORST: A:** Assuring the caller that the FSO will advocate on their behalf feels good in the moment, but the FSO may not be able to follow through on their promise. Unknown information, such as if the caller was rejected due to involvement in criminal activity, means this response has increased negative outcomes.

2. BEST: D: Materials from the State Department are mission-critical because they define the FSO's foreign policy objectives in their new position. Learning and understanding key objectives provides the FSO with understanding of how to prioritize their time and energy. **WORST: B:** The prior FSO's documentation may be of use, but their challenges in the position do not mean you will face the same conflicts. It is better to understand your own objectives and to spend time familiarizing yourself with the current conditions faced by your position.

3. BEST: C: Although the use of an explanation intended for nonspecialists will lack some detail, this type of simple explanation is a good introduction to the new rules until the FSO can dedicate more significant time to getting up to date. **WORST: B:** Staff who are competent in US law are not necessarily competent in the laws of the host nation, because each nation's legal system, structure, and traditions have a great deal of variance. In addition, as a staff in the consulate, the FSO is expected to seek continuing education on topics relevant to their work on their own initiative.

4. BEST: A: Because no American citizens were involved in the accident, the accident's impact on the FSO's duty is likely to be low. Ensuring that correct information is sent to the State Department in a timely manner serves US foreign policy by helping higher officials make informed policy decisions. **WORST: B:** Concern for the host nation's citizens over American interests is inappropriate in the course of an FSO's duties.

5. BEST: D: Seeking volunteers first increases the feeling of investment in the team and the FSO's leadership decisions. **WORST: A:** Although taking on the missing person's duties might seem to demonstrate responsibility and competence, extra work in an already demanding position increases the danger that the FSO will burn out.

6. BEST: B: This choice is the best explanation for the decision because the threats' credibility and source indicate increased danger. **WORST: D:** Feelings of insecurity are worth the official's attention but do not on their own merit a change of security protocols.

7. BEST: C: Choice *C* is best because it indicates that the coworker's suggestion is inferred from the data rather than from broad principles (such as in Choice *B*). **WORST: A:** An appeal to authority is a logical fallacy that does not draw a valid conclusion.

8. BEST: C: The lack of deviation from normal patterns is the best evidence for unreliability because such deviation would be the most difficult element to conceal from analysts. For example, Choice *D* could merely indicate that insurgent activity took place during normal working hours. **WORST: B:** An informant's anonymity is a common protective factor. Choice *B* does not make the reported information more reliable or less reliable.

9. BEST: A: Choice *A* is the best piece of information for inferring this conclusion because it uses multiple sources. If the same information comes from multiple sources, that information is more likely to be true. **WORST: C:** Although enforcing a curfew may give cause for increased anti-government activity, this action does not itself indicate that a terrorist attack is imminent.

10. BEST: B: This choice is best because it provides the necessary information directly to the representative in a way that does not overstep the FSO's role or make a demand on the representative's time and resources. **WORST: D:** Passing the decision on to a member of the representative's staff requires that staff person to perform additional work and may come across as insensitive or rude, harming rapport between the representative and the Foreign Service.

11. BEST: B: In general, it is best to follow the chain of command rather than calling a more senior official or department upon immediately hearing about an emergency. **WORST: D:** Escalation to calling an authority in the US government should be decided by a team or someone with authority, not by a single FSO.

12. BEST: A: A subject matter expert is the best choice because they can provide the best information. Expertise also indicates that it will be easier for them to complete the task quickly. **WORST: C:** As team leader, your responsibility is to ensure that the task is completed. Giving the task to a team member who is more suited shows greater seriousness than assigning it to yourself.

13. BEST: D: Expending additional Foreign Service resources by bringing in additional FSOs is justified here because it facilitates communication without causing embarrassment or loss of standing by the local leader. **WORST: B:** Hiring a translator specifically for the leader may come across as condescending and rude. This will hinder completion of the search and rescue operation.

14. BEST: C: Choice *C* is best because its explanation describes why completing that task is important. The other choices do not describe time-sensitive reasons for prioritizing that task. **WORST: D:** Although diligence is valuable, prioritizing a task for the sake of impressing a superior isn't a strong justification for priority. Rather, the FSO should prioritize tasks in terms of time sensitivity and how important they are for completing assigned objectives.

15. BEST: C: Even while participating in a culture that does not value punctuality, acting in a punctual way shows respect to those you meet. **WORST: B:** Bringing a laptop, briefcase of documents, or other work supplies that are not needed for the scheduled meeting can be seen as condescending. Finding something to do while waiting, such as email correspondence on a smartphone, is typically inoffensive.

Presuming that you will need to fill fifteen to thirty minutes before local attendees arrive demonstrates negative valuation of the local culture.

16. BEST: B: Oral communication is the best method to use because it is generally quickest. In addition, offering to reschedule is professional because it is the option that is most considerate of the other FSO's time. **WORST: A:** Although an apology is indeed appropriate, waiting until arrival when other options are available is disrespectful and shows a lack of consideration for the FSO's time.

17. BEST: D: It is important for the team's leader to take responsibility for delays and creatively devise alternative plans of action, even if the delay is not due to failed decision-making. Proactive communication and collaboration is the best course of action. **WORST: C:** It's unwise to assume you can "just do more work," because an FSO's workload is often intense. For the team leader to take on staff duties typically results in the leader's tasks being incomplete.

18. BEST: A: Working together to support the project expresses teamwork and helps establish camaraderie with your coworkers. **WORST: C:** Providing assistance outside your expertise is unprofessional and can lead to the project's failure by including incorrect information. In addition, it is important to establish workplace boundaries, and bringing work into nonwork situations is generally unprofessional.

19. BEST: A: This choice is best because the team leader may not have noticed their employee's challenges. A private word without the struggling individual's knowledge may alleviate their stress before they reach full burnout. **WORST: C:** Ignoring a teammate's difficulties is NOT an example of professional behavior. Remember that all members of the Foreign Service are part of one team, even if they are divided into smaller cohorts.

20. BEST: D: New team members can be integrated quickly through a combination of formal and informal mentoring processes. Choice *D* is best because it describes a course of action that will immediately begin helping the teammate integrate. **WORST: C:** Critical evaluation of a teammate's work, even if well intended, can hinder their integration into the team through negative emotional experiences. Unless directly requested, it's best to leave criticism to the team leader.

21. BEST: B: Although relationships with citizens of the host nation are important, the FSO should be watchful that they do not prioritize the well-being of local relationships over Foreign Service interests. This choice is best because it raises concern directly but maintains discretion. **WORST: A:** The maxim "See something, say something" is relevant in this situation. The friendship may be appropriate, but without acting on the concern the FSO cannot be certain.

22. BEST: E: Questions are a useful tool to provide someone a chance to explain themselves more thoroughly and to help the FSO understand a new teammate's method of making choices. Choice *E* is best because these questions ease the process by which the leader and team will come to understand one another. **WORST: D:** Unquestioning support often has long-term negative consequences because criticism helps generate more durable and reliable thinking. Without criticism, the leader's decisions can't be revised and improved if needed.

23. BEST: B: Finding mutual agreement about who will complete which portion of the missing leader's tasks allows the team to return to work quickly, thus supporting completion of the project on time. **WORST: A:** Waiting for another team member to act is the worst option because an FSO should strive to be proactive. The other choices are better because they each indicate that the FSO is moving to address the situation.

24. BEST: B: Following the superior's lead makes a safe assumption that they are familiar with this nation's social norms. **WORST: D:** Although recognizing one's errors is an important step in correcting behavior, this isn't an effective tactic in formal situations. It's better to observe before acting so that you avoid offense rather than acting with a willingness to apologize should you accidentally offend.

25. BEST: D: Avoiding eye contact is common when someone is uncomfortable, and a deep breath is often an unconscious means of steadying oneself. The comparative mildness of this body language indicates that the contact likely isn't feeling a stronger emotion (like Choice *A*). **WORST: B:** Fear is the least likely option because the contact's body language does not indicate "flight" (e.g., looking at doorways as avenues of escape).

26. BEST: A: This is the most important official to get accurate information to because a senator is an elected representative, working in generally a more "senior" body of Congress, and they are on a relevant committee. **WORST: B:** As an American diplomat, your responsibility is to prioritize American interests, not German interests.

27. BEST: B: Choice *B* is best because this body language expresses confidence and honesty. This provides physical subtext supporting the decision of the FSO's superiors. **WORST: D:** The described body language is better for deescalating hostile situations rather than delivering an important message. In particular, avoiding eye contact often indicates mistrust or dishonesty. This could imply that the local leader is not trusted or is not being treated as an equal by the American government.

28. BEST: A: When additional information is unclear or not immediately available, it is best to follow established emergency procedures. Deviating from procedure—even for positive reasons, such as helping others—often increases risk rather than increasing safety. **WORST: C:** The function of alarms and procedures is to avoid independent judgment calls. The FSO should avoid making their own decision and instead follow the plan.

FSOT Practice Test #2

Part One: Job Knowledge

1. How many justices sit on the modern Supreme Court?
    a. Three
    b. Six
    c. Twelve
    d. Nine

2. While Congress has the authority to declare war, who serves as commander in chief of the United States military?
    a. Chief justice
    b. Secretary of defense
    c. President
    d. Secretary of state

3. If a president pocket vetoes a new law, what are they doing?
    a. Signing the bill into law
    b. Directly rejecting the bill
    c. Taking no action at all
    d. Sending the bill back to the Senate for debate

4. What is the significance of the Nineteenth Amendment?
    a. It gave women the right to vote.
    b. It protects people against unreasonable search and seizure by the government.
    c. It explains that people have the right to bear arms.
    d. It prohibits cruel and unusual punishment.

5. An athlete records her times for a series of runs as 25, 18, 23, 28, 30, 22.5, 23, 33, and 20 minutes. What is the athlete's approximate mean time?
    a. 26 minutes
    b. 19 minutes
    c. 25 minutes
    d. 23 minutes

6. Media relations refers to the relationship between which two parties?
    a. Television media and radio media
    b. An organization or government and various media outlets
    c. Online social media and print media
    d. One country's media and another country's media

7. In media relations and journalism, what is meant by the term *evergreen content?*
    a. Evergreen content is content that has an eco-friendly message.
    b. Evergreen content is content that receives the most clicks and therefore earns the most revenue.
    c. Evergreen content is content that can be rolled out at any time and is not designed for a specific day or time of year.
    d. Evergreen content is content over a certain length, which is usually dependent on the context of the media entity and their publication(s).

180

8. What is the purpose of a CSV file?
   a. It changes the orientation of the page that the database is on.
   b. It separates emails into different folders for easier organization.
   c. It generates a visual graph of data, like a sales chart or customer report.
   d. It is used for importing and exporting data from a database.

9. Before inserting any formula in Excel, what symbol must come before it?
   a. Plus sign
   b. Equal sign
   c. Minus sign
   d. Asterisk

10. The League of Nations was the precursor to what international organization?
    a. North American Free Trade Agreement
    b. International Criminal Police Organization
    c. North Atlantic Treaty Organization
    d. United Nations

11. The Louisiana Purchase affected the United States in what way?
    a. It doubled the size of the nation and increased its wealth.
    b. It allowed France to greatly expand their territory in North America.
    c. It resulted in the signing of the Treaty of Paris in 1783.
    d. It resulted in selling parts of Louisiana to Great Britain.

12. President Ronald Reagan sent military forces to what Caribbean nation in 1983?
    a. Haiti
    b. Grenada
    c. Jamaica
    d. Saint Lucia

13. The Tet Offensive marked a major turning point in which military conflict?
    a. Spanish-American War
    b. Gulf War
    c. Vietnam War
    d. Korean War

14. In Excel, what is one way to manually select multiple, individual cells to insert into a formula?
    a. Holding the Delete key
    b. Pressing the spacebar
    c. Holding the CTRL key
    d. Pressing the ESC key

15. Which formula in Excel returns the smallest value of the selected cells?
    a. MINE
    b. MIN
    c. MINI
    d. MINIMUM

16. What caused the Korean War?
    a. Soviet and North Korean forces invaded South Korea.
    b. Chinese and North Korean forces invaded South Korea.
    c. North Korean forces invaded South Korea.
    d. South Korean forces invaded North Korea.

17. What treaty ended the American Revolution?
    a. Treaty of Paris
    b. Treaty of Ghent
    c. Treaty of Alliance
    d. Treaty of Versailles

18. What was included in the Connecticut Compromise?
    a. Two legislative bodies with different methods of representation
    b. Two legislative bodies with the same method of representation
    c. One legislative body with representation based on population
    d. One legislative body with one vote per state

19. What was the domino theory?
    a. An economic theory that caused the Great Depression
    b. An American foreign policy approach to contain communism
    c. A framework for analyzing how military alliances caused World War I
    d. A British attempt to integrate French Canada into the British Empire

20. A country's entire railway system is provided by only one company. What is this company referred to as?
    a. Monopoly
    b. Oligopoly
    c. Duopoly
    d. Perfect competition

21. A worker who has recently left a company voluntarily and has not yet found a new job is experiencing what type of unemployment?
    a. Cyclical
    b. Frictional
    c. Structural
    d. Institutional

22. What would cause a left shift in a demand curve?
    a. Huge increase in the population
    b. Recession
    c. Overall increase in population income
    d. Shortages

23. In economics, the terms *freely floating, fixed, pegged,* and *managed float* all refer to what concept?
    a. Rate of inflation
    b. Mixed economic system
    c. Exchange rate regimes
    d. Supply and demand

182

24. An athlete records her times for a series of runs as 25, 18, 23, 28, 30, 22.5, 23, 33, and 20 minutes. What is the athlete's median time?
   a. 23 minutes
   b. 17 minutes
   c. 28 minutes
   d. 19 minutes

25. Collaborative management finalizes all team decisions based on what?
   a. Opinions of all team members delivered to the team leader
   b. A majority vote from team members
   c. A final decision from the leader
   d. Metrics and data based on each team member's performance

26. What is the primary focus of transformational management?
   a. Maximum productivity
   b. A balance of productivity and team satisfaction
   c. Greater employee freedom
   d. Employee skill growth

27. In delegative management, managers only assign projects and provide feedback, leaving team members free to determine what?
   a. Their workflow
   b. Project parameters
   c. Working hours
   d. Social interactions

28. A manager practicing visionary management is trying to do what for their team?
   a. Make sure everyone's input is valued
   b. Be inspirational and motivating
   c. Provide all basic human needs
   d. Micromanage every step of their work

29. You are giving a speech to a crowd of people at a public venue. Feeling nervous, you try to focus on making eye contact with a few different individuals, so you perceive the crowd as smaller than it really is. Which tip for public speaking does this situation exemplify?
   a. Practice
   b. Clear direction
   c. Hyper-fixation
   d. Keep calm

30. You are giving a motivational speech to the graduating class of a university. While sharing an anecdote about your own college experience, you tell a small joke and the audience laughs with a short applause break before you smile and continue your speech, tying the anecdote into your current topic. Which tip for public speaking does this situation exemplify?
   a. Respect
   b. Clear direction
   c. Practice
   d. Awareness

31. When is NOT an appropriate time to practice an upcoming speech?
    a. For a few minutes in the morning while in the shower
    b. For an hour or two alone in your office
    c. While walking down the street, addressing random pedestrians
    d. Five minutes before walking onstage, practicing a few key moments

32. Carla is starting a cake-decorating business and wants to know how long it will take her to start making a profit. She knows the original investment is $100. After that investment, she can begin making cakes and selling them for $20 each. How many cakes will she need to sell to break even on her investment?
    a. 5
    b. 100
    c. 10
    d. 2

33. What is one way to repeat a formula in multiple cells?
    a. Clicking the lower corner of the cell with the formula and dragging it to select other cells
    b. Pressing Backspace while selecting a formula
    c. Holding the Tab button and selecting multiple cells with a formula
    d. Double-clicking on a cell

34. What is the function of the "Slide Show" button in PowerPoint?
    a. It deletes unwanted slides in a presentation.
    b. It changes the overall look and theme of the slide.
    c. It changes the alignment of the text on each slide.
    d. It creates a full-screen presentation of the slides.

35. Which statement most accurately describes the CC and BCC functions of email?
    a. The CC and BCC functions enable users to have up to two additional recipient lists, and emails placed on CC and BCC fields can only see and respond to other recipients placed in the same fields.
    b. The CC and BCC functions both enable recipients to receive a copy of the email, even though their email addresses are not entered in the To field. However, recipients whose email addresses are entered in the CC field will receive additional Reply All emails and their addresses will be visible to all recipients; neither fact is true for recipients whose email addresses are entered in the BCC field.
    c. The CC and BCC functions both enable recipients to receive a copy of the email, even though their email addresses are not entered in the To field. However, emails entered in the BCC field will receive additional Reply All emails and their addresses will be visible to all recipients, whereas neither is true for those entered in the CC field.
    d. The CC and BCC functions enable all recipients to see the email addresses of other recipients, as well as which field those addresses have all been entered in. These functions enable the sender of an email to lay out the hierarchy of recipients, from the most essential recipients in the To field and the least essential in the BCC field.

184

36. What is the purpose of the non-red lines that sometimes appear under certain words and phrases in text on a word document?
    a. Those lines appear under misspelled words and alert the user to the spelling errors.
    b. Those lines appear to indicate that the user has edited the formatting of the text.
    c. Those lines appear under grammatical errors in text and alert the user to such errors.
    d. Those lines are purely decorative and are added by users to emphasize certain words or phrases.

37. According to the Twenty-Second Amendment, what is the maximum number of terms that a president can serve?
    a. One
    b. Two
    c. Three
    d. Four

38. According to the Interstate Commerce Act of 1887, who has the authority to regulate interstate commerce?
    a. Secretary of agriculture
    b. President
    c. Supreme Court
    d. Congress

39. How many senators currently serve in Congress?
    a. 50
    b. 100
    c. 150
    d. 200

40. Which of the following powers is exclusive to the federal government in the United States?
    a. Regulate immigration
    b. Regulate local government
    c. Implement welfare and benefit programs
    d. Levy taxes

41. Which of the following is a characteristic of a perfectly competitive market?
    a. All of the products are the same quality, size, and shape.
    b. There are barriers to entry and exit.
    c. Market influences are present.
    d. There is no product transparency.

42. Which of the following is one of the main factors for production?
    a. Property taxes
    b. Scarcity
    c. Entrepreneurship
    d. Elasticity

43. A businessman spends $1,000 to purchase a new coffee machine for his coffee shop. The money that he spent on this new machine is referred to as what?
    a. Operating cost
    b. Variable cost
    c. Sunk cost
    d. Fixed cost

44. A country is experiencing a severe, long-term period of economic decline where the GDP falls approximately 10 percent each year. This country is undergoing a what?
    a. Deflation
    b. Recession
    c. Shortage
    d. Depression

45. The population of coyotes in the local national forest has been declining since 2000. The population can be modeled by the function $y = -(x - 2)^2 + 1600$, where y represents number of coyotes and x represents the number of years past 2000. When will there be no more coyotes?
    a. 2020
    b. 2040
    c. 2012
    d. 2042

46. In what way did Native American and European colonists' family structures differ?
    a. Men served as the primary provider of resources.
    b. European colonists lived more sustainably.
    c. Native Americans included broader kinship networks.
    d. European colonists were more likely to honor their elders.

47. What event exposed the Articles of Confederation as a deeply flawed system of government?
    a. Publication of The Federalist Papers
    b. John Brown's raid at Harper's Ferry
    c. Whiskey Rebellion
    d. Shays' Rebellion

48. Which of the following presidential administrations conquered and annexed the most territory from a foreign power?
    a. Polk administration
    b. Madison administration
    c. Monroe administration
    d. Jackson administration

49. What is the Space Race's legacy?
    a. The United States dismantled its space exploration program after beating the Soviets to the Moon.
    b. The superpowers' relations improved, and the United States withdrew from the Vietnam War.
    c. The underlying technology led to the Digital Revolution.
    d. The Soviet Union collapsed due to its repeated failure to put a man on the Moon.

50. The US government has many requirements for federal employees who manage teams, and they can easily be found online. Which US government agency posts these requirements online for the benefit of managers and agency heads?
    a. US Government Accountability Office
    b. Department of Foreign Affairs
    c. US Staffing Department
    d. Federal Managers Agency

51. How often do an agency's strategic plans need to be rewritten and reissued?
    a. Every year
    b. Every two years
    c. Every four years
    d. Every eight years

52. What is the primary purpose of the various Equal Employment Opportunity laws?
    a. To give every American citizen an equal consideration for federal employment
    b. To prevent discrimination based on a variety of factors such as gender, race, and age
    c. To make sure every federal agency has an equal number of job positions
    d. To prevent managers from firing employees without adequate reason

53. Which law made it illegal to pay men and women different wages for the same work?
    a. Equal Pay Act of 1963
    b. Pregnancy Discrimination Act of 1978
    c. Title VII of the Civil Rights Act of 1964
    d. Title I of the Americans with Disabilities Act of 1990

54. Which period of history immediately followed the end of the American Civil War?
    a. War on Terror
    b. Industrial Revolution
    c. Reconstruction
    d. Prohibition Era

55. Which president was the first to visit China, marking a major milestone in Sino-American relations?
    a. Harry Truman
    b. Ronald Reagan
    c. Gerald Ford
    d. Richard Nixon

56. What was a major achievement during the Han dynasty?
    a. The Han dynasty installed the world's first representative government.
    b. The Han dynasty defeated Alexander the Great's legendary military.
    c. The Han dynasty invented a new, more powerful form of concrete.
    d. The Han dynasty connected the Far East with the West for the first time.

57. How did large-scale agriculture facilitate European colonization in the Americas?
    a. Large-scale agriculture increased American exports to Europe, and the colonies received military aid in return.
    b. Large-scale agriculture led to the development of new technologies that were applied to the military.
    c. Large-scale agriculture supported the development of major cities in the American South, and Native Americans couldn't pierce the city's defenses.
    d. Large-scale agriculture produced a food surplus that supported a larger population, permanent settlements, and a centralized government.

58. Mass media can be described as a powerful tool for doing what?
    a. Gauging public opinion
    b. Sharing information
    c. Shaping public interests
    d. Controlling the population

59. Which theory of mass media states that it is both what the media covers and how the media covers it that influences the public?
    a. Framing theory
    b. Harvest theory
    c. Agenda-setting theory
    d. Cultivation theory

60. You are planning a media campaign to encourage older locals to participate in an upcoming fundraiser for the city government. Which of the following media outlets would be the best way to reach your intended audience of older, locally involved citizens?
    a. City newspaper
    b. Television news
    c. Social media
    d. Radio news

Part Two: English Expression and Usage

Type A: Sentence Selection
Directions: For each item in this section, select the one sentence that best meets the requirements of standard written English.

1. Select the sentence that best meets the requirements of standard written English.
    a. The military reported that the average number of new recruits has fallen dramatically within the last five years.
    b. I glanced, at my watch and noticed that I was late.
    c. One of the best ways to begin a conversation are to shake hands.
    d. Three of my favorite vacation destinations are New York City; Paris; and Los Angeles.

2. Select the sentence that best meets the requirements of standard written English.
    a. These people reports that daily production has fallen below an acceptable level.
    b. We need to be attentive, showing respect, and polite when talking to the principal.
    c. My teacher highly recommends learning mandarin chinese because of its practical use.
    d. Everyone was curious about the large yellow blimp that appeared overnight.

3. Select the sentence that best meets the requirements of standard written English.
    a. Walking along the beach while the sun is shining.
    b. The school board unanimously voted to implement the new dress code immediately.
    c. Periods of economic hardship effect everyone, even the extremely wealthy.
    d. It is very disappointing that the Negotiations did not go as planned.

4. Select the sentence that best meets the requirements of standard written English.
    a. He frantically yelled for his son: but he did not hear a response.
    b. They're family is originally from Boston and moved to Orlando many years ago.
    c. The coldest season of the year is the perfect time to wear your winter clothing.
    d. I spoke with president Carter many times while he was in office.

5. Select the sentence that best meets the requirements of standard written English.
    a. This watch isn't mine" it is my grandfather's.
    b. I was relieved when I finally quit my job because that meant less hours spent on the computer.
    c. The political situation in Africa is quickly deteriorating.
    d. He noted that this airport was more cleaner than the one in his hometown.

6. Select the sentence that best meets the requirements of standard written English.
    a. The governor announces that he will not seeking reelection and would step down by the year's end.
    b. The mayor is much loved by his community and has been mayor for the past 3 years.
    c. Alot of the new interns at the news station graduated from the local community college.
    d. World leaders met and discussing the issue of climate change at the pristine fishing village.

7. Select the sentence that best meets the requirements of standard written English.
    a. While wandering through the forest, I encountered a strange new creature.
    b. Dreaming of a more good life was the only thing that was motivating him.
    c. My trip to mount Rushmore was both exciting and educational.
    d. I don't have many time to spend on this project.

8. Select the sentence that best meets the requirements of standard written English.
    a. I'm sure that we will has another chance to win money at the casino.
    b. He gave the taxi driver, something that works so much, a very low tip.
    c. Food from this restaurant is usually too spicy, while that restaurant is too bland.
    d. I cannot understand how to solve this problem.

9. Select the sentence that best meets the requirements of standard written English.
    a. Apologizing when you know you were wrong is the right way to conduct yourself.
    b. I couldn't handle the amount of work who my boss gave to me, so I was thinking of leaving.
    c. I would like another plate of desert, if you may.
    d. Now that I think about it, gambling and rampant alcoholism destroyed mine family.

10. Select the sentence that best meets the requirements of standard written English.
    a. Whatever he did, nothing seeming to be working.
    b. The amount love I feel right now is indescribable.
    c. Fear is reserved for those who don't have the courage to take the first step.
    d. The chef reported that he had created this dish with an excessive amounts of butter.

11. Select the sentence that best meets the requirements of standard written English.
    a. He listed three different foods he didn't like; celery, sushi, and tuna.
    b. This establishment has served the community since 1975.
    c. The movie was extremely expensive to make, the director started to regret it.
    d. Give me one more yet another chance and I will prove to you that I can finish the project.

12. Select the sentence that best meets the requirements of standard written English.
    a. The students are all getting bored of the class they are so patient for sticking with it for so long.
    b. He remained undifferent to the complaints of his boss.
    c. It was already agreed beforehand which every boy going to the party would bring their own costumes.
    d. The latest, greatest, and hottest sunglasses are now available for sale on our website.

13. Select the sentence that best meets the requirements of standard written English.
    a. Itll be extremely disappointing if I don't pass this class after all this effort.
    b. After all the time I spent getting everything ready for the perfect birthday, I remembered that my mothers birthday was actually next week.
    c. Sometimes, I enjoy taking long walks during cool summer days and contemplating life.
    d. Its extremely cold today in New Haven.

14. Select the sentence that best meets the requirements of standard written English.
    a. Grits is traditional eaten in the South.
    b. The way that your driving really makes me think you never learned properly.
    c. They're is no way I failed that grammar test after studying for the last month.
    d. The service here in particular is outstanding.

15. Select the sentence that best meets the requirements of standard written English.
    a. College professors in general are highly educated and knowledgeable in their field.
    b. I had the chance to become a doctor, being a lawyer, or studying to be a dentist, but I gave it all up to pursue singing.
    c. As a young girl, my father took me on a memorable trip about the Grand Canyon.
    d. Please take a look at my work, Doctor. Williams.

16. Select the sentence that best meets the requirements of standard written English.
    a. With no money left in his account, he knew he had to start looking for a job.
    b. The main tenants of this organization are trust, honor, and loyalty.
    c. The recent outbreak of the diseases malaria is highly concerning to this area.
    d. Irate group members wont contribute to the project.

17. Select the sentence that best meets the requirements of standard written English.
    a. Her wasn't exactly sure when the party was, but that didn't stop her from preparing.
    b. War has been such a terrible blight on society.
    c. I was prepared to except any job offer at this point.
    d. There was shouting in the room they said that there was a fire.

190

Type B: Sentence Correction

Directions: For each item in this section, select the one underlined word or phrase that needs to be changed to make the sentence correct, or indicate that none of the underlined parts are in error.

18. A long time ago, <u>the legendary Michael</u> Jordan played basketball for the Chicago Bulls <u>and lead</u> the team to <u>great success.</u>
    a. NO ERROR
    b. the legendary Michael
    c. and lead
    d. great success

19. As a teacher, <u>it is my responsibility</u> to make sure that all of <u>my students'</u> are well taken care of and <u>do well in school.</u>
    a. NO ERROR
    b. it is my responsibility
    c. my students'
    d. do well in school

20. <u>The department</u> head <u>expressed</u> his displeasure over the <u>lack of enthusiasm</u> for team meetings.
    a. NO ERROR
    b. The department
    c. expressed
    d. lack of enthusiasm

21. <u>Recently,</u> my father <u>has been</u> constantly <u>loosing his keys</u> and wasting time searching for them.
    a. NO ERROR
    b. Recently,
    c. has been
    d. loosing his keys

22. The recent discovery of a new way to modify cancer cells <u>have completely</u> changed <u>the way that</u> we <u>view cancer and its</u> treatment.
    a. NO ERROR
    b. have completely
    c. the way that
    d. view cancer and its

23. Once <u>you have finished</u> the assignment, please make sure to <u>send them to me</u> using the new link to <u>our school's website</u>.
    a. NO ERROR
    b. you have finished
    c. send them to me
    d. our school's website

24. There was absolutely <u>no reason to become</u> upset over the increase <u>in our workload</u> because we are being <u>paid extremely well</u> for our work.
    a. NO ERROR
    b. no reason to become
    c. in our workload
    d. paid extremely well

25. Nick expressed <u>his love for</u> his new girlfriend, Judy, by <u>buying her, chocolates</u>, flowers, and <u>a stuffed animal</u>.
    a. NO ERROR
    b. his love for
    c. buying her, chocolates
    d. a stuffed animal

26. I decided to purchase <u>much lottery tickets</u> after seeing <u>another news article</u> about a <u>lucky grocery</u> shopper winning the lottery.
    a. NO ERROR
    b. much lottery tickets
    c. another news article
    d. lucky grocery

27. I felt guilty when I began my interview with a new startup company because I told them that <u>I had been working</u> at a major marketing firm <u>for 2007</u> even though this <u>wasn't true.</u>
    a. NO ERROR
    b. I had been working
    c. for 2007
    d. wasn't true

28. No matter <u>what anyone says</u> to me, I will never <u>give up on</u> my <u>dream of becoming</u> a professional volleyball player.
    a. NO ERROR
    b. what anyone says
    c. give up on
    d. dream of becoming

29. I still remember the look on my family members' faces when my cousin announced her surprise <u>wedding with a</u> photographer that <u>she had met</u> at <u>my birthday party</u>.
    a. NO ERROR
    b. wedding with a
    c. she had met
    d. my birthday party

30. My uncle <u>told me stories</u> about his motorcycle <u>journey across America</u>, where he saw <u>everything to</u> rolling hills to flat plains.
    a. NO ERROR
    b. told me stories
    c. journey across America,
    d. everything to

192

31. I concluded that people which graduated from college have a higher chance of getting hired than someone who did not finish college.
   a. NO ERROR
   b. people which graduated
   c. chance of getting
   d. someone who did not

32. Nothing gets the crowd more excited than a word from their idol standing on the stage.
   a. NO ERROR
   b. more excited
   c. a word from
   d. standing on the

33. When I compared different rental car prices for my upcoming trip, I was upset when I learned how more expensiver an electric car would be.
   a. NO ERROR
   b. for my upcoming
   c. more expensiver
   d. would be

34. One of my biggest regrets is never being able to see the beauty of the Las Vegas city lights before I left this country permanent.
   a. NO ERROR
   b. of my biggest
   c. being able to see
   d. country permanent

Type C: Sentence Correction II
Directions: For the items in this section, select the one word or phrase that needs to be used in place of the underlined text to make the sentence correct, or indicate that the underlined text is not in error.

35. The celebration started with a speech from the guest speaker and finished with a colorful and vibrant display of fireworks.
   a. NO ERROR
   b. vibrating
   c. shaking
   d. viral

36. Given the huge amount of majors offered at the local university, it's no wonder enrollment has increased.
   a. NO ERROR
   b. mass of
   c. number of
   d. quality of

193

37. It was obvious from the author's tone of voice what he was trying to <u>elude</u> to.
    a. NO ERROR
    b. engage
    c. elevate
    d. allude

38. This is the perfect <u>every day</u> watch to wear on your wrist because of its durability, stylish looks, and affordability.
    a. NO ERROR
    b. every, day
    c. everyday
    d. every-day

39. Students <u>whom</u> are not accustomed to the heavy workload assigned by the biology teacher may not be able to pass the course.
    a. NO ERROR
    b. who
    c. which
    d. whim

40. The founding of the city of Rome is attributed to <u>two</u> legendary brothers named Romulus and Remus.
    a. NO ERROR
    b. to
    c. too
    d. bilateral

41. The psychologist noted that the family's situation became extremely complicated when the <u>ex husband</u> began to demand more and more from the mother.
    a. NO ERROR
    b. ex/husband
    c. ex;husband
    d. ex-husband

42. Even though the patient may be <u>conscientious</u> and speaking to you, it is still extremely important to check for head injuries at this time.
    a. NO ERROR
    b. conflagrant
    c. conscious
    d. confluence

43. Perfumery is a <u>true</u> wonderful profession that blends science and artistry.
    a. NO ERROR
    b. truly
    c. verified
    d. authenticated

194

44. The miraculous success of the early space program showed the world that it was <u>feasible</u> to send humans to space.
    a. NO ERROR
    b. infallible
    c. fealty
    d. featured

45. She didn't want to support another streaming <u>services</u>, but she was too lazy to go shopping anywhere else.
    a. NO ERROR
    b. service
    c. assistance
    d. subservience

46. The submarine <u>circumference</u> the entire globe, traveling from the Atlantic to the Pacific and back.
    a. NO ERROR
    b. will be circled
    c. circumstances
    d. circumnavigated

47. I have a friend <u>who's</u> father is the captain of a luxury cruise ship famous for its casino and dining options.
    a. NO ERROR
    b. who
    c. whom
    d. whose

48. In Shanghai, <u>they're</u> is a tower called the Pearl Tower which has a big round base and a pointed tip.
    a. NO ERROR
    b. their
    c. there
    d. them

49. I had <u>had</u> way too much food already, but my grandmother insisted that I eat more.
    a. NO ERROR
    b. has
    c. have
    d. his

50. I originally planned to walk home, <u>on the one hand</u> my feet got so sore I eventually called a taxi.
    a. NO ERROR
    b. but
    c. contrasting
    d. moreover

51. People don't realize how often you can fail as a writer, even after <u>you getting</u> a good job or book deal.
   a. NO ERROR
   b. you get
   c. you got
   d. you will get

Type D: Paragraph Organization

Directions: For each item in this section, select the ordering of sentences that results in the clearest, most well-organized paragraph.

52.
(1) My grandfather was a veteran and an adventurer, and he told me so many exciting stories from his life.
(2) For example, he once took a road trip all across the United States on his trusted motorcycle.
(3) Some of my fondest childhood memories are from spending time with my grandfather.
(4) After this road trip, he even went backpacking across Europe.
   a. 1, 2, 3, 4
   b. 2, 3, 4, 1
   c. 3, 1, 2, 4
   d. 1, 4, 3, 2

53.
(1) Fugu, or pufferfish, is considered a delicacy in Japanese cuisine.
(2) Tetrodotoxin causes paralysis, and victims eventually die of asphyxiation.
(3) Due to the extreme care that must be taken to remove the poison from the fish, only specially licensed chefs are authorized to prepare the fish.
(4) However, fugu can be extremely dangerous to consume because of the tetrodotoxin produced in the fish.
   a. 1, 4, 2, 3
   b. 2, 3, 1, 4
   c. 1, 3, 2, 4
   d. 3, 4, 2, 1

54.
(1) However, for James, Christmas is even more special.
(2) During a romantic dinner at home, James proposed to his girlfriend, asking her to marry him.
(3) James could still remember the tears of happiness in her eyes and her head nodding in agreement to his proposal.
(4) Many people consider Christmas to be their favorite holiday of the year.
   a. 4, 1, 2, 3
   b. 2, 4, 3, 1
   c. 2, 1, 3, 4
   d. 4, 3, 1, 2

55.

(1) Some people experience itchiness and a red rash, but severe razor burn can cause razor bumps to appear.

(2) Razor burn is an uncomfortable and irritating rash that sometimes appears after shaving.

(3) Razor bumps are caused by ingrown hairs, which are hairs that curl back and start to grow into the skin.

(4) Usually, these bumps will disappear on their own.

    a.   2, 3, 4, 1

    b.   2, 1, 3, 4

    c.   3, 2, 4, 1

    d.   3, 1, 4, 2

56.

(1) Seasonal affective disorder, also known as seasonal depression, is related to the change of seasons.

(2) Symptoms include low energy, feelings of hopelessness, and difficulties concentrating.

(3) These symptoms usually occur around the same time every year.

(4) This depression most commonly occurs during the transition from warmer seasons to colder seasons.

    a.   4, 1, 2, 3

    b.   2, 3, 1, 4

    c.   1, 2, 3, 4

    d.   1, 4, 2, 3

57.

(1) After that, we will leave for the airport at least three hours before our flight.

(2) My girlfriend and I carefully went over our itinerary again.

(3) First, we will wake up early in the morning to check our luggage.

(4) Finally, we will wait at the gate and finish the report that we are working on.

    a.   2, 3, 1, 4

    b.   1, 3, 4, 2

    c.   3, 1, 2, 4

    d.   3, 4, 1, 2

58.

(1) All of the teams had arrived at the gymnasium for the annual basketball tournament.

(2) Many people were disappointed by this answer and noted that the heat in the building was becoming unbearable.

(3) After the teams arrived, everyone started to notice that the gymnasium was unusually hot.

(4) When people asked what was going on, tournament organizers explained that the air conditioning unit had stopped working and could not be fixed in time.

    a.   3, 1, 4, 2

    b.   4, 2, 3, 1

    c.   1, 3, 4, 2

    d.   1, 2, 3, 4

Type E: Paragraph Revision

Directions: This section consists of several sentences that compose a paragraph. Read the paragraph carefully, and then answer the question that follows it.

59. The team initially expected the project to only take a few weeks to complete. The project was so simple that even novices would have been able to complete it. The team ran into many unexpected difficulties. Their project manager resigned halfway through the project, and they received fewer than expected resources. Before they knew it, the deadline had approached, and they had very little to show for it. What transition word would improve the flow between the second and third sentence?

    a. Obviously
    b. However
    c. Undoubtedly
    d. Moreover

60. Marcus could scarcely believe his eyes when he read the acceptance letter. For years now, he had been dreaming of the day when he would be able to walk through the doors of this prestigious acting school. For Marcus, this was a huge step in his acting journey. He was confident that under the <u>tutelage</u> of so many elite actors, he would improve his acting skills more than he could ever imagine.

As used in the sentence, what word is closest in meaning to the underlined word?

    a. Guidance
    b. Threat
    c. Cacophony
    d. Neglect

61. Watchmaking is truly a magnificent art. It fascinates me how so many tiny, moving parts can come together to create a mechanical wonder. It's almost as if the finished watch has its own heartbeat, beating with every second. The idea of working tirelessly on a single masterpiece in a dedicated workshop seems almost romantic to me.

What word best describes the author's tone?

    a. Perplexed
    b. Loathsome
    c. Admiring
    d. Hostile

62. John Snow was an English physician considered to be the father of modern epidemiology. His detailed notetaking and evidence-based observations distinguished him from leading contemporaries. He did not believe the prevailing theory that certain diseases were caused by breathing "bad air." His most significant contribution to epidemiology was using graphs and diagrams to support his observations that an outbreak of cholera was not due to breathing toxic air but drinking contaminated water from a communal water pump.

Which of the following statements would the author of this paragraph most likely agree with?

    a. John Snow's work and observations ultimately did not have a significant impact on the development of epidemiology.
    b. John Snow was showing disrespect by going against a theory that many of his contemporaries agreed with.
    c. John Snow's willingness to go against the popular theories at the time helped revolutionize the study of medicine and diseases.
    d. John Snow was a strong supporter of the current theory for the spread of disease.

63. Michael Jackson was a music industry legend recognized for his unique music and dancing techniques. People would line up for hours for the chance to see him perform. His concerts would sell out in record time. His music is listened to by millions of people every day. Although he found himself in numerous controversies later in his life, the passion he had for music never left him. In fact, he was planning an epic comeback tour that would show the world that Michael Jackson was far from finished.
Which of the following sentences would most likely be found at the end of the paragraph?
    a. Michael Jackson was born on August 29, 1958, in Gary, Indiana.
    b. Before his success as a solo artist, Michael Jackson was a member of The Jackson 5, a group that consisted of him and his brothers.
    c. As the youngest member of The Jackson 5, Michael Jackson was adored by everyone for his energy and youth.
    d. Unfortunately, Michael was never able to show the world the fruits of his labors, as he died suddenly in 2009.

64. He knew what he was supposed to do, but he didn't know if he had the strength to go through with it. The decision constantly weighed on his mind, and he spent many sleepless nights considering every possibility. After all, making the wrong decision meant that he would be burdened with a lifetime of debt. However, he knew that the deadline was approaching, and he needed to act quickly.
What is the main purpose of the third sentence?
    a. It emphasizes the importance of this decision and the effect that it would have on him.
    b. It clarifies that the decision would not play a huge role in his life.
    c. It provides clues as to what the author would ultimately decide to do.
    d. It contrasts the previous sentence's claim that the decision was important.

65. When you compare how much it would cost to update the company's old system with simply buying new software, it's obvious what decision the board will take. Our company is known for its innovation and dedication to providing excellent service. This new software will allow us to help more people than ever. Although it will take time to implement the new software, its benefits are well worth the effort.

Based on the paragraph, what can be inferred about the company's current software?
    a. Most workers disagree with the company's decision to move away from the old software.
    b. The current software would be too expensive to update to justify its cost.
    c. The software is very easy to use and well-liked by the current workforce.
    d. There is no one available that knows how to update the current software.

Part Three: Situational Judgment

Directions: For each question in this section, select the BEST and WORST response to each scenario.

1. You've been at your post in a new host nation for two weeks and have been invited to a casual dinner at a local official's home. How would you prepare for this event?
    a. Skim a week's worth of the local newspaper to gather familiarity with current events.
    b. Ask a culture expert on staff for pointers on semi-formal etiquette.
    c. Inquire with the host about other guests so you can brainstorm potential conversation topics.
    d. Consciously choose not to prepare in order to come across as authentic rather than artificial.

2. An earthquake strikes the city that hosts the consulate where you work. Several consulate buildings were damaged. After a self-assessment, you find yourself unharmed. What do you do first?
   a. Use a smartphone or other device to look up the Foreign Service's environmental disaster protocol.
   b. Begin searching the rubble for survivors in need of medical assistance.
   c. Call a Foreign Service office in another city to inform them that your consulate needs emergency assistance.
   d. Gather other mobile survivors in a safe place and begin a head count to determine how many people are missing.

3. The election result in your host nation is a surprise victory for the local Socialist Party. Independent observers indicate that the election was fair and democratic. How should you respond to this change in the political climate?
   a. Reach out to the party's leadership and congratulate them on their victory.
   b. Begin further research into the election conditions to confirm that there was no foul play.
   c. Hold a team meeting with your coworkers to brainstorm strategies for furthering American interests under the new administration.
   d. Do nothing, because that shows respect to the host nation's right of self-determination.

4. Protests break out in the capital of your host nation where you work with the security department of the US Embassy. The demonstrators are angry about economic inequality and have come into conflict with local police at government buildings. What action do you recommend to ensure continued security of the embassy?
   a. Approve use of force if the embassy is threatened, but continue using standard security equipment.
   b. Provide combat gear to security personnel as a deterrent.
   c. Call in additional security personnel until the protests end.
   d. Begin drafting an evacuation plan in case the protests grow and become more violent.

5. While grabbing lunch with coworkers at a local restaurant, you overhear some other customers complaining about the American presence in your host nation. Is this a piece of reliable information indicating significant anti-American sentiment in the local population?
   a. No, because the comments did not express violent intent.
   b. No, because one person's or group's opinion doesn't necessarily indicate a national opinion.
   c. Yes, because the opinion comes from a local source.
   d. Yes, because voiced discontent indicates that more individuals believe the same way.

6. The committee overseeing renovations of the embassy's meeting and conference rooms is selecting a contractor to perform the work. Their final selection is an American contractor's proposal, which has a higher cost and implements more current telecommunications technology. The proposal is still within the project's budget. What is the best explanation for not choosing a cheaper contractor?
   a. The cost isn't important, as long as it's under the original budget.
   b. The proposal offers the best value for the project's cost.
   c. Use of a local contractor at an embassy is a security risk.
   d. An American contractor provides higher quality than local contractors.

200

7. Your team's data collection has determined that the average cost of food in your host nation has increased by 20 percent over the last three months. Which of the following statements best represents a valid conclusion drawn from these data?
   a. The average citizen's quality of life has decreased because they are spending more income on food.
   b. Production from local agriculture has decreased.
   c. A company is hoarding supplies as part of a price-gouging tactic.
   d. This represents an economic opportunity for American exports of foodstuffs.

8. Due to an upcoming election in the host nation, your team's leader has decided to implement mandatory overtime for the next two weeks on a rotating schedule so that at least one staff member is available 24/7 for gathering information and analyzing new data. What is the most reasonable explanation for their decision?
   a. It's important to have an FSO on duty in case an official overseas in America requires current information.
   b. Overtime will provide the team a chance to both monitor the election and continue working toward normal objectives.
   c. Working extra hours for a limited time isn't a major stressor.
   d. Putting overtime on a rotating schedule will ensure that the workload is split more evenly instead of one or two team members constantly monitoring.

9. The frequency of peaceful political demonstrations in the host nation has linearly increased over the last six months in anticipation of an election, which will take place in four weeks. This is more protests than have taken place in the last ten years. Which of the following is a valid conclusion from that information?
   a. The election is politically divisive.
   b. Your team should monitor the election for fraud.
   c. The demonstrations will escalate to violence prior to the election.
   d. The citizens of the host nation consider this election to be the most important in a decade.

10. Your objective is to collect raw data about the political climate in your host nation. Which of the following methodologies is most efficient?
   a. Allocate time each day to skim local news stations for political coverage.
   b. Devise a five-question survey and distribute it through social media.
   c. Sift through official sources to collate the local government's data about how representatives vote.
   d. Sit in on public sessions of the elected assembly.

11. You discover a colleague who has passed away unexpectedly in their sleep. Who do you inform first?
   a. Their relatives or spouse
   b. Their listed emergency contact
   c. The embassy's security
   d. An emergency health service

12. Which of the following statements defines a "decisive leader" best?
   a. An individual who makes complex decisions quickly
   b. An individual with confidence in their own judgment
   c. An individual who takes time to analyze the situation before making a choice
   d. An individual who uses creative problem-solving to devise solutions
   e. An individual who implements procedures effectively during a crisis

13. Which of the following tasks is the most time-sensitive?
    a. Report on efficacy of current security policies.
    b. Gather information for political situation analysis.
    c. Schedule a meeting with the ambassador to discuss operational progress.
    d. Meet with local officials about a trade agreement.
    e. Summarize the week's news from local TV stations.

14. You witness a local official you've been working with receive a wad of paper money during an interaction with a local factory owner and put it in their pocket. You suspect that this is a bribe but aren't sure. Later, the local official advocates for giving that person's factory a new development project. The official's argument seems well reasoned and appears not to include bias. What course of action do you take?
    a. Confront the official and ask if the factory owner bribed them.
    b. Seek advice from a superior who has been in the country longer and is more familiar with the culture.
    c. Report the bribe to your supervisor in the Foreign Service and let them handle an investigation.
    d. Confirm the factory owner's receipt of the development project because the arguments in favor seem sound to your own judgment, regardless of a possible bribe.

15. You agreed to attend a meeting in the afternoon with officials of the host nation's government but later realize that if you attend this meeting, you won't be able to complete a weekly report for your supervisor on time. How do you handle the situation?
    a. Call the meeting's organizer, apologize, and explain why you're unable to attend.
    b. Complete as much of the report as possible before the meeting, and submit incomplete work if necessary.
    c. Contact your supervisor, explain the circumstances, and attend the meeting.
    d. Call the meeting's organizer and offer to meet with them at a later date.

16. A new staff member at your consulate asks a question that you anticipate will take fifteen minutes to answer. However, you have a meeting with the consul in ten minutes. What course of action do you take?
    a. Provide a basic explanation in hopes of attending the meeting on time.
    b. Direct the staff member to send an email with their question so you can respond in writing later in the day.
    c. Direct the staff member to ask you again sometime after the meeting adjourns.
    d. Answer the staff member's questions to demonstrate support for the new team member, and apologize to the consul for your tardiness.

17. You see a coworker put a small plastic bag with white powder in their backpack after leaving the restroom. Their behavior has been unusual lately—restless, anxious, and working long hours to complete high-priority assignments—and you suspect that the powder was a stimulant, such as cocaine. What is an appropriate response?
    a. Confront the coworker directly after the incident, asking them what was in the bag.
    b. Ask the coworker if they need assistance in the workplace because you've seen them working late into the night.
    c. Wait for an opportunity to look in the coworker's backpack and confirm what you saw.
    d. Report what you saw to your supervisor, and follow their directions for addressing your coworker's behavior.

18. Your office happens to be in a passcode-protected wing of an embassy. This section has privileged archives and computer infrastructure, including some information that requires security clearance for access. Your team's offices do not have any of this information. While working after-hours, a coworker's significant other enters the office, retrieves your coworker's coffee thermos, chats with you for a few minutes, and then leaves. They are not a staff member in the embassy. What is the correct response to this situation?

    a. Ask your team's supervisor who is permitted to know the wing's passcode.

    b. Report to your team's supervisor that the significant other came into the office on their own after-hours.

    c. Ask your coworker tomorrow if their significant other was let into the wing by another embassy staffer.

    d. Suggest that the passcode should be changed more frequently as an update to security protocols.

19. You've been assigned to join a group of medical professionals from the host nation as an observer on behalf of the United States while they provide humanitarian aid during civil strife. What action do you take to establish rapport with the team?

    a. Ask how you can help if a crisis situation emerges.

    b. Use knowledge of local customs to host an appropriate social function to introduce yourself.

    c. Focus on small talk during downtime or travel.

    d. Simply observe the unrest and report it to the Foreign Service rather than trying to establish rapport.

20. One of your coworkers at the consulate has grown increasingly pessimistic, irritable, and apathetic over the last month. What direct action can you take to support your burned-out teammate?

    a. Invite them to join a group for drinks after work.

    b. Offer to pick up some of their duties so they can take a breather.

    c. Encourage them to ask the team's leader to give them fewer duties.

    d. Actively listen to their complaints and validate their frustrations.

21. After four years of working at a consulate, you are assigned to a different team at a new consulate in the same host nation. The other members of this team have been working together for approximately six months. What best facilitates integration with the new team?

    a. Focus on completing work tasks to demonstrate competence and reliability.

    b. Follow the supervisor's lead on the team-building process.

    c. Seek opportunities to socialize with coworkers outside the office.

    d. Ask a coworker for additional briefings about the team's area of activity, even though you feel you have a grasp of the subject matter.

22. You arrive at the office a few minutes late and see that one of your coworkers is rummaging through one of your desk drawers. They greet you and explain that they were just looking for a pen. You feel that this is a violation of personal boundaries in the office and have expressed this to your coworker on prior occasions. How do you resolve this conflict?

    a. Have a conversation with your team's leader later in the day and ask for their intervention.

    b. Directly tell the coworker that going through your desk is unprofessional and inappropriate.

    c. Write a formal complaint to your supervisor explaining why you feel this situation is unprofessional.

    d. Appeal to your coworkers, asking if they feel that this behavior is acceptable.

23. What body language indicates to a coworker that you are listening?
 a. Maintain eye contact and continue typing on a project related to the conversation.
 b. Maintain eye contact with hands in lap.
 c. Make occasional eye contact, with verbal acknowledgment of their discussion, while continuing to type.
 d. Make occasional eye contact while pacing or moving around the room.

24. Your team is close to finishing a project, and it's not yet clear if you'll achieve the deadline. One of your teammates seems anxious about completing the project on time. How do you provide support?
 a. Privately ask the team leader if the group is able to get an extension if necessary.
 b. Encourage the teammate to vent.
 c. Provide encouragement about their accomplishments when working with them on shared portions of the project.
 d. Reassure the teammate that their concerns aren't as worrisome as they perceive.

25. You're meeting with a middle-aged man whose son was killed during insurgent activity. Your objective is to express sincere condolences for the man's loss. How do you present yourself physically in this conversation?
 a. Sit down close to the man, facing him directly, reaching out to touch his hand.
 b. Sit down close to the man, positioned at an angle, while speaking slowly and softly.
 c. Stand together, speak clearly and directly, with one hand on his shoulder.
 d. Stand together, voice raised slightly, with your brow furrowed and jaw tense.

26. An air raid siren has gone off, and you've led a group of civilians into a reinforced shelter. What body language can you use to help the civilians remain calm?
 a. Crouch against the wall with your head covered to prepare for a potential building collapse.
 b. Speak in a slow, loud voice, with hands held behind your back.
 c. Walk among the crowd, using a small amount of physical touch.
 d. Lean against a wall, with hands in pockets.
 e. Speak quietly, encouraging others to stay quiet too.

27. While you're on a fact-finding mission about civil strife as a neutral observer in the host nation, you see a young man lingering near a police station. The man's head turns frequently, observing his surroundings. He leans back on a wall, keeping both hands concealed in the pockets of a large coat. What do you do?
 a. Alert a member of your security detail of a possible risk.
 b. Continue to observe from where you are.
 c. Approach and initiate conversation with the young man.
 d. Call the police station and inform them of the man's presence.
 e. Walk down the street to increase the distance between you and the police station.

28. You have a negotiation meeting with some local officials scheduled in one hour at a restaurant that has a reserved private room in the back for business purposes. The restaurant calls and cancels the reservation due to closing the restaurant for the day following a technical malfunction in the kitchen. How do you respond to this situation?
 a. Invite the officials to your consulate for the meeting.
 b. Ask the restaurant to remain open, without kitchen service, during the meeting.
 c. Rent out a conference room at the local community center for the meeting.
 d. Offer to meet the officials at their offices.

204

Test #2 Answer Explanations

Part One: Job Knowledge

1. D: Congress sets the number of justices. There are currently nine justices sitting on the Supreme Court, consisting of one chief justice and eight associate justices. Choices *A*, *B*, and *C* are not the correct number of justices on the Supreme Court currently.

2. C: In addition to being the head of state, the president is also the commander in chief of the United States military. Choice *A* is the head of the judicial branch. Choice *B* oversees the entire Defense Department but is primarily responsible for policymaking and is not the commander in chief of the military. Choice *D* heads the State Department and is the president's chief advisor on foreign affairs.

3. C: A pocket veto is a type of veto where a president takes no action on an upcoming bill. If Congress is not in session, and ten days have passed, the bill does not become law. Choice *A* is signing a bill into law, which is not the purpose of a veto. Choice *B* is a regular veto. Here, the president makes a conscious decision to reject a bill. Choice *D* is not a veto. Instead, the president has the option to send bills back to the Senate for further debate or revision.

4. A: The Nineteenth Amendment is significant because it gave women the right to vote for the first time. Choice *B* is the Fourth Amendment. Choice *C* is the Second Amendment. Choice *D* is the Eighth Amendment.

5. C: The mean is found by adding all the times together and dividing by the number of times recorded.

$$25 + 18 + 23 + 28 + 30 + 22.5 + 23 + 33 + 20 = 222.5$$

$$\frac{222.5}{9} = 24.722$$

Rounding to the nearest minute, the mean is 25 minutes.

6. B: Media relations specifically refers to the relations between an organization or government and various media outlets. It doesn't refer to the relations between two types of media or two different countries' media, so Choices *A*, *C*, and *D* are all incorrect.

7. C: Choice *C* is correct because evergreen content is content that can be released to the public at any time and therefore is not time sensitive. The term *evergreen* is used because the content, much like evergreen trees, stays "fresh" all year round. Choices *A*, *B*, and *D* are incorrect because they all refer to content that may be time sensitive.

8. D: A CSV file is a pure text document that can be exported and used to move data to another location. Choice *A* is a feature in the "Page Layout" tab of most word-processing software. Choice *B* describes a contacts list in email servers. Choice *C* is an output of a database and displays the information in the user's desired manner.

9. B: The equal sign must come before every formula in order for Excel to recognize the formula. Choices *A*, *C*, and *D* are not symbols that come before a formula in Excel. However, the plus or minus sign can be

205

used inside of the formula to describe what users would like Excel to do with the information provided to it.

10. D: The failed League of Nations was an early precursor to the modern-day United Nations. Choices *A*, *B*, and *C* did not involve the League of Nations. The North American Free Trade Agreement (NAFTA) was a deal between the United States, Canada, and Mexico to reduce trade barriers and increase economic growth. The International Criminal Police Organization, also known as Interpol, encourages worldwide police and safety efforts. The North Atlantic Treaty Organization (NATO) is a military alliance involved in international peacekeeping efforts.

11. A: In 1803, the United States purchased large amounts of territory from France, greatly increasing the size and strength of the nation. Choice *B* is incorrect because France gave up territory to the United States and did not gain any in return. Choice *C* is incorrect because the Treaty of Paris (1783) was signed much earlier than the Louisiana Purchase and ended hostilities between American colonies and Great Britain. Choice *D* is incorrect because territory was sold to the United States, not Great Britain.

12. B: President Ronald Reagan sent military forces to Grenada following conflict involving the prime minister of Grenada, Maurice Bishop. One of the goals of the invasion was to protect US citizens living in Grenada at the time. Choices *A*, *C*, and *D* were not involved in military conflict with the United States during the Reagan presidency.

13. C: The Tet Offensive was a series of military campaigns launched by North Vietnamese forces in 1968 during the Vietnam War. Although a military defeat for the North Vietnamese, news of the offensive greatly shifted American public perception of the war and resulted in a loss of public support. Choice *A* was a military conflict between Spain and America in 1898. Choice *B* was a military campaign launched as a result of the invasion of Kuwait by Iraq. Choice *D* involved conflict between North Korea and South Korea from 1950 to 1953.

14. C: Holding the CTRL key allows users to select multiple cells by left-clicking them. For formulas, any cell selected in this way will be used in the formula's calculation. Choice *A* will delete the information already written in a formula. Choice B will add a space between formula values. Choice *D* will cancel the current action in Excel.

15. B: MIN is the correct formula notation to return the smallest value in the selected cells. Choices *A*, *C*, and *D* are not valid formulas to enter into Excel and will not be recognized.

16. C: The Korean War started with North Korea invading South Korea, so Choice *C* is correct. The United States entered the war to protect its ally and prevent communism spreading across Asia. China didn't enter the conflict until General MacArthur led the American military across the 38th parallel. The Soviets provided material support to communist North Korea, but they never formally entered the war.

17. A: The Treaty of Paris concluded the American Revolution, securing American independence. Thus, Choice *A* is the correct answer. The Treaty of Ghent ended the War of 1812. The United States and France signed the Treaty of Alliance during the American Revolution, and French support turned the tides of war for the Americans. The Treaty of Versailles ended World War I, and its failure to establish a lasting peace partially caused World War II.

18. A: Delegates at the American Constitutional Convention agreed on the Connecticut Compromise, establishing two legislative bodies. Representation in one house was based on population (House of

206

Representatives), and the other granted each state two votes (Senate). As such, Choice *A* is the correct answer. The New Jersey Plan proposed a single legislative body with one vote per state, but it was rejected in favor of the Connecticut Compromise.

19. B: American Cold War foreign policy followed the domino theory, the idea that if one country turned communist, so would all of the neighboring countries. Consequently, the United States regularly intervened militarily to contain communism, which happened in Korea and Vietnam. Therefore, Choice *B* is the correct answer. None of the other answer choices are related to American foreign policy in the Cold War era.

20. A: A company that is the sole provider of a good, such as a railway system, is a monopoly. Choice *B* refers to several different major companies that compete against each other to provide a good or service. Choice *C* is a situation when only two major companies are the main competition against each other. Choice *D* is the opposite of a monopoly. In a state of perfect competition, there are numerous companies that provide a good or service, and consumers have a wide range of options to choose from.

21. B: Frictional unemployment occurs when people voluntarily leave a job and are in the process of searching for a new one. Choice *A* is unemployment that changes based on the supply and demand of a good, such as oil. Choice *C* occurs when a change in technology results in a loss of jobs. Choice *D* is long-term unemployment based on government, society, and incentives. For example, high minimum wage laws could lead to a decreased demand in labor.

22. B: A recession will cause a left shift in the demand curve because there is an overall decrease in spending due to general economic decline. Choices *A* and *C* would cause a right shift in the demand curve because more people will have the resources to purchase more goods and services. Choice *D* is incorrect because a shortage indicates that there is a high demand for a good or service, which would cause a right shift in the demand curve.

23. C: Choice *C* is correct because the terms *freely floating, fixed, pegged,* and *managed float* all refer to exchange rate regimes. Exchange rate regimes are ways in which a monetary authority may attempt to regulate the value of their currency as compared to other currencies and the world market in general.

24. A: To find the median of a data set, you must list the numbers from smallest to largest and find the number in the middle. If there are two numbers in the middle, add the two numbers together and divide by 2. Putting this list in order from smallest to greatest yields 18, 20, 22.5, 23, 23, 25, 28, 30, and 33, where 23 is the middle number, so 23 minutes is the median.

25. B: A collaborative manager makes all decisions based on a full team vote, with majority vote being the deciding factor. Input filtered through the team leader is a consultative manager's method of decision-making, so Choice *A* is incorrect. Choice *C* is incorrect because a single decision made by the team lead is how an autocratic manager makes decisions. Metrics and data are important, but they are not the decision-maker; rather, they inform the decisions that are made by the team, so Choice *D* is incorrect compared to Choice *B*.

26. D: Transformational management's primary focus is to push the team to constantly improve their work with each new project, so it can best be described here as focusing on employee growth. Maximized productivity is a focus of autocratic management, so Choice *A* is incorrect. A balance of productivity with satisfaction isn't the focus of transformational management since it carries a high risk of employee

207

burnout and frustration, so Choice *B* is incorrect. Greater employee freedom is more a focus of laissez-faire management, so Choice *C* is incorrect.

27. A: Delegative management leaves employees free to determine their own workflow for completing projects; managers only provide requirements on a project and review the completed work. Project parameters are still determined by managers and higher-ups, so Choice *B* is incorrect. Working hours and social interactions, depending on the exact job in question, may be accurate, but some jobs may not allow employees under delegative management to determine these things themselves. Thus, in a broader sense they are less correct than Choice *A*, making Choices *C* and *D* incorrect.

28. B: Leaders practicing visionary management do little directly for their team members, instead trying to inspire and motivate them into performing excellent work. Making sure everyone's input is considered is part of democratic management styles, so Choice *A* is incorrect. These managers don't try to provide every need possible for their employees since visionary management is a type of laissez-faire management, so Choice *C* is incorrect. Micromanagement is a characteristic of autocratic management, so Choice *D* is incorrect.

29. D: Focusing on a few distinct individuals during a speech is a method of keeping calm while speaking in public. It isn't a method of practice or maintaining a clear direction, so Choices *A* and *B* are incorrect. Hyper-fixation would be a more extreme and potentially harmful version of this practice, so Choice *C* is incorrect.

30. B: Sharing a short anecdote and appropriate joke that tie into the topic of your speech indicate having a clear direction. By having a clear sense of knowing what your speech is about, even diversions meant to keep the audience engaged are appropriate and naturally continue the speech. It's not an obvious example of respect or practice, so Choices *A* and *C* are incorrect. An on-topic anecdote could be a sign of awareness, but it isn't always, so choice *D* is incorrect as Choice *B* is more appropriate.

31. C: Practicing your speech at random in public can be awkward for bystanders, so it is the least appropriate answer. Choices *A* and *B* are good times to practice your speech, so they are both incorrect. Choice *D* is incorrect because while it may seem like there's not enough time, even a few minutes of practice can help relax nerves and re-energize you before the speech.

32. A: The equation used to model this situation is $y = 20x - 100$, where 20 is price of each cake and 100 is the original investment. The value of x is the number of cakes and y is the money she makes. If this line is plotted on the graph, the x-intercept will be the number of cakes she needs to make in order to recoup her investment and break even. The x-intercept occurs when the y-value is zero. For this equation, setting $y = 0$ and solving for x gives a value of 5 cakes. 100 cakes would yield a profit of $1,900, ten cakes would yield a profit of $100, and 2 cakes would still leave her in the negative (-$10).

33. A: Clicking the lower corner of the cell with the formula and dragging it to select multiple cells will put this formula in the selected cells. Choice *B* will delete the formula and information in a cell. Choice *C* moves the cell cursor to the cell one column to the right. Choice *D* will allow users to enter information into a cell.

34. D: The "Slide Show" button creates a full-screen presentation of the created slides. Choice *A* occurs when users manually delete a slide. Choice *B* is found in the "Design" tab and lets users change the background of the presentation. Choice *C* is found in the "Paragraph" tab and can align text on the slide left, right, or center.

35. B: The CC and BCC functions, which respectively stand for carbon copy and blind carbon copy, are both functions which enable the sender of the email to add recipients not explicitly listed in the To field. Whereas those recipients listed in the "CC" field will be visible to all recipients and will receive future emails sent out as "Reply All," neither is true for those recipients entered in the "BCC" field. Therefore, the correct answer is Choice *B*. Choices *A*, *C*, and *D* all incorrectly describe the CC and BCC functions.

36. C: In most common word processing software, a default function displays non-red (often blue) lines under certain sections of text to alert the user to perceived grammatical mistakes. Therefore, the correct answer is Choice *C*. Choice *A* is incorrect because the lines that appear under misspelled words are usually red. Choice *B* is incorrect because when a user turns on a function that shows changes in edited text, that change is typically displayed in the font color, not in underlining. Choice *D* is incorrect because those lines appear only due to the editing of the text directly by the user.

37. B: The Twenty-Second Amendment states that the president may serve a maximum of two terms. The only president to ever serve more than two terms in office was Franklin Roosevelt, who served four terms in office. Choices *A*, *C*, and *D* are not the maximum number of terms that a president can serve.

38. D: Congress has the important responsibility of regulating trade with foreign nations, Indian tribes, and between states. The Interstate Commerce Act of 1887 was originally designed to regulate the railroad industry. However, many of its principles were applied to other trades and businesses as well. Choices *A*, *B*, and *C* do not regulate interstate trade.

39. B: According to the Constitution, each state will have two senators representing them. Since there are 50 states, there are 100 senators serving in Congress. Choices *A*, *C*, and *D* are not the correct number of senators currently in Congress.

40. A: The power to regulate immigration is exclusive to the federal government; so, Choice *A* is the correct answer. The powers to regulate local government and implement welfare programs are reserved to the states. Both the federal and state governments enjoy the power to levy taxes.

41. A: In a perfectly competitive market, all products are homogenous and the same regardless of seller. Choice *B* is incorrect because there are no barriers to entry or exit in a perfectly competitive market. Choice *C* is incorrect because there are no market influences in a perfectly competitive market. Choice *D* is incorrect because consumers have access to all information and have complete product transparency.

42. C: The four main factors for production are labor, land, capital, and entrepreneurship. Entrepreneurship is important because it encourages new business and economic growth, which will drive production of goods and services. Choices *A*, *B*, and *D* are not one of the main factors for production.

43. C: The cost of the new equipment is considered a sunk cost. A sunk cost is an investment where the money cannot be retrieved. It is not used to calculate future business expenses because the business has already paid for it. Choice *A* is the cost of running the business, such as rent and basic utilities. Choice *B* varies with the level of output or sales. For example, a business may need to spend more on packaging if they are receiving a high number of orders. Choice *D* does not vary with an increase or decrease in output or sales. For example, if the insurance on a business remains at $100 a month, that is a fixed cost.

44. D: An economic depression is a severe, long-term period of economic decline. Choice *A* is a period of time where the prices of goods decrease and consumer purchasing power increases. Choice *B* is similar to a depression but lasts for a much shorter period of time and is not as severe. Choice *C* is when demand is greater than the supply of a good or service.

45. D: There will be no more coyotes when the population is 0, so set y equal to 0 and solve the quadratic equation:

$$0 = -(x - 2)^2 + 1,600$$

Subtract 1,600 from both sides and divide by -1. This results in:

$$1600 = (x - 2)^2$$

Then, take the square root of both sides. This process results in the following equation:

$$\pm 40 = x - 2$$

Adding 2 to both sides results in two solutions: $x = 42$ and $x = -38$. Because the problem involves years after 2000, the only solution that makes sense is 42. Add 42 to 2000; therefore, in 2042 there will be no more coyotes.

46. C: Native Americans traditionally lived in extended kinship networks. As such, Native Americans defined family as the nuclear family, extended family, tribal members, and/or entire nation. Fictive (non-blood related) kin were also commonly included as family members. In contrast, European colonists' families typically only included the nuclear and extended family. Therefore, Choice *C* is the correct answer. Men served as the primary provider of resources in both family structures, the European colonists didn't live more sustainably than Native Americans, and Native Americans also honored their elders.

47. D: From 1786 to 1787, Revolutionary War veteran Daniel Shays led an armed insurrection in western Massachusetts, and the government's inability to quash the rebellion exposed the Articles of Confederation's flaws. Thus, Choice *D* is the correct answer. The *Federalist Papers* were published during the ratification process, and, at that time, the Articles of Confederation was widely considered to be untenable. The question was what form of government would replace it. John Brown's raid at Harper's Ferry increased regional tension before the Civil War, and President George Washington's suppression of the Whiskey Rebellion demonstrated the strength of the US Constitution.

48. A: James K. Polk won the 1844 presidential election based on his promise to complete America's manifest destiny. Polk annexed the present-day American Southwest and California from Mexico, and his administration settled border disputes with Great Britain in the Oregon territory. None of the administrations in the other answer choices annexed a comparable amount of territory; therefore, Choice *A* is the correct answer.

49. C: During the Space Race, the United States and Soviet Union invested in computer-based technology to advance their rocket and satellite capabilities. These advancements in computing power led to the Digital Revolution, so Choice *C* is the correct answer. The United States never dismantled its space exploration program, and the Soviet Union collapsed more than a decade after they gave up trying to put a man on the Moon. Although the Space Race improved the superpowers' relationship, this didn't influence the American withdrawal from Vietnam. Instead, mounting domestic protests caused the United States to leave Vietnam.

50. A: The US Government Accountability Office (GAO) is responsible for posting all the management requirements with which federal agencies must comply. The Department of Foreign Affairs does not have anything to do with these accountability requirements, so Choice *B* is incorrect. US Staffing Department and Federal Managers Agency are both false names, so Choices *C* and *D* are incorrect.

51. C: An agency's strategic plans must be reevaluated and reissued every four years, specifically in the second year of every presidential term. Annually and biannually are too frequent, so Choices *A* and *B* are incorrect. Every eight years is too rarely, so Choice *D* is incorrect.

52. B: The primary purpose of the various Equal Employment Opportunity (EEO) laws is to prevent any discriminatory hiring practices, such as discriminating against applicants based on their gender, race, age, and other factors. They do not give Americans equal consideration for federal job positions, since work experience and skills are still considered, so Choice *A* is incorrect. They do not try to equalize the number of job positions in every federal agency, so Choice *C* is incorrect. While many of these laws offer protections from being fired based on discrimination, EEO laws make this a secondary goal after preventing discriminatory hiring practices, so Choice *D* is incorrect.

53. A: The Equal Pay Act of 1963 made it illegal to provide unequal pay based on gender. Choice *B* is incorrect; the Pregnancy Discrimination Act of 1978 made it illegal to discriminate in hiring based on an applicant's pregnancy status. Choice *C* is incorrect; Title VII of the Civil Rights Act of 1964 made it illegal to discriminate in hiring based on an applicant's race, color, religion, national origin, and many other factors. Choice *D* is incorrect; Title I of the Americans with Disabilities Act of 1990 made it illegal to discriminate in hiring based on the applicant's status as a qualified person with a disability.

54. C: The Reconstruction era immediately followed the end of the Civil War. One of the major challenges of this era was integrating newly freed slaves and granting them rights as citizens. Choice *A* is a 21st century effort to combat terrorism following the September 11th attacks. Choice *B* was characterized by major industrial innovations like the steam engine and lasted from around 1760 to 1840. Choice *D* is most known for banning the sale and production of alcohol from 1920 to 1923.

55. D: Richard Nixon's visit to China in 1972 marked the first time a president had visited mainland China. It was a major turning point in normalizing relations between the United States and China. Choice *A* did not visit China, and his administration was criticized for "losing" China to communism in 1949. Choice *B* was the third president to visit China. Choice *C* was the second president to visit China.

56. D: The Han dynasty created the Silk Road, a series of trade routes that linked the Far East and West for the first time in world history. Thus, Choice *D* is the correct answer. The Greeks installed the first representative government; Indian rulers defeated Alexander the Great's legendary military; and the Romans invented a superior type of concrete.

57. D: The European system's large-scale production of crops and livestock produced a food surplus that sustained permanent settlements and centralized government. Thus, Choice *D* is the correct answer. The European colonies didn't trade agriculture for military aid; agriculture didn't lead to military technological advancements; and the American South didn't urbanize for several centuries.

58. C: Mass media is an incredibly powerful tool for shaping public interest in various topics and events. It can be helpful for gauging public opinion or sharing information, but those uses are not nearly as potent, so Choices *A* and *B* are incorrect. Choice *D* is incorrect because while it may be possible in some situations to use state-controlled media to control the population, the modern mass media is extremely difficult if not impossible to control in this way.

59. A: Framing theory states that what the media chooses to cover and how it is covered are elements that influence the public's opinion of news and events. Harvest theory is a false term, so Choice *B* is incorrect. Agenda-setting theory is only partially correct, focusing only on what the media chooses to cover, so Choice *C* is incorrect. Cultivation theory focuses on how the elements of framing theory can influence the public into believing whatever the media states, so it is a more extreme version of framing theory, making Choice *D* incorrect compared to Choice *A*.

60. A: Older citizens who are involved with local politics and events are most easily reached through a local established news source like the city's newspaper. Television and radio news may be used to reach your intended audience, but less so compared to the newspaper, so Choices *B* and *D* are incorrect. Social media is the least likely choice here to reach older, locally involved citizens, so Choice *C* is incorrect.

Part Two: English Expression and Usage

1. A: Choice *B* incorrectly places a comma after glanced. Choice *C* uses *are* instead of *is* which does not agree with the subject. Choice *D* uses semicolons instead of commas to separate a list.

2. D: Choice *A* uses *reports* instead of *report*, which does not match the plural subject. Choice *B* does not maintain the parallel structure of the list. Choice *C* does not capitalize the proper noun, *Mandarin Chinese*.

3. B: Choice *A* is an example of a sentence fragment. Choice *C* incorrectly uses *effect* instead of *affect*. Choice *D* incorrectly capitalizes *negotiations*.

4. C: Choice *A* uses a colon instead of a comma. Choice *B* mixes up *they're* with *their*. Choice *D* does not capitalize the *President* title.

5. C: Choice *A* uses parts of a quotation mark instead of a semicolon to separate the sentences. Choice *B* uses *less* instead of *fewer* for the countable noun. Choice *D* incorrectly uses the word *more* with a comparative word.

6. B: Choice *A* is missing the verb *be* before *seeking*. Choice *C* spells the phrase *a lot* wrong by not including a space. Choice *D* does not use the correct tense for *discussing*.

7. A: Choice *B* uses *more good* instead of *better* as the comparison word. Choice *C* does not capitalize the proper noun *Mount Rushmore*. Choice *D* uses *many* instead of *much* to match with *time*.

8. D: Choice *A* does not match the plural subject *we* with *have* instead of *has*. Choice *B* incorrectly uses *something* to describe a person. Choice *C* incorrectly compares the food of one restaurant directly with another restaurant, instead of with another restaurant's food.

9. A: Choice *B* uses the incorrect pronoun *who* instead of *which* to describe work. *Who* refers to people, not things. Choice *C* mixes up the word *desert*, or a dry and empty area, with *dessert*, a sweet food normally eaten after a meal. Choice *D* does not use the possessive noun *my* to describe *family*.

10. C: Choice *A* uses *seeming* instead of *seems*, which creates an incomplete sentence. Choice *B* is missing the preposition *of*. Choice *D* uses the plural *amounts* instead of the singular *amount* to describe the butter.

11. B: Choice *A* uses a semicolon instead of a colon to separate a list. Choice *C* uses a comma instead of a semicolon to separate two independent clauses, creating a comma splice. Choice *D* inserts the words *yet* and *another* into the sentence which causes it to not make sense.

12. D: Choice *A* is a run-on sentence and needs a period to separate the two clauses. Choice *B* does not use the correct prefix for the word *indifferent*. Choice *C* uses the word *which* instead of *that* to introduce a clause.

13. C: Choice *A* is missing an apostrophe to create the contraction *It'll*. Choice *B* is missing an apostrophe in *mothers* to denote possession. Choice *D* uses *its* instead of *it's* to complete the sentence. *Its* is a possessive word, while *it's* is the contraction of *it is*.

14. D: Choice *A* needs to use an adverb, *traditionally*, to describe *eaten*. Choice *B* uses the possessive *your* instead of the contraction *you're*. Choice *C* mixes up the contraction *they're* with the adverb *there*.

15. A: Choice *B* does not correctly use parallel structure in the list in the sentence. Choice *C* incorrectly describes the father as a young girl instead of the daughter. Choice *D* places a period after the word doctor, which is only applicable when it is abbreviated to *Dr.*

16. A: Choice *B* uses *tenants*, or people who live on a property, instead of *tenets*, or beliefs. Choice *C* uses the plural of the word *diseases* instead of the singular *disease*. Choice *D* is missing an apostrophe for the contraction *won't*.

17. B: Choice *A* uses the possessive *her* instead of the subject *she* in the sentence. Choice *C* uses *except* instead of *accept*. Choice *D* is a run-on sentence and needs a period to separate the two sentences.

18. C: Choice *C* uses the present tense *lead* instead of the past tense *led*.

19. C: Choice *C* incorrectly places an apostrophe at the end of *students*. *Students* is not possessive in this sentence.

20. A: The sentence contains no errors.

21. D: Choice *D* uses the word *loosing* instead of *losing*.

22. B: Choice *B* does not use the singular word *has* to modify the singular subject of discovery. It instead uses the plural modifier *have*.

23. C: Choice *C* uses the plural word *them* instead of *it* to refer to the singular assignment.

24. A: The sentence contains no errors.

25. C: Choice *C* inserts an extra comma before *chocolates* and disrupts the flow of the sentence.

26. B: Choice *B* uses *much* to describe lottery tickets instead of *many*. *Much* does not modify counting nouns.

27. C: Choice *C* uses *for* to describe the 2007 start date. *Since* should be used to indicate that 2007 was when the job was first started.

28. A: The sentence contains no errors.

29. B: Choice *B* uses the incorrect preposition *with* to talk about marrying someone. The correct preposition is *to*.

30. D: Choice *D* does not use the word *from* to talk about a range of different things. The phrase should be *everything from rolling hills to flat plains*.

31. B: Choice *B* uses the incorrect pronoun *which* to refer to people. *Which* is used to refer to things, not people. The correct preposition is *who*.

32. A: The sentence contains no errors.

33. C: Choice *C* uses the incorrect comparative form of the word *expensive*. The correct comparison is *more expensive*.

34. D: Choice *D* is missing the adverb *permanently* to describe leaving and uses *permanent*, an adjective, instead.

35. A: The underlined text contains no errors. Choices *B* and *C* mean shaking or trembling and are not used to describe fireworks. Choice *D* refers to a virus.

36. C: Choice *C* replaces *amount of* for *number of*, which corrects the initial mistake in the phrase. *Amount of* refers to a mass or an uncountable measure. *Majors* is a counting noun and needs a phrase such as *number of* to correctly measure it.

37. D: Choice *D* correctly substitutes *allude* for *elude* when describing the author's text. *Elude* usually refers to the act of running away from something, while *allude* means to suggest or hint. Choice *B* means to begin something, while Choice *C* means to raise something.

38. C: Choice *C* correctly uses *everyday*, which is an adjective that means daily, instead of *every day*, which means each day. Choices *B* and *D* include unnecessary punctuation.

39. B: Choice *B* uses the correct relative pronoun *who* to describe the students. *Whom* is the objective form of *who* and is used as an object for verbs and phrases. Choice *C* is a relative pronoun for things or objects. Choice *D* refers to a sudden desire or need.

40. A: The underlined text contains no errors. The word *two* describes the pair of brothers that helped found the city of Rome. Choice *B* is a preposition used to describe movement to somewhere, while Choice *C* means additionally or also. Choice *D* refers to having two sides but is not used to describe brothers in this context.

41. D: Choice *D* correctly uses a hyphen to separate *ex* and *husband*. When *ex* is used as a prefix, such as with *ex-husband*, it needs to be connected to the main noun with a hyphen. Choices *B* and *C* do not use the correct punctuation to connect *ex* and *husband*.

42. C: Choice *C* means being awake and aware of one's surroundings, which describes the patient in the sentence. Choice *B* means on fire or blazing. Choice *D* describes a merging between two things.

43. B: Choice *B* correctly changes *true*, an adjective, to *truly*, an adverb. The word *truly* is used to modify the verb *is* and emphasizes the sentence about perfumery. Choices *C* and *D* both mean true but are used in different contexts than this sentence.

44. A: The underlined text contains no errors. If something is feasible, it means that it is possible to do. Choice *B* describes when someone or something is never wrong. Choice *C* means loyalty. Choice *D* means to show off or display something.

45. B: Choice *B* correctly changes the plural *services* to the singular *service*. The word *another* is used to describe singular nouns only. Choice *C* means helping others, while the *service* in this sentence refers to an amenity. Choice *D* refers to obeying something without question.

46. D: Choice *D* is a word usually used to describe travelling all the way around something. In this case, the submarine circled around the whole world. Choice *B* is a passive phrase that does not match the tense of the sentence. Choice *C* refers to events or situations.

47. D: Choice *D* correctly uses the possessive word *whose* to describe the relationship between the friend and his father. *Who's* is a contraction of the phrase *who is*. Choice *B* is a relative pronoun and does not describe the possessive. Choice *C* acts as a direct object and not as a possessive.

48. C: Choice *C* uses the correct word *there* to describe a location or position. *They're* is a contraction of the phrase *they are*. Choice *B* is used to show possession. Choice *D* is the objective form of *they*.

49. A: The underlined text contains no errors. *Had had* is a valid phrase when the sentence is in the past perfect tense and the main verb is *have*. Choice *B* is in the present tense. Choice *C* is the base form of the verb *have*, not the past participle. Choice *D* is a possessive word.

50. B: Choice *B* contrasts the initial plan to walk home and the change in this plan. *But* is used to introduce something that is the opposite of what was previously stated. *On the one hand* is a comparative phrase that cannot be used alone. Choice *C* does not match the tense or structure of the sentence. Choice *D* is a word used to add additional information.

51. B: Choice *B* matches the parallel structure of the sentence that the word *getting* interrupts. Choices *C* and *D* do not match the parallel structure in the sentence.

52. C: Sentence 3 establishes the main topic of the sentence, the speaker's memories of their grandfather. Sentence 1 describes the grandfather. Sentence 2 is an example of a story from the grandfather's life. Sentence 4 provides additional information that references the road trip from the previous sentence.

53. A: Sentence 1 introduces the topic of fugu. Sentence 4 contrasts fugu's status as a delicacy and the fact that it contains poison. Sentence 2 provides more information about the poison. Sentence 3 references the fact that the poison is dangerous and concludes by saying that only trained chefs are allowed to handle the fish.

54. A: Sentence 4 begins the paragraph by generalizing common opinions regarding Christmas. Sentence 1 builds on this to explain that Christmas is even more special for James. Sentence 2 explains why Christmas is special to James. Sentence 3 provides more detail to the previously mentioned scene and concludes the paragraph.

55. B: Sentence 2 introduces the topic of razor burn to begin the paragraph. Sentence 1 provides more detail about razor burn and introduces the concept of razor bumps. Sentence 3 explains the cause of razor bumps. Sentence 4 provides more detail on these bumps.

56. D: Sentence 1 introduces the topic of seasonal depression and should be first. Sentence 4 provides more detail about the depression. Sentence 2 further explores the topic by listing symptoms. Sentence 3 provides more detail about these symptoms.

57. A: Sentence 2 begins the story about a trip to the airport. Sentence 3 lists the first thing the couple will do. Sentence 1 uses the transition *after that* to explain their next steps. Sentence 4 concludes the paragraph with the transition *finally*.

58. C: Sentence 1 mentions the teams arriving for the tournament. Sentence 3 introduces a problem that happened after all the teams had arrived. Sentence 4 shares more details about the problem. Sentence 2 describes the response to those details and should be the last sentence in the story.

59. B: Choice *B* contrasts the initial confidence the team had with the unexpected result that followed. *However* improves the flow between the sentences and completes the paragraph. Choices *A* and *C* are used for emphasis. Choice *D* is used to add additional information.

60. A: Choice *A* means teaching or guiding someone. Marcus believes his acting skills will improve because experienced actors will mentor him, and he will be under their *tutelage*. Choice *B* means a danger or warning. Choice *C* is a harsh mix of sounds. Choice *D* is ignoring someone or something.

61. C: Choice *C* demonstrates the respect that the author has toward the art of making watches. He admires the craft and has a very positive opinion about it. Choice *A* signals confusion. Choice *B* describes hatred or extreme dislike. Choice *D* describes negative or antagonistic behavior.

62. C: Choice *C* describes the impact John Snow's work had on the development of epidemiology and matches the author's statement that John Snow was the father of modern epidemiology. Choices *A* and *B* do not consider the impact of John Snow's work. Choice *D* is incorrect because John Snow worked to disprove the prevailing theory, not support it.

63. D: Choice *D* refers to the previous sentence's remarks about a series of comeback tours, and contrasts Michael Jackson's desire to perform again with his sudden death. Choices *A*, *B*, and *C* reference earlier periods of Michael Jackson's life and do not follow the flow of ideas established in the sentence about comeback tours.

64. A: Choice *A* emphasizes how important the decision would be. The phrase *after all* also builds upon the previous sentence's description of how difficult making the decision would be. Choice *B* does not properly explain that the decision is important. Choice *C* is incorrect because the sentence does not give any clue or indication about what the actual decision will be. Choice *D* incorrectly states that the sentence is used to contrast details, but it is actually used to provide more detail.

65. B: Choice *B* is supported by the first sentence in the paragraph, which compares the old and new software. The paragraph also states that the new software will provide more benefits to the company overall. Choices *A*, *C*, and *D* cannot be supported by evidence from the paragraph. The paragraph does not mention workers' opinions about the decision or their personal feelings about the software. There is also no mention of who would be doing the updating.

Part Three: Situational Judgment

1. BEST: A: A bit of brief research allows the FSO to get some understanding of what the other guests may discuss or may consider interesting without overdoing preparations by outlining specific talking points, questions, jokes, etc. **WORST: C:** Asking the host for a guest list could be seen as prying or even outright rude, depending on the local culture.

2. BEST: D: Removing yourself and other people from harm's way makes it easier for emergency responders to provide medical assistance or rescue trapped individuals. **WORST: A:** The FSO needs to act immediately in moments of crisis because they are often called upon to be leaders without warning. Looking up protocol delays action.

3. BEST: A: A simple letter of congratulations can help smooth relations between the United States and the new regime without implying support or condemnation. This shows integrity by adapting to an unexpected political situation. **WORST: B:** Ignoring the independent observers implies American dissatisfaction with the election outcome and could imply to the new regime that the FSO is considering undermining their government.

4. BEST: C: Additional guards without an overt change in gear or weaponry increases safety without seeking to intimidate the host nation's citizens. It is easy to escalate security measures but difficult to deescalate if their intensity is inappropriate. **WORST: B:** The use of military gear to intimidate protesters to leave the embassy alone is unnecessarily provocative, especially if the demonstrators are upset about the host nation's government, not American involvement in the area.

5. BEST: B: Demographic opinions generally require polls or other data-collection tools for accuracy rather than the voiced opinion of a handful of individuals. **WORST: A:** Antagonistic sentiment, such as an anti-American feeling in the populace, can be meaningfully expressed without violent statements. Violent statements are a further escalation of discontent.

6. BEST: B: Good value for cost is the core goal of a cost–benefit analysis. The additional value provided by the American contractor is the best justification for choosing their proposal. **WORST: D:** The nation of origin doesn't thereby guarantee the quality of the work.

7. BEST: A: Choice *A* is the most valid conclusion because it does not make assumptions about the causes and effects of the provided data. For example, Choice *B* is less valid because no explanation has been provided for the production shortage. Further information is needed to draw such a conclusion. **WORST: C:** Although price gouging often happens during supply shortages, this practice usually is not the cause of the shortage.

8. BEST: A: This answer best represents a rational decision to move to 24/7 monitoring because it accounts for differing time zones between the United States and the host nation. **WORST: C:** Choice *C* is the worst answer because the stress of mandatory overtime is not trivial.

9. BEST: D: The quantity and frequency of demonstrations logically indicates that the host nation's people have strong opinions about the election but does not provide enough data to draw a more meaningful conclusion. **WORST: B:** The existence of demonstrations does not therefore indicate that a political faction intends to corrupt the electoral process.

10. BEST: B: The survey is most efficient because it uses modern tools to minimize the FSO's time gathering data while obtaining a large sample size. **WORST: D:** Choice *D* is inefficient because attending a session in person requires travel time, and assembly sessions are often long. It is additionally flawed due to the FSO's status as an American official, which may draw undesirable attention.

11. BEST: D: It's always best to handle a health crisis by calling an appropriate authority to the scene. **WORST: A:** Handling contact with the deceased's relative, spouse, etc., is the duty of those in a position of authority. The FSO should do so only if the task is delegated to them as someone familiar with the deceased individual.

12. BEST: A: A decisive leader needs to be able to act effectively and quickly. Decisiveness requires the individual to make snap decisions based on known information. Quick decisions are necessary when responding to a crisis. **WORST: C:** Slowing down the decision-making process to complete rigorous analysis can be useful, but it does not demonstrate decisiveness.

13. BEST: A: Choice *A* is the most time-sensitive because it deals with embassy security. In general, security concerns and threats to the safety of staff and/or American citizens is always a priority. Work concerned with security issues should be completed as quickly as possible. **WORST: E:** A news summary sourced from information available to the public is not very time sensitive. Routine tasks and tasks that make use of easily obtained information are usually not time sensitive.

14. BEST: B: Some countries have a business culture where exchanges of money, which would be considered bribes in the United States, are common. Unless you are very familiar with the local culture, it is best to seek advice from a more experienced FSO on how to proceed in a culturally informed way and then act on the learned information. **WORST: A:** A direct confrontation without prior research and information gathering can harm your working relationship with the local official. It is best to seek information before acting hastily.

15. BEST: C: The most professional response is to own up to your scheduling mistake and follow through on your word with the local government. This maintains good relationships with the local officials. **WORST: D:** Failing to follow through on your word and additionally asking to reschedule can be perceived as disrespectful of the other party's time.

16. BEST: B: Instructing the staff member to send an email or write a note, memo, etc., provides an actionable direction to the staffer that will get them the information they need while allowing you to be punctual to meeting the consul. **WORST: D:** Punctuality to meetings, especially with senior officials in the Foreign Service or the host nation, is an important aspect of professional behavior as an FSO. The new staff's inquiry should be answered but isn't important enough to justify tardiness.

17. BEST: D: In any case involving possible drug use in the workplace, the best answer is to submit an anonymous report to an authority with supervising power over the individual in question. **WORST: C:** Invading another FSO's privacy is a violation of personal boundaries and can land you in trouble, even if you had good intentions.

18. BEST: B: Any possible security breach should be reported immediately to the responsible authorities. This may be the team's supervisor, a member of the Bureau of Diplomatic Security, or a higher official, as appropriate to the FSO's position within the embassy. **WORST: D:** This choice, although a valid security protocol for passwords, security codes, etc., does the least to immediately address the potential security risk demonstrated by this incident. In addition, if the coworker told their significant other the passcode, a changed code could be leaked again if corrective action is not taken.

19. BEST: C: Building rapport in an unobtrusive way is important because it increases the observer's safety in potentially dangerous situations. **WORST: A:** When acting as a neutral observer, the FSO's duty is to avoid intervening in crisis situations.

20. BEST: D: Active listening is a reliable first tool when dealing with stress and burnout because it provides an immediate response while helping the FSO determine other useful methods of support for the individual. **WORST: A:** Social activity can help reduce stress, but an invitation to go drinking risks encouraging alcohol consumption as a maladaptive coping mechanism.

21. BEST: D: Asking for support from teammates in small ways helps build relationships because of the psychological "Ben Franklin" effect. This phenomenon impacts rapport building because it indicates that individuals are more likely to feel positively toward people they have assisted in some way. **WORST: B:** Although the FSO should generally follow the supervisor's guidance, team building is a situation where proactive effort is more effective.

22. BEST: C: A formal complaint is appropriate because this situation has occurred several times and the teammate's behavior has not changed. **WORST: D:** Seeking approval or disapproval from the team as a whole group is more likely to spread strife in the team than to solve the problem of professional boundaries.

23. BEST: B: Eye contact and remaining still is the most effective way to communicate attention to someone you're speaking with. **WORST: C:** Continuing to work while filling gaps in the conversation with verbal invitations for the other person to keep speaking communicates a lack of attention. This physical language can lead the other person to feel disregarded and unimportant.

24. BEST: C: Positive reinforcement can boost the teammate's self-esteem and confidence, which reduces the frequency of anxiety. **WORST: D:** Choice *D* doesn't actually reassure the teammate. Instead, this minimizes their worries. Minimizing a coworker's concerns worsens anxiety rather than reducing it.

25. BEST: B: Acting slowly, quietly, and patiently demonstrates gentleness and togetherness. This effectively expresses empathy for the man because the physical subtext implies sharing his sorrow. **WORST: D:** Although anger is a common emotion expressed after death, it is not an appropriate emotion to present when consoling a grieving parent.

26. BEST: C: Choice *C* is best because being close to people, combined with physical touch, is an effective means of reassuring individuals during crisis. **WORST: A:** Assuming an emergency preparedness position may be correct from the perspective of personal safety, but doing so reduces your ability to engage with the civilians to ameliorate fear and panic.

27. BEST: E: As a neutral observer, it is important to avoid putting yourself at risk and also to avoid putting others at risk with your actions. The young man's behavior may seem suspicious, but there is nothing in the description that indicates overt danger. Thus, distance and continuing to observe interactions between local police and citizens is the best choice. **WORST: C:** If this situation turns out to involve an insurgent, a foreigner approaching the individual puts themselves at inappropriate risk.

28. BEST: C: During a negotiation, it's important to meet in a neutral space so that all participants feel comfortable, without pressure based on their surroundings. A change of venue, even at additional cost, is preferable to using one party's offices. **WORST: D:** Meeting at either the American or the local offices are both poor choices. However, Choice *D* is the worst because it imposes on the local officials to find a way to make the meeting work or to reject your offer. This is more likely to be perceived as rude than offering to make use of your own meeting spaces.

FSOT Practice Test #3

Part One: Job Knowledge

1. What is an advantage of online social media?
   a. Accessible while driving
   b. Strong local ties
   c. Dedicated audience
   d. Quick, creative messaging

2. What makes public diplomacy different from regular diplomacy?
   a. It is conducted between a home government and a foreign government.
   b. It is conducted between a home government and a foreign public citizenry.
   c. It is conducted between two private individuals of a foreign public citizenry.
   d. It is conducted out in the open in public venues.

3. When were Jim Crow laws prevalent in the Southern United States?
   a. 1608-1783; from around the time of the Jamestown being established to the end of the American Revolution
   b. 1787-1865; from the end of the American Revolution to the end of the Civil War
   c. 1877-1954; from the end of Reconstruction to the Supreme Court's ruling in *Brown v. Board of Education*
   d. 1955-1975; from the start of America's involvement in the Vietnam War to its eventual exit

4. What does Article 5 of the North Atlantic Treaty establish?
   a. Article 5 of the North Atlantic Treaty establishes that any member of NATO should consider an attack against any other member of NATO as if it were an attack on itself.
   b. Article 5 of the North Atlantic Treaty establishes that any member of NATO may call for a general meeting if circumstances have arisen that the member believes threatens its national sovereignty.
   c. Article 5 of the North Atlantic Treaty establishes the geographical confines within which the majority of a country must lay in order for that country to be eligible for membership.
   d. Article 5 of the North Atlantic Treaty establishes the role countries not directly bordering the North Atlantic Ocean may be allowed to play in the operation and functioning of NATO.

5. Most rules regarding day-to-day operations of federal agencies come from what law?
   a. Civil Rights Act of 1964
   b. Title II of the American Agency Functions Act of 1975
   c. Administrative Procedure Act of 1946
   d. Agency Administration Act of 1902

6. How does a negative externality affect groups that were not involved in the production or consumption of a product?
   a. It results in an increase in satisfaction in the third party.
   b. It results in one company becoming the sole provider of a good.
   c. It results in indirect harm to the group.
   d. It results in a general decrease in society's economic growth.

7. Which mass media theory claims that followers of news media will begin to believe whatever the media tells them about a story or event?
   a. Agenda-setting theory
   b. Cultivation theory
   c. Zeitgeist theory
   d. Doctor theory

8. What is the usual effect of inflation?
   a. Increased regulation and decreased growth
   b. Decreased regulation and increased growth
   c. Increased prices and decreased currency values
   d. Decreased prices and increased currency values

9. An agency may decide, for various reasons, to not comply with a request for information from the public. How long do they have to decide and respond to such a request?
   a. Ten days
   b. Sixty days
   c. Fourteen days
   d. Twenty days

10. When a user deletes an email, where does it get sent?
   a. Inbox
   b. Folder
   c. Archive
   d. Trash

11. Which of the following would be least likely to cause difficulties in public diplomacy?
   a. Failed shipping agreements
   b. Different cultural customs
   c. Language barriers
   d. Declining governmental relations

12. Under which United States president were the first atomic weapons deployed?
   a. Harry S. Truman
   b. Dwight D. Eisenhower
   c. Franklin D. Roosevelt
   d. John F. Kennedy

13. In representative democratic politics, what is meant by the term *gerrymandering*?
   a. Gerrymandering is the process by which an elected representative may attempt to delay a legislative vote by means of a prolonged speech.
   b. Gerrymandering is the process by which votes are counted and allotted to various national electors, who then vote on behalf of the constituency they represent.
   c. Gerrymandering is the process by which the boundaries of electoral districts are manipulated and redrawn in order to favor a particular political party.
   d. Gerrymandering is the process by which a tied vote in a legislative body is resolved and usually involves a final decision being made by either the executive or the judiciary.

221

14. To what does the term *Second World* refer?
    a. The Second World refers to countries that were part of the so-called Communist Bloc during the mid to late twentieth century, including the Soviet Union, China, and Cuba.
    b. The Second World refers to countries that were part of the alliance between the US, Western European states, and various satellite states during the mid to late twentieth century.
    c. The Second World refers to countries that were allied with neither the Communist Bloc nor the alliance between the US and various Western European powers. The Second World includes many countries in the developing world, such some countries in Africa and South America.
    d. The Second World refers to the Americas, and all the countries contained therein, and it specifically refers to the Americas in relation to the "First World" (Europe, Asia, and Africa).

15. Which federal retirement plan is similar to a privately offered 401k Plan?
    a. Federal Retirement Plan
    b. Thrift Savings Plan
    c. Social Security
    d. Basic Benefit Plan

16. In the context of the Constitution, what is meant by the term *president pro tempore*?
    a. The president pro tempore is an unelected member of the public who serves as a non-voting member of Congress.
    b. The president pro tempore is the term used for the president when they are present in either house of Congress (for example, during the State of the Union).
    c. The president pro tempore is the term used by the vice president if and when they are performing a duty or obligation on behalf of the president themselves.
    d. The president pro tempore is a member of the Senate who presides over the Senate in the absence of the vice president.

17. When sending emails, when would using a BCC be appropriate?
    a. When sending many emails, but you don't want users to know who else it was sent to
    b. When sending emails to multiple people, and it doesn't matter if they see who else it was sent to
    c. When the email is too long and needs to be broken into separate emails
    d. When sending a single email to only one person

18. Given limited resources, what term illustrates the different quantities of a product that society can make when two or more goods depend on the same resource?
    a. Marginal cost
    b. Budget constraint
    c. Opportunity cost
    d. Production possibilities frontier

19. Which pairing of public officials and their term lengths is NOT correct?
    a. Representative in the House of Representatives—two years
    b. Senator—six years
    c. Ambassador—three years
    d. President—four years

222

20. What is the Schengen Area?
  a. The Schengen Area is a demilitarized zone along the border of Finland and Russia that has been in place since the fall of the Soviet Union.
  b. The Schengen Area is an area consisting of 27 European nations, within which passports and other kinds of border control measures have been abolished.
  c. The Schengen Area is the area around an embassy in which the laws of the nation presiding over the embassy take precedence.
  d. The Schengen Area is an area of open sea in the South Pacific that represents the largest portion of the globe not internationally recognized as belonging to any nation.

21. Why is the image of a salad bowl considered to be a more appropriate metaphor for the diversity found in the United States, rather than a melting pot?
  a. In contrast to a melting pot, in which all ingredients are combined into something distinct and new, the image of a salad bowl emphasizes that individuals of different cultural backgrounds can participate in American culture without necessarily needing to leave their own culture behind.
  b. In contrast to a melting pot, which may contain both meat and non-meat products, the image of a salad bowl emphasizes the heavy agricultural background of many of the individuals who have contributed to the culture of the United States.
  c. In contrast to a melting pot, which is an antiquated term that not many contemporary Americans intuitively relate to, the salad bowl is a much more recognizable object in American life and is therefore considered to be a more appropriate metaphor.
  d. In contrast to a melting pot, which can often require hours of work in order to successfully incorporate all the flavors, the salad bowl can be used to prepare and serve meals quickly, emphasizing the fact that Americans of all races and creeds no longer have to work as hard as their ancestors did to achieve success.

22. In media, what is meant by the term *embedded journalists*?
  a. Embedded journalists are journalists who are employed by, under contract with, or otherwise associated with a specific media company.
  b. Embedded journalists are journalists who assist in the writing of articles and exposés, but they typically do not get their own bylines.
  c. Embedded journalists are journalists who write only about a specific topic or industry.
  d. Embedded journalists are journalists who are attached to military units during an armed conflict.

23. In foreign affairs, what is meant by the term *plenipotentiary*?
  a. A plenipotentiary is a public official, usually a diplomat, who has been invested with the full powers to act on behalf of the president.
  b. A plenipotentiary is a meeting that occurs between two or more heads of states.
  c. A plenipotentiary is a public official of a foreign nation who provides support and advice to diplomatic officials of one's own nation.
  d. A plenipotentiary is an official legal hearing through which an ambassador or other diplomat can be stripped of their position.

24. In order for a treaty to be considered a Concordat, who must be a signatory?
  a. More than half of all globally recognized heads of states
  b. The reigning British monarch
  c. The Pope
  d. The current American president

25. What is the consequence of economic comparative advantage?
  a. Countries increase tax rates to subsidize more industries.
  b. Countries enforce high tariffs on products they can't produce efficiently.
  c. Countries specialize at what they can do most efficiently relative to their competitors.
  d. Countries increase spending to stimulate economic growth.

26. A foreign country seeks diplomatic aid from your home country regarding a refugee crisis they are having. What type of diplomatic goal are they seeking in negotiations?
  a. Economic
  b. Militaristic
  c. Humanitarian
  d. Environmental

27. Which of the following is NOT a part of diplomatic negotiations?
  a. Persuasive arguments
  b. Concessions
  c. Rewards
  d. Retaliation

28. By default, where are all received emails located?
  a. Desktop
  b. Inbox
  c. Archive
  d. Junk

29. What does the doctrine of mutual assured destruction posit?
  a. The doctrine of mutual assured destruction posits that the only way for a country or countries to undergo a decolonial process is with the careful dismantling of the system in concert with the previous colonial leaders.
  b. The doctrine of mutual assured destruction posits that any nuclear exchange between two nuclear powers would result in the complete destruction of both parties.
  c. The doctrine of mutual assured destruction posits that the length and cost of a war is proportional to the personal hatred the leaders of both armies feel towards the other side.
  d. The doctrine of mutual assured destruction posits that the only way for a legitimate, full-blown war to occur is for a majority of politicians from both sides to agree to the declaration of war.

30. What is the general process in the United States government for a treaty to be passed?
  a. A member of the House of Representatives introduces the proposed treaty, which then has to pass simple majorities in the House and Senate before the president decides whether to approve or veto the treaty.
  b. A member of the Senate introduces the proposed treaty, which then has to pass a simple majority in the Senate before the president decides whether to approve or veto the treaty.
  c. The president introduces the treaty, which then must pass a two-thirds vote in the Senate before taking effect.
  d. The president has full control over the drafting and implementation of treaties, and no consent from Congress is required.

31. What is the government's role in a centrally planned economic system?
    a. The government distributes resources based solely on merit.
    b. The government allows the private market to set all prices based on supply and demand.
    c. The government makes all decisions related to production, distribution, and price.
    d. The government balances a private and public sector to stabilize the economy.

32. In most common spreadsheet software, what does adding a formula to a cell enable you to do?
    a. Adding a formula enables you to create graphs and other visual representations of the information contained in the spreadsheet.
    b. Adding a formula enables you to edit the cell. Without first placing a formula in a cell, you cannot permanently edit it.
    c. Adding a formula enables you to alter the look of a cell, making it possible to change the color, outline, and opacity of the cell, among other things.
    d. Adding a formula enables you to make calculations based on the inputs of other cells, making it possible to add totals and find averages.

33. What is a potential benefit of using the advanced search features of a database?
    a. The advanced search features of a database enable you to specify the exact phrasing of your search terms, ensuring the right terms are searched.
    b. The advanced search features of a database enable you to add additional search terms in order to search for resources that contain all of the keywords.
    c. The advanced search features of a database enable you to exclude certain search terms so that resources containing that keyword are not in the results.
    d. All of the above are potential benefits of using the advanced search feature of a database.

34. Some information is forbidden from being made publicly available upon request. Which of the following is NOT one of those items of information?
    a. Confidential financial information
    b. Personnel medical files
    c. Information being compiled for criminal investigation that has no impact on the investigation procedure
    d. Information related to national defense

35. Which statement most accurately describes the difference between Memorial Day and Veterans Day?
    a. Memorial Day is for the remembrance of military personnel who have died in service of their country, whereas Veterans Day celebrates all military personnel, living and dead.
    b. Memorial Day is an international holiday, whereas Veterans Day is celebrated only in the United States.
    c. Memorial Day recognizes current members of the armed forces, whereas Veterans Day recognizes only those who have previously served.
    d. Memorial Day is a general day of remembrance for veterans who have died, whereas Veterans Day is a day of remembrance specifically for veterans who died in service.

36. What type of relationship is there between age and attention span as represented in the graph below?

Attention Span

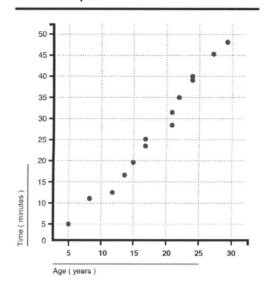

Age (years)

a. No correlation
b. Positive correlation
c. Negative correlation
d. Inverse correlation

37. In emails, what is an attachment?
a. The email address of the recipient
b. An extra layer of security added to each email
c. A user-created folder that helps to organize emails
d. A document that is added to an email

38. Which statement most accurately describes the difference in how the CIA and the FBI are allowed to conduct themselves?
a. Whereas the FBI mainly operates inside the United States, the CIA is prohibited from collecting information about any United States citizen or resident.
b. Whereas the FBI only operates in law enforcement, the CIA operates in both the areas of law enforcement and intelligence gathering.
c. Whereas the FBI is under the supervision of the Justice Department, the CIA is under the supervision of the Department of Homeland Security.
d. Whereas FBI agents are required to obtain warrants in order to enter and search a property, no such warrant is needed for the CIA to enter and search a property.

39. Which American military incident is correctly linked with the conflict it helped to incite?
a. The attack on Fort Sumter—Revolutionary War
b. The Gulf of Tonkin incident—Vietnam War
c. The assassination of Archduke Ferdinand—World War II
d. 9/11—Gulf War

40. A public official pushing for military intervention may be referred to as what?
    a. A war dog
    b. A war hyena
    c. A war vulture
    d. A war hawk

41. Which military action may be taken in response to the establishment of a no-fly zone?
    a. Preemptive attacks to prevent airspace violations
    b. Reactive attacks targeting aircrafts violating the no-fly zone
    c. Continuous surveillance of airspace
    d. All of the above are examples of military actions that may be taken in response to the establishment of a no-fly zone.

42. In common American political parlance, what does the term *lame duck* mean?
    a. A lame duck is any executive who oversees a political body in which the majority of the members are of a different political party than the executive.
    b. A lame duck is an elected official in the final months of their term, usually after their successor has been elected.
    c. A lame duck is a proposed bill that lacks adequate support from political parties or blocs.
    d. A lame duck is an elected official who loses their first bid at re-election and never serves in public office again.

43. When sending an email to multiple recipients, what symbol is used to separate each email address?
    a. Comma
    b. Period
    c. Semicolon
    d. Percent

44. In emails, what does CC stand for?
    a. Continual Control
    b. Control Caps
    c. Carbon Copy
    d. Cannot Create

45. Paul took a written driving test, and he answered 12 questions correctly. If he answered 75% of the total questions correctly, how many questions were on the test?
    a. 25
    b. 15
    c. 20
    d. 16

46. *Semper Fidelis* is the official motto for which branch of the United States military?
    a. The Marines
    b. The Coast Guard
    c. The Navy
    d. The Air Force

47. What is the best definition of scarcity in a consumer economy?
    a. An increased supply of a product
    b. An increased demand for a product
    c. The limited availability of a particular commodity
    d. The excess production of a particular commodity

48. Every year, a federal agency must file a report regarding all cases of public requests for information. Who is this report submitted to?
    a. The US Attorney General
    b. The Speaker of the House
    c. The President
    d. The White House Chief of Staff

49. What agency enforces worker health and safety standards?
    a. Federal Health Administration
    b. Workplace Safety Administration
    c. Federal Internal Safety Agency
    d. Occupational Safety and Health Administration

50. What are the two means by which an amendment to the Constitution may be proposed?
    a. By a two-thirds majority vote in the House of Representatives OR by a two-thirds majority vote in the Senate
    b. By a two-thirds majority vote in the Senate OR by a two-thirds majority on a national ballot
    c. By a two-thirds majority vote in the House of Representatives and the Senate OR by a constitutional convention called for by two-thirds of state legislatures
    d. By a two-thirds majority on a national ballot OR by presidential executive order

51. What are the three points of the rhetorical triangle?
    a. Ethos, logos, pathos
    b. Audience, message, speaker
    c. Intention, implementation, effect
    d. Argument, evidence, solution

52. Triple the difference of five and a number is equal to the sum of that number and 5. What is the number?
    a. 5
    b. 2
    c. 5.5
    d. 2.5

53. What are the first ten amendments of the United States Constitution known as?
    a. Bill of Rights
    b. Articles of Confederation
    c. The Declaration of Independence
    d. The Magna Carta

54. Which executive department was established most recently?
    a.   Department of Energy
    b.   Department of Veterans Affairs
    c.   Department of Homeland Security
    d.   Department of Commerce

55. Which domain is likely to be used by a website run by a nonprofit group?
    a.   .com
    b.   .edu
    c.   .org
    d.   .gov

56. In PowerPoint, what is a transition?
    a.   A link to an outside picture, document, or website that can be inserted on a slide
    b.   An option that changes the size of text on each slide
    c.   An animation that plays in between each slide in a presentation
    d.   A shortcut to save progress on a presentation

57. What does the acronym OPEC stand for?
    a.   Overseas Populations of Expat Citizens
    b.   Organization of the Petroleum Exporting Countries
    c.   Organization of People Excited for Change
    d.   Organization for Pacific Emergent Countries

58. Which of the following best describes commodities?
    a.   Physical, tangible items
    b.   Activities based on labor or skill
    c.   Raw materials or agricultural products
    d.   High-demand products

59. Which type of graph best represents a continuous change over a period of time?
    a.   Stacked bar graph
    b.   Bar graph
    c.   Pie graph
    d.   Line graph

60. What official journal publishes all new rules, regulations, and reports that come from the US government?
    a.   Federal News Bulletin
    b.   Consumer Price Index
    c.   American Agency News
    d.   Federal Register

Part Two: English Expression and Usage

Type A: Sentence Selection
Directions: For each item in this section, select the one sentence that best meets the requirements of standard written English.

1. Select the sentence that best meets the requirements of standard written English.
    a. I don't know how I will do it, but I know that this couldnt be the end of my journey to be a doctor.
    b. While relaxing in the pool, a drink was enjoyed by the wealthy businessman.
    c. Unfortunate, the registration period has closed.
    d. Driving while tired is just as dangerous as drinking and driving.

2. Select the sentence that best meets the requirements of standard written English.
    a. The cool winter whether has me in chills.
    b. He did so good on his math exam that he jumped out of his seat.
    c. I could feel tears welling up in my eyes when I learned the ultimate fate of the airplane.
    d. With nothing else to do, I decided to watch around the world in 80 days.

3. Select the sentence that best meets the requirements of standard written English.
    a. Excuse, me sir, but I believe you have dropped your wallet.
    b. The only thing I want right now is a sweet, delicious mango smoothie.
    c. There has been a big debate over if or not we should return to working in the office.
    d. Among my peer, I am the most capable and talented.

4. Select the sentence that best meets the requirements of standard written English.
    a. Moving abroad gives us the chance to experience different cultures.
    b. It is a dangerous game to be play with fire.
    c. Something that I;ve always wanted to learn was how to fight like a professional.
    d. Sharp looks, intelligence, and wealth; she has it all.

5. Select the sentence that best meets the requirements of standard written English.
    a. I feel so much happiness wherever the grocery store has its weekly sale.
    b. The weather today was chilly and insuitable for swimming.
    c. I apologize for the amount of time it took for me to respond to this text.
    d. They weren't able to meet the increased demand do to being understaffed.

6. Select the sentence that best meets the requirements of standard written English.
    a. My brother's are named Jack and William.
    b. She was less than impressed by the company's lack of empathy and communication.
    c. The car slow inched towards the edge.
    d. My vacation to orlando, Florida was extremely memorable.

7. Select the sentence that best meets the requirements of standard written English.
    a. I wake up in the morning and brushed my hair.
    b. It is extremely important to wear a helmet whenever you ride a motorcycle.
    c. This country's economy was greatly effected by the global recession.
    d. My brother and myself presented my parents with a new car.

230

8. Select the sentence that best meets the requirements of standard written English.
   a. After he had finish his work, he felt relieved.
   b. Sometimes, I enjoy riding, my bike in the mountains.
   c. It doesn't matter if or not you didn't know about the rules.
   d. My business was extremely successful despite the lack of support from my partner.

9. Select the sentence that best meets the requirements of standard written English.
   a. A healthy diet consists of food from a variety of sources.
   b. The debate between dr. Williams and his staff was in regards to how long they needed to stay with the patient.
   c. He couldnt even remember why he came here in the first place.
   d. I was shocked when I met the actor themselves walking down the street.

10. Select the sentence that best meets the requirements of standard written English.
    a. Ever for the economy crashed, I have been unable to find a job.
    b. The memories I have of the mountains will stay for me forever.
    c. Music is a passion that I intend to pursue in college.
    d. For example the cheapest produce in the area is located at a store very far from here.

11. Select the sentence that best meets the requirements of standard written English.
    a. She graciously accepted the flowers from her boyfriend however she secretly preferred chocolate instead.
    b. Daydreaming about a better future kept Sarah motivated to complete her graduate degree.
    c. So many teams enter this tournaments only to fail after the first round.
    d. Patients who are unable to make their appointment needs to contact the office.

12. Select the sentence that best meets the requirements of standard written English.
    a. The news reporter looked at him phone and sighed at his new assignment.
    b. I shocked when I learned who was responsible for the recent uptick in crime.
    c. I begged and pleaded for another chance, but they informed me that the decision was final.
    d. I just got off the phone with my brother, which is a firefighter in California, and told him how much I missed him.

13. Select the sentence that best meets the requirements of standard written English.
    a. Six weeks ago, Lulu brought this kitten home, she was so fond of her.
    b. Lulu brought this kitten home only six weeks ago and she was so fond of her.
    c. Lulu brought this kitten home only six weeks ago, and she was so fond of her.
    d. Lulu was only five years old, and brought this kitten home only six weeks ago, and she was so fond of her.

14. Select the sentence that best meets the requirements of standard written English.
    a. There isn't a sound heard accept for the birds outside and your own hands tapping on the computer keyboard.
    b. There isn't a sound heard expect for the birds outside and your own hands tapping on the computer keyboard.
    c. There isn't a sound heard accept for the birds outside, and your own hands tapping on the computer keyboard.
    d. There isn't a sound heard except for the birds outside and your own hands tapping on the computer keyboard.

15. Select the sentence that best meets the requirements of standard written English.
    a. Despite what he says, he have never been to New York City.
    b. The rainy London weather made the entire trip miserable; and it felt like wasted time.
    c. Time was at a premium during their tour of paris; they only had four hours before the flight.
    d. The neon lights of Las Vegas were a dazzling sight for the new visitor.

16. Select the sentence that best meets the requirements of standard written English.
    a. Find a quiet place to set up, John, and settle down into your work.
    b. Remember to pick up the bread, and milk before the snowstorm.
    c. She would saunter around from table to table, talked with the diners and occasionally pulling up a chair to gab a little longer.
    d. She picked one of the City's Parks at random and headed there for a walk.

17. Select the sentence that best meets the requirements of standard written English.
    a. The vast industrialization of Europe which took place between 1760 and 1840 was perhaps the most significant watershed period in the history of Europe.
    b. The vast industrialization of Europe, which took place between 1760 and 1840 was perhaps the most significant watershed period in the history of Europe.
    c. The vast industrialization of Europe, which took place between 1760 and 1840, was perhaps the most significant watershed period in the history of Europe.
    d. The vast industrialization of Europe which took place, between 1760 and 1840, was perhaps the most significant watershed period in the history of Europe.

Type B: Sentence Correction
Directions: For each item in this section, select the one underlined word or phrase that needs to be changed to make the sentence correct, or indicate that none of the underlined parts are in error.

18. Sarahs dedication to her education is heartwarming, especially when you consider the difficulties that her family experienced to support her.
    a. NO ERROR
    b. Sarahs dedication
    c. heartwarming, especially
    d. family experienced

19. One of the biggest benefits of working at this company is the immediate access to there renowned online learning platform.
    a. NO ERROR
    b. of the biggest
    c. immediate access
    d. there renowned

20. Scholars of ancient history generally agree that this individual was the worst ruler to ever take control of the Roman Empire.
    a. NO ERROR
    b. generally agree that
    c. the worst ruler
    d. control of

232

21. This marketing strategy is <u>usually only</u> reserved for <u>highly desirable</u> luxury goods like watches, <u>the perfume</u>, and designer purses.
    a. NO ERROR
    b. usually only
    c. highly desirable
    d. the perfume

22. <u>My brother and me</u> have <u>always shared</u> a close bond <u>with each other</u>.
    a. NO ERROR
    b. My brother and me
    c. always shared
    d. with each other

23. Based <u>on mine personal</u> experiences, <u>inspiration can</u> come from even <u>the smallest</u> places.
    a. NO ERROR
    b. on mine personal
    c. inspiration can
    d. the smallest of

24. <u>When asked</u> what his favorite colors were, the child <u>smiled and said</u> that he liked <u>red and blue</u> the most.
    a. NO ERROR
    b. When asked
    c. smiled and said
    d. red and blue

25. <u>If you have</u> any questions <u>regarding the</u> contract, please speak to <u>Mister. Ramos in</u> Building 5.
    a. NO ERROR
    b. If you have
    c. regarding the
    d. Mister. Ramos in

26. The <u>corporation's workforce</u> can be divided into <u>two groups;</u> people who have seen the video and <u>people who have</u> not.
    a. NO ERROR
    b. corporation's workforce
    c. two groups;
    d. people who have

27. Marcus <u>became extremely</u> agitated <u>where he was</u> getting ready for his wedding; he even snapped at <u>his best friend</u> of 20 years.
    a. NO ERROR
    b. became extremely
    c. where he was
    d. his best friend

28. I normally <u>don't buy</u> expensive <u>accessories,</u> but I <u>couldn't resisted</u> when I saw them available at a huge discount online.
    a. NO ERROR
    b. don't buy
    c. accessories,
    d. couldn't resisted

29. The constant rainstorms <u>have made</u> it extremely <u>difficult for me</u> to connect <u>to my online</u> classes.
    a. NO ERROR
    b. have made
    c. difficult for me
    d. to my online

30. There are transitional words and phrases <u>that emphasize</u> a point, <u>demonstrating</u> an opposing point of view, present a condition, introduce examples <u>in support of</u> an argument, and so much more.
    a. NO ERROR
    b. that emphasizes
    c. demonstrate
    d. in supporting of

31. Transitional words act as a <u>bridge; connecting</u> <u>ideas and</u> strengthening a paper's <u>coherency</u>.
    a. NO ERROR
    b. bridge connecting
    c. ideas, and
    d. coherance

32. <u>"Please sit down" the teacher said.</u>
    a. NO ERROR
    b. 'Please sit down,' the teacher said.
    c. "Please sit down", the teacher said.
    d. "Please sit down," the teacher said.

33. It was <u>springtime</u> once again in the <u>Arctic, and</u> just like countless times before, signs of life <u>were beginning</u> to reappear.
    a. NO ERROR
    b. spring time
    c. arctic, and
    d. was beginning

34. The only sounds for <u>months over</u> end <u>are the distant</u> cries of a <u>lone wolf</u> or the howling wind ravaging through the land.
    a. NO ERROR
    b. months on
    c. is the distant
    d. loan wolf

Type C: Sentence Correction II

Directions: For the items in this section, select the one word or phrase that needs to be used in place of the underlined text to make the sentence correct, or indicate that the underlined text is not in error.

35. The football captain tried to rally his team after their crushing loss by shouting <u>we'll win next time.</u>
   a. NO ERROR
   b. we will be won next time.
   c. "we'll win next time."
   d. (we'll win next time.)

36. Barack Obama <u>(the 44th President of the United States)</u> was born in Honolulu, Hawaii.
   a. NO ERROR
   b. the 44th President of the United States
   c. [the 44th President of the United States]
   d. ;the 44th President of the United States;

37. We agreed that I would present the initial research <u>findings,</u> and my partner would present the research methods.
   a. NO ERROR
   b. findings;
   c. findings/
   d. findings:

38. The candidate and the <u>interviewer,</u> went into the office to discuss the benefits of working at this company.
   a. NO ERROR
   b. interviewer"
   c. interviewer:
   d. interviewer

39. After losing his chess championship to the rookie player, the former champion explained that he could <u>of</u> won if he had tried harder.
   a. NO ERROR
   b. off
   c. have
   d. an

40. I was pleasantly surprised when I learned that my dog didn't mind <u>to go</u> to see the veterinarian.
   a. NO ERROR
   b. went
   c. going
   d. will go

41. Historians confidently agree that the reign of this monarch was the <u>worst</u> the nation had ever seen.
   a. NO ERROR
   b. most bad
   c. worse
   d. baddest

235

42. When asked why her son showed little enthusiasm for his own birthday party, <u>Jack</u> explained that he simply was not feeling well.
    a. NO ERROR
    b. Jack's mother
    c. Jack's
    d. Jack already

43. Desperate to do anything to improve his financial situation, he eventually became a <u>cellar</u> at the local flea market.
    a. NO ERROR
    b. catacomb
    c. chamber
    d. seller

44. When I compare the food between the two new restaurants, I think the soup at the first restaurant tastes much <u>more good</u> than the soup at the other restaurant.
    a. NO ERROR
    b. better
    c. well
    d. good

45. In Japan, there aren't any freshwater lakes bigger <u>then</u> Lake Biwa.
    a. NO ERROR
    b. compared
    c. as
    d. than

46. To qualify for the next event, swimmers needed to have <u>swum</u> in five other sanctioned events.
    a. NO ERROR
    b. swim
    c. swam
    d. swimming

47. One famous story she used to tell was of her younger years in Italy, and how once she won a <u>national beauty contest</u>.
    a. NO ERROR
    b. National Beauty Contest
    c. National beauty contest
    d. national Beauty contest

48. <u>For what its worth,</u> the train arrived two hours late.
    a. For what its worth,
    b. For what it's worth,
    c. For what its worth
    d. For what it's worth

236

49. After lunch <u>I went swimming, played with my dog, and cleaning up my room.</u>
    a. I went swimming, played with my dog, and cleaning up my room.
    b. I went swimming, playing with my dog, and cleaning up my room.
    c. I was going swimming, played with my dog, and cleaned up my room.
    d. I went swimming, played with my dog, and cleaned up my room.

50. When writing an academic paper, <u>spelling, punctuation, and content development are key.</u>
    a. spelling, punctuation, and content development are key.
    b. students should consider spelling, punctuation, and content development.
    c. spelling, punctuation, and content development, are key.
    d. being key are spelling, punctuation, and content development.

51. <u>Transitions are an extremely important part of writing. Without proper transitions, a paper might seem choppy and disconnected.</u>
    a. Transitions are an extremely important part of writing. Without proper transitions, a paper might seem choppy and disconnected.
    b. Transitions are an extremely important part of writing without which, a paper might seem choppy and disconnected.
    c. Transitions are an extremely important part of writing. Additionally, without them, a paper might seem choppy and disconnected.
    d. Transitions are an extremely important part of writing without them, a paper might seem choppy and disconnected.

Type D: Paragraph Organization
Directions: For each item in this section, select the ordering of sentences that results in the clearest, most well-organized paragraph.

52.
(1) She reminisced about that special day that she had spent with her friends.
(2) My mother said that she and her friends were absolutely crazy about Elvis at the time.
(3) When I asked my mother about the most memorable concert she had ever been to, she said that it was when she saw Elvis for the first time.
(4) They admired his good looks, powerful vocals, and exciting dance moves.
    a. 2, 3, 1, 4
    b. 2, 4, 1, 3
    c. 1, 4, 2, 3
    d. 3, 1, 2, 4

53.
(1) The pizza uses the freshest ingredients and a specially made cheese found only in Italy.
(2) The best item on the menu is the pizza.
(3) They immigrated to the United States from Italy years ago and brought their amazing recipes with them.
(4) I know the owners of the new Italian restaurant that opened next to the movie theater.
    a. 4, 1, 3, 2
    b. 4, 3, 2, 1
    c. 2, 3, 1, 4
    d. 1, 4, 2, 3

54.

(1) This increased demand meant more opportunities to make money and live a better life.

(2) The numerous factories that appeared at this time demanded huge workforces.

(3) Factories are one of the main reasons that cities grew rapidly during the Industrial Revolution.

(4) However, labor laws were extremely primitive and rudimentary, leading to long work days and unsafe working conditions.

    a. 3, 1, 4, 2
    b. 4, 1, 2, 3
    c. 3, 2, 1, 4
    d. 1, 2, 3, 4

55.

(1) Meera's parents were extremely proud of her and expected a lot from her because she would be the first person in their family to graduate from college.

(2) Meera did her best to meet her parents' high expectations, joining multiple clubs and achieving high grades.

(3) However, her hard work paid off when she received her diploma and saw her parents' faces light up with smiles.

(4) She was constantly busy, and some people wondered why she was working so hard.

    a. 1, 2, 4, 3
    b. 3, 1, 2, 4
    c. 1, 4, 3, 2
    d. 2, 1, 3, 4

56.

(1) Before the printing press, bookmaking was an extremely laborious and long process.

(2) However, the printing press made it possible to create books extremely quickly and cheaply.

(3) This led to the spread of knowledge and the creation of a global market for books.

(4) The invention of the printing press revolutionized human society.

    a. 3, 1, 4, 2
    b. 4, 1, 2, 3
    c. 2, 1, 3, 4
    d. 4, 3, 2, 1

57.

(1) Luckily, they were able to clear security with enough time to catch their flight to New York.

(2) Stephen and Amy had been married for a long time, but they felt that they had not seen enough of the world.

(3) After years of planning, they decided to visit New York City for the first time.

(4) When they arrived at the airport, they were worried that they might miss their flight because of how long security checks were taking.

    a. 1, 2, 3, 4
    b. 2, 1, 4, 3
    c. 3, 2, 1, 4
    d. 2, 3, 4, 1

58.

(1) While he tried to clean it up, he spilled his boss's drink onto the computer.

(2) Jeremy told me that his first day at the new office did not go well.

(3) His boss was in a foul mood for the rest of the day as he worked with the IT department to salvage files from the computer's hard drive.

(4) He spilled his coffee all over his boss's desk during their meeting.

    a. 3, 1, 4, 2

    b. 2, 1, 4, 3

    c. 3, 2, 1, 3

    d. 2, 4, 1, 3

Type E: Paragraph Revision

Directions: This section consists of several sentences that compose a paragraph. Read the paragraph carefully, and then answer the question that follows it.

59. The situation on the battlefield is becoming increasingly dire. Morale is extremely low. Without additional resources or manpower, the enemy will be able to break through our lines and encircle our forces. If this happens, the enemy will have a clear path toward the capital. We must not allow this to happen, and we will fight until the last man to prevent this.

What is the main purpose of the fourth sentence?

    a. To show why the author feels hopeful that they will succeed

    b. To explain an event that happened in the past because of the current situation

    c. To contrast the previous sentence with an event that is unlikely to happen

    d. To provide details about a hypothetical situation if the current situation is not addressed

60. I could hardly contain my excitement when I learned about my friend's marriage to her longtime boyfriend. I can still remember when they started casually dating in high school. I never expected that they would be together for so long. However, they have tackled every challenge in life together, from finding their purpose to balancing school and family responsibilities. I simply could not be happier for them.

The author's tone is best described as what?

    a. Sorrowful

    b. Pessimistic

    c. Jubilant

    d. Apprehensive

61. The sunset was particularly gorgeous today. I admired the myriad colors in the sky and the gentle sway of the wind. It felt like I was in a dream, free from the worries of everyday life. I felt as if I was caught in an <u>ephemeral</u> moment in time, experiencing life's beauty for only a brief second. An inner calm washed over me like waves on the beach. Everything seemed perfect at that moment.

As used in the sentence, the underlined word is closest in meaning to what?

    a. Fleeting

    b. Eternal

    c. Disorderly

    d. Peerless

62. Japan has one of the world's most advanced train networks. Its train system is important because it makes it possible to travel all around the country affordably. For example, it only costs around $150 US to travel from Tokyo to Osaka. The <u>crown jewel</u> of Japanese train prowess is the Shinkansen. This advanced railway network has transported billions of people safely and quickly since 1964.

What is the purpose of the underlined word in the paragraph?
   a. To explain why the Shinkansen is unsustainable in the long run
   b. To emphasize the most impressive aspect of the Japanese train system
   c. To express the author's dissatisfaction over the overuse of trains in Japan
   d. To provide an example of why trains have had a minimal impact on life in Japan

63. Gelato is a frozen treat that is enjoyed by people around the world. Created in the 16th century by Bernardo Buontalenti, gelato is frequently compared to ice cream. Although gelato and ice cream share several common characteristics, the main difference between the two sweet treats is the amount of milk used. Gelato in general uses more milk than cream, so it contains less fat and calories overall. Additionally, gelato does not normally contain egg yolks, which is a common ingredient in ice cream.

According to the paragraph above, what can be implied about gelato?
   a. Gelato was created before ice cream.
   b. Gelato and ice cream are identical creations.
   c. Gelato is not as popular as ice cream in North America.
   d. Gelato is generally a healthier alternative to ice cream.

64. It had been a disastrous week for Alexander. He realized too late that he was procrastinating on assignments that would take much longer to complete than he'd anticipated. Therefore, he didn't have a lot of time to study for his final exams. He tried to "study" on Saturday, but he ended up spending all that time catching up on previous assignments instead. He could feel dread building up inside of him with every passing day.

Why does the author use quotation marks around the word *study* in the fourth sentence?
   a. To show Alexander's optimism that he would finish his work on time
   b. To indicate Alexander's unwillingness to start studying for his exams
   c. To emphasize that Alexander attempted to allocate time to study for his exams but was ultimately unable to
   d. To explain the cause of Alexander's sense of dread

65. Novelist H.G. Wells is known for his many classic books such as *The Time Machine* and *The War of the Worlds*, but one of his lesser-known creations was a game called *Little Wars*. First published in 1913, *Little Wars* was a wargame played with miniature soldiers on the floor. It included rules to launch small dowel rods from a toy cannon at miniature enemy figures to knock them over. While *Little Wars* wasn't the first wargame in history, it shows another way in which H.G. Wells was a creative innovator.

Why does the author include the names of two of H.G. Wells' novels?
   a. Little Wars is an extension of The War of the Worlds.
   b. Those that enjoy Little Wars will also enjoy the selected novels.
   c. The titles are familiar to a wide audience and help introduce H.G. Wells.
   d. The selected novels lend authority to H.G. Wells as a key military strategist.

Part Three: Situational Judgment

Directions: For each question in this section, select the BEST and WORST response to each scenario.

1. Three new FSOs are joining your team, and you've been assigned to provide their basic orientation to the team's duties and roles completing Foreign Service objectives in the host nation. How do you prepare to orient these staff members?
    a. Use materials from previous staff orientations to provide a similar presentation.
    b. Work on an "FAQ" document based on the questions you had upon arrival at this position.
    c. Develop a one-day orientation program providing a basic introduction to your team's current objectives.
    d. Research pedagogical techniques to provide more effective instruction.

2. While educating a new staff member about the culture of your host nation, the trainee shares that they learn most effectively through hands-on experience. How do you respond to this situation?
    a. Take a walk to a local market, mall, or other commercial space with the trainee.
    b. Advise the trainee that prior education is preferable to hands-on experience because it helps avoid social embarrassment.
    c. Invite the trainee to observe you in a meeting with local officials.
    d. Ask a local liaison to host an informal dinner to help the trainee practice the local culture's etiquette.

3. At a social function, a local official you don't know very well asks your opinion about a controversial election back in the United States. What's an appropriate response?
    a. Indicate that it's not appropriate for an FSO to discuss US domestic politics.
    b. Express trust in the institutions laid in place by the Constitution.
    c. Share your personal views with the official to build rapport through honesty.
    d. Discuss how the consulate leadership expects the election to alter—or not alter—American foreign policy in the host nation.

4. You travel into a rural province of your host nation for the purpose of a disaster relief program and are invited to spend the night at a local official's house. This is a culturally normative expression of hospitality, and you accept. During the night, an adult in the household propositions you for sex. How do you respond?
    a. As you see fit, because this choice falls into the category of private life, not public service.
    b. Decline, and share that information privately with your host.
    c. Decline, but do not disclose the proposition to anyone.
    d. Decline, and describe the proposition anonymously in your final report.
    e. Decline, report the proposition to your superior in the Foreign Service, and find a culturally acceptable reason to stay elsewhere in the future.

5. You have helped a local family get an American visa for asylum. The day the family leaves the host nation, they gift you a small silver heirloom. How do you respond?
    a. Take the gift, and find a gift of your own to provide in return.
    b. Decline, and encourage the family to save their resources for their new life.
    c. Thank them for the gift, and document it in your reports.
    d. Decline, saying that the Foreign Service's standards don't allow you to receive gifts.
    e. Accept the gift on behalf of the Foreign Service rather than as a personal memento.

6. A local news corporation publishes an exclusive report describing political corruption among senior elected officials in the host nation's government. Which of the following additional statements provides additional information that makes the report more reliable?
    a. The corporation specializes in political news.
    b. The corporation has a reputation for journalistic integrity.
    c. The report's claims are supported by your team's collected data about local election funds.
    d. Opposition politicians are calling for a formal investigation into alleged corruption.

7. Military saber-rattling has escalated between your host nation and one of its neighbors. Both nations have increased the number of armed forces on their border. Your consulate is stationed in a major city thirty miles from the border. There is minimal history of anti-American belligerence from the neighboring nation. Based on this information, do you recommend evacuation of the consulate's staff to your superiors?
    a. No, because international law dictates that neutral diplomats shall not be harmed during military actions.
    b. No, because American citizens in the region may need evacuation assistance in case of an invasion.
    c. Yes, because the consulate's security is not adequate to operate in a conflict zone.
    d. Yes, because the city's proximity to the border increases the risk of bombardment.

8. An FSO on a fact-finding trip in a rural area of their host nation chooses to spend several nights at a local friend's home. They brush off the concerns of their security team. Why was this a poor decision?
    a. The FSO didn't listen to expert advice.
    b. The FSO's decision wasn't based on data.
    c. The FSO didn't follow standard safety protocol.
    d. The FSO made an emotional decision.

9. A local contact tips you off that a major industrial company is going to make an announcement in three days that is likely to impact American trade interests in the host nation. Which of the following statements best describes why the contact's information is reliable?
    a. The individual has provided accurate information multiple times in the past.
    b. The individual showed an internal document outlining the announcement.
    c. Another member of your team reported that a different individual delivered similar information.
    d. You've fostered a relationship with this individual for several years.

10. Your team receives a new objective from a superior and, as team leader, it is your job to distribute the tasks required for completing this objective among your team members. Which of the following tasks do you assign to yourself?
    a. Monitor public digital communications (e.g., social media).
    b. Collate data from your team and other teams that are working on the same objective.
    c. Organize the team's schedule for completing goals related to the objective.
    d. Compose the report sharing your team's findings.

11. While fielding the embassy's emergency phone, you receive a call reporting a hostage situation involving an American citizen. Who do you pass this information to first?
    a. The head of security
    b. Your immediate superior
    c. The American ambassador
    d. The local authorities

12. You have several reports due at the end of the week. Each report is due to a different individual or group. Which recipient's report do you prioritize completing first?
   a. Your immediate superior
   b. A senior official in the local government
   c. An American congressperson
   d. A contracted company working for the consulate

13. It is the start of the month, and you've received new tasks from your supervisor. Which of the following work assignments should you focus on completing first?
   a. Complete your in-progress report on environmental policies, which is due at the end of the week.
   b. Review letters of recommendation to determine which candidate to schedule an interview with next week.
   c. Prepare for your presentation on environmental regulations to a senior official.
   d. Review gathered data on regulation compliance by local companies, and begin analysis on which companies to partner with when seeking contractors later this month.

14. As team leader, what's the most effective way to communicate with your subordinates when distributing new tasks?
   a. Catch up with team members during the workday, and assign new tasks orally.
   b. Distribute tasks and explain objectives with written documentation during a weekly meeting.
   c. Maintain a physical or digital project management board for team members to check independently.
   d. Notify each subordinate of new tasks by email.

15. The vendor of a food stall that is set up on your embassy's street is arguing with a security agent when you return to the embassy from a meeting. The food stall is popular with embassy staff, and you're acquainted with the vendor. The vendor asks you to intercede on his behalf. The security guard says the vendor was trying to sneak into the embassy, whereas the vendor admits that he sought entry but did so seeking to set up in the courtyard. How do you respond to this situation?
   a. Defer to the security agent.
   b. Apologize to the vendor but inform them that strangers are only permitted on official business.
   c. Compromise by inviting the vendor to set up their stall closer to the entrance.
   d. Vouch for the vendor with security, and get them special permission to set up in the courtyard.

16. You work in a secure wing of your consulate. The usual cleaning service provider has been ill for several days, and you feel that the office needs cleaning because the US ambassador to your host nation is scheduled to visit in a few days. What's the best way to handle this situation?
   a. Advocate privately to your team's leader that the office's cleanliness needs to be addressed.
   b. Do research, and suggest hiring a new service provider.
   c. Take the initiative and begin cleaning the office when you have some downtime.
   d. Suggest that the team divides up the cleaning tasks and completes them the day before the ambassador's visit.
   e. Call the service provider and ask them to send a replacement employee.

17. Your office receives a phone call from a local number saying there is a bomb outside your building. The speaker's voice is high-pitched, and you hear giggling in the background. What do you do?
    a. Ask the caller for more information.
    b. Inform the caller that this is an embassy, and the threat could cause an international incident.
    c. Report the call to your supervisor.
    d. Report the call to the head of security.
    e. Note in a memo that a prank bomb threat was called in to the embassy.

18. You are making an eight-hour flight back to the United States to make a presentation to senior government officials and representatives about the political tensions in your host country prior to a major election. Due to a weather delay, you have one hour between when the plane lands and when the meeting is scheduled. How do you prepare for the meeting?
    a. Grab a nap after the flight to be as rested as possible for the presentation.
    b. Review your presentation points one last time.
    c. Skim the latest news from your host country to check if the political situation has changed.
    d. Request a delay or rescheduled meeting so you can be at your sharpest for the presentation.
    e. Use the time to shower, groom, and refresh yourself in your hotel room.

19. While collaborating with a public official representing the host nation, you inadvertently offend them through a breach of the local culture's etiquette. How do you mend the relationship?
    a. Calmly explain that you're from a culture where that behavior is appropriate in the workplace.
    b. Orally apologize for the breach in etiquette, and promise not to repeat the mistake.
    c. Remove yourself from the situation, and send the official a written apology.
    d. Ask your superior to reach out to the official's superior, and explain that the offense was not intentional.

20. A coworker in your team at the local consulate confronts you in the hallway outside the office. They insist that you have been getting preferential assignments and that you're trying to make their work look shoddy. What's the most appropriate way to resolve this conflict?
    a. Excuse yourself, and reach out to your supervisor to request conflict mediation.
    b. Listen to your coworker's complaints and describe your perspective.
    c. Privately ask a teammate if they believe that you need to correct your office behavior.
    d. Ignore the complaint because the team's time is better spent on Foreign Service work than office drama.

21. You have been assigned to be the leader of a newly established team at an embassy in a host nation where you haven't been previously posted. What action do you take to encourage building rapport among your employees?
    a. Host an informal gathering at your residence to provide an opportunity for socialization.
    b. Hold a short team meeting where each member of the team has a chance to briefly describe their set of skills and their prior diplomatic assignments.
    c. Seek out positive reinforcement opportunities and give praise in a public place where other employees are present.
    d. Actively seek employee input on how they believe the team can most effectively achieve its objectives.

244

22. The local official you've been working with on disaster prevention plans has retired from diplomatic service, and a new official takes their place. What's the best way to establish a new working relationship without slowing down your work?
    a. Ask your retiring colleague to write a letter of introduction for you, addressed to the new official.
    b. Request a meeting with the new official at their office to review current progress on the project.
    c. Invite the new official to dinner at the embassy to meet you and your team.
    d. Write and email a document explaining the responsibilities the new official is inheriting from their predecessor.

23. You've been working a little longer into the evening for the last month to complete your fourth high-priority report on the host nation's political situation for various senior officials in Washington, DC. A colleague comments that you've been irritable lately. You've noticed trouble focusing and reduced energy and suspect that you're experiencing burnout. What's the best way to address this?
    a. Establish firmer boundaries for working hours.
    b. Request a leave of absence to rest and recover energy.
    c. Express to your superior that you've been feeling overwhelmed with your workload.
    d. Make use of self-care techniques, such as time management and exercise, to cope until work returns to normal.

24. One of your coworkers receives a phone call during the workday informing them of a family member's death. How do you support your grieving coworker?
    a. Verbally express condolences and support.
    b. Give them space, and avoid broaching the subject unless they do so first.
    c. Quietly organize a card or small gift with other coworkers.
    d. Extend no-pressure invites to social activities.

25. You're attending an environmental disaster preparedness meeting along with a variety of nongovernmental officials, elected representatives, appointed policymakers, and subject matter experts. Which of the following individuals is most important to sway to your department's perspective on proposed evacuation plans?
    a. A senior elected representative
    b. Your immediate superior
    c. A nongovernmental official sponsoring the plan's funding
    d. A junior subject matter expert
    e. The meeting's chair or moderator leading the discussion

26. A woman standing outside the American Embassy has her arms crossed, stands with her feet close together while leaning against a wall, and her head moves frequently. She doesn't appear to be looking at particular individuals, vehicles, etc. What emotion does this body language best describe?
    a. Anxiety
    b. Anger
    c. Fear
    d. Joy

27. After your first meeting negotiating with a group of local officials, a coworker privately informs you of a breach you made in local etiquette. They believe that this is why the meeting ended earlier than was scheduled. How do you address this situation?
   a. Seek out the local officials before they leave the building, and apologize.
   b. Write a letter of apology admitting the mistake, and send it to the officials' office.
   c. Schedule a refresher on etiquette with a culture expert.
   d. Ask your superior to reach out on your behalf to demonstrate that the offense was taken seriously.

28. You fall ill, and due to your embassy's policies concerning contagious illness, you are required to be away from the workplace for one week. Many of your duties for this week involved in-person contacts and meetings. How do you handle this situation?
   a. Message each individual you would have met with and request to reschedule.
   b. Attend meetings that don't take place at the embassy so you won't fall behind.
   c. Use teleconferencing tools to attend as many appointments as possible.
   d. Coordinate with your supervisor to help a coworker attend in your place.
   e. Rest at home, and trust your team to handle the situation until you're feeling well.

Test #3 Answer Explanations

Part One: Job Knowledge

1. D: Social media's strongest advantage is easy access to quick and highly creative messaging with short-form posts. Being accessible while driving is an advantage of radio media, so Choice *A* is incorrect. Strong local ties are an advantage of newspaper print media, so Choice *B* is incorrect. A dedicated audience is an advantage of specific or niche online news blogs, so Choice *C* is incorrect.

2. B: Public diplomacy is conducted between a home country's government or government officials and the public citizens of a foreign country. Discussions between two countries' governments is simply referred to as diplomacy, so Choice *A* is incorrect. Discussions between two private individuals, even in a foreign country, is not a type of diplomacy at all, so Choice *C* is incorrect. Public diplomacy is not necessarily defined by being conducted out in public, so Choice *D* is incorrect.

3. C: Jim Crow laws upheld and furthered racial segregation in the American South. These laws arose after the end of Reconstruction, when federal involvement in the affairs of southern states largely subsided and white southerners began to institute a more overt system of segregation and racial oppression. Such laws continued into the mid-twentieth century, when a federal ruling in *Brown v. Board of Education of Topeka* made it illegal to discriminate on the basis of race. Therefore, the correct answer is Choice *C*.

4. A: The North Atlantic Treaty Organization, commonly called NATO, is a multinational military alliance dedicated to protecting its member states. Formed during the Cold War in opposition to the Communist Bloc, Article 5 of NATO establishes that every member of NATO should treat an attack on any other NATO member as if it were an attack on itself. Such a provision provides a strong deterrence to any state looking to invade and expand. Therefore, the correct answer is Choice *A*.

5. C: The Administrative Procedure Act of 1946 is responsible for many of the rules governing the day-to-day operations and transparency requirements of federal agencies. The Civil Rights Act of 1964 has rules preventing discriminatory hiring practices but otherwise has nothing to do with day-to-day federal agency operations, so Choice *A* is incorrect. Choices *B* and *D* are both false terms, so they are both incorrect.

6. C: A negative externality indirectly harms groups that were not involved in the production and consumption of a product. For example, pollution caused by the production of a new technology indirectly harms the health of others. Choice *A* is an example of a positive externality, where a group benefits indirectly. Choice *B* is a monopoly. Choice *D* is a recession.

7. B: Cultivation theory states that the more an audience follows a particular media outlet's coverage of events, the more susceptible they are to believe whatever that media outlet tells them about events. Agenda-setting theory is not as complex, stating only that the public is influenced by the stories the media chooses to cover, so Choice *A* is incorrect. *Zeitgeist theory* and *doctor theory* are both false terms, so Choices *C* and *D* are incorrect.

8. C: Inflation is a period of increased prices and decreased currency values, so Choice *C* is the correct answer. Most countries designate a central bank or government agency to set and enforce monetary policies to control inflation and interest rates. Regulation typically correlates with growth, but that relationship is not inflation.

9. D: An agency has twenty days from the day it receives a request for information to determine if they will comply with the request. Ten and fourteen days are too brief, so Choices *A* and *C* are incorrect. Sixty days is far too long, so Choice *B* is incorrect.

10. D: Deleted emails are sent to the Trash, where there is an option to permanently delete them. Choice *A* is where almost all emails are sent initially. Choice *B* organizes files and emails. Choice *C* is where emails are stored for future reference.

11. A: Failed shipping agreements are the least likely to impact public diplomacy within a foreign country. Language barriers and different cultural customs are two of the most common difficulties with public diplomacy, so Choices *B* and *C* are incorrect. Declining relations between a home government and foreign government can also make public diplomacy with that foreign public significantly more difficult, so Choice *D* is incorrect.

12. A: The United States deployed the first atomic weapon on August 6, 1945, when a bomb code-named "Little Boy" was dropped on the Japanese city of Hiroshima. At the time, the president of the United States was Harry S. Truman, who had assumed the presidency a few months prior in April 1945, when then-president Franklin D. Roosevelt died. Therefore, the correct answer is Choice *A*.

13. C: In representative democratic politics, the term gerrymandering refers to the intentional redrawing or redesigning of electoral constituencies by a political official in order to benefit themselves and/or their political party. By redrawing the borders of these constituencies, politicians can attempt to include or excise specific neighborhoods, streets, or even houses that they suspect may be supporting them or their opponent. Therefore, the correct answer is Choice *C*. Choice *A* is incorrect because it describes filibustering. Choice *B* is incorrect because it describes the electoral college. Choice *D* is incorrect because it describes, among other situations, the vice president casting a vote to break a tie in the Senate.

14. A: The concept of the First, Second, and Third Worlds arose in the twentieth century during the Cold War, to show which side countries were on in the Cold War. Countries in the First World were those that had aligned themselves with the United States and with Western European countries against the Soviet Union. Countries in the Second World were generally those that were either a member of or friendly with the "Communist Bloc." The Third World, as a consequence, consisted of countries that were not aligned with either the First World or the Second World, and included much of Africa and South America. Therefore, the correct answer is Choice *A*.

15. B: A Thrift Savings Plan allows federal employees to choose how much and how often they deposit into the plan and how they receive funds when they retire, similar to a 401k plan from private employers. Federal Retirement Plan is a false term, so Choice *A* is incorrect. Social security is available to most private sector, federal, state, and local employees and is a system where a portion of your paycheck is withheld and automatically deposited for benefits later, so Choice *C* is incorrect. A Basic Benefit Plan is a retirement plan where the benefits vary depending on how many years you worked for the federal government and your highest average pay, so Choice *D* is incorrect.

16. D: In the Constitution, it was originally intended that the vice president would preside over all Senate affairs. However, given the multitude of responsibilities of the vice president, the Constitution also included a provision allowing the Senate to choose a member from their chamber to preside over the Senate in instances where the vice president cannot. This person is then given the title president pro tempore, meaning "president for a time." Therefore, the correct answer is Choice *D*.

17. A: BCC, which stands for Blind Carbon Copy, is a method of sending emails to many recipients. Recipients will not know who else the email was sent to. Choice *B* is an example of CC. CC and BCC both send emails to many recipients, but in a CC everyone can see who else received the email. Choices *C* and *D* are not appropriate situations for a BCC.

18. D: The production possibility frontier is a curve that shows how much of a product can be made when two or more goods are competing for the same resource. Choice *A* is the increase in production costs associated with creating more product. Choice *B* is similar to a production possibility frontier but focuses on what an individual can afford to create, rather than general society. Choice *D* calculates the benefits that are lost when one alternative is chosen over another.

19. C: Choice *C* is correct because ambassadors do not have a specified term length. They are generally appointed by the president and serve on their authority, and how long they serve is up to the discretion of the president or presidents whom they might serve under. Choice *A* is incorrect because Congressional rules set the term for a member of the House of Representatives at two years. Choice *B* is incorrect because the term for members of the Senate is set at six years. Choice *D* is incorrect because the president is elected to a four-year term (and they may serve a maximum of two terms).

20. B: The Schengen Area, named after Schengen, Luxembourg, refers to an area of Europe encompassing 27 European nations, within which all forms of border control have been abolished. The Schengen Area makes it possible for individuals in member states to travel freely through most of Europe without needing to apply for visas or pass security checkpoints. Therefore, the correct answer is Choice *B*.

21. A: For many years, the common metaphor used to describe the vast cultural diversity of the United States was a melting pot, with the idea being that people from all over the world would come to America and assimilate, blending like ingredients in a melting pot. However, in more recent years there has been an emphasis on recognizing and valuing the distinctive cultural qualities and attitudes of individuals who immigrate to the United States. Additionally, there has been pushback against the promotion of the idea that assimilation should be the norm or even desired among Americans. That recognition has led to the creation of a new metaphor for the diversity of the United States, namely that of a salad bowl. In a salad bowl, unlike in a melting pot, the constituent elements that make up the meal still retain their unique character, and assimilation is not the goal. Therefore, the correct answer is Choice *A*.

22. D: Choice *D* is the correct answer because an embedded journalist is one who reports from a war zone and is attached to a specific military unit. Such journalistic practices often involve careful coordination between the media entity, the journalist themselves, and the military unit to which the journalist is attached. Choice *A* is incorrect because embedded journalists do not have to be associated with a specific media company. Choice *B* is incorrect because embedded journalists can have their own byline. Choice *C* is incorrect because embedded journalists are not limited to writing about a specific topic or industry.

23. A: The term *plenipotentiary*, which comes from the Latin for "full of power," refers to an official who has been invested with the power of their government, usually to act on behalf of that government in a foreign country. In the United States, plenipotentiaries are typically diplomats and serve on behalf of the president in the drafting and signing of treaties and international resolutions. Therefore, the correct answer is Choice *A*.

24. C: A Concordat is a specific form of political treaty between a sovereign state and the Roman Catholic Church. Generally, these agreements are made between the Holy See and other nations in order to help resolve or alleviate secular matters affecting both the sovereign state and the Roman Catholic Church (for example, wars, economic depression, political corruption, and so on). Therefore, the correct answer is Choice *C*.

25. C: Comparative advantage is the principle that countries produce the goods and services that have the least opportunity cost. When a country has a comparative advantage, they'll specialize in that industry because it's more efficient. Thus, Choice *C* is the correct answer. A country might implement the other three policies, but it's less likely when the country enjoys a comparative advantage.

26. C: Aid with a refugee crisis is a humanitarian diplomatic goal. It does not carry any economic impact, so Choice *A* is incorrect. Choices *B* and *D* are incorrect since the negotiations are only relating to the refugees themselves and not the source of the crisis, be it a war or environmental disaster.

27. D: Diplomacy does not include any form of violence as a part of negotiations, or else it would not truly be diplomacy. Persuasions, concessions, and rewards are all tactics that can be used in diplomatic negotiations, so Choices *A*, *B*, and *C* are all incorrect.

28. B: All emails that users receive can be found in their inbox by default. Choice *C* is where emails are stored for the user to look at in the future. Choice *D* is where unsolicited advertisements are sent.

29. B: The doctrine of mutual assured destruction came about after the Second World War and continued through the Cold War, as nuclear weapons proliferated in the United States and the Soviet Union. The doctrine proposed that, given the power of these weapons and the infrastructure dedicated to them, any full nuclear exchange between two countries possessing them would result in the complete destruction of both parties. Such a doctrine was meant to illustrate that it would be irrational to use such a weapon at all, as can be doubly understood when looking at its acronym—MAD. However, it was considered necessary to have enough arms to remain a credible threat; MAD would fall apart if one country had dominance. Therefore, the correct answer is Choice *B*.

30. C: The process of passing a treaty, like many aspects of American governance, involves the careful balancing of different branches of the government, specifically the executive and legislative branches. While the president is given the constitutional authority to make and propose treaties, it is only after passing with a two-thirds vote in the Senate that the treaty is ratified. Therefore, the correct answer is Choice *C*.

31. C: The government makes all decisions related to production, distribution, and price in a centrally planned economic system; therefore, Choice *C* is the correct answer. This allows communist governments to oversee price control, and, as a result, the production and distribution of resources is less efficient but more equitable. If a government distributes resources solely based on merit and allows private markets to set prices, then the economy is operating under a free-market system. A government that balances a private and public sector is characteristic of a mixed economic system.

32. D: Choice *D* is correct for the following reasons. In most common spreadsheet software, including Excel and Google Sheets, adding a formula to a cell enables that cell to process inputs from other cells and represent them as output, depending on the specific formula entered and the specific cells selected. Choices *A* and *C* are incorrect because the options for visual representations of data and aesthetic alterations are usually in the toolbar above the spreadsheet; these options are not typically editable within the spreadsheet itself. Choice *B* is incorrect because the cells of a spreadsheet are usually editable by default, and no action is required to make them editable.

33. D: Choice *D* is correct because Choices *A*, *B*, and *C* all describe benefits of advanced search features. Most databases, including publicly accessible ones like Google Scholar, provide tools for qualifying their search terms. You can specify the exact phrasing of your search terms, as in Choice *A*. Using quotation marks around a search term (for example, "United Arab Emirates") ensures that those words in that specific order are searched for, and sources with those words in that order are prioritized over sources that contain the words separately. You can add or exclude search terms, as in Choices *B* and *C*. The addition and subtraction symbols before terms (for example, +Europe or -Germany) enable users to add or exclude search terms, helping to ensure that results contain all the desired information and none of the undesired information. Therefore, the correct answer is Choice *D*.

34. C: Information being compiled for criminal investigation may be disclosed if it can be determined that it does not interfere with police or legal proceedings. Confidential financial information, medical files, and information related to national defense must not be disclosed, and files containing this information must be scrubbed of forbidden information before being publicly disclosed. Thus, Choices *A*, *B*, and *D* are all incorrect.

35. A: Memorial Day and Veterans Day are both nationally recognized holidays in the United States, and both honor the individuals who have served in the United States Armed Forces. However, Memorial Day is a more solemn day dedicated to the remembrance of those who died in service of their country, and Veterans Day is a more joyous celebration of all those who have served, both living and dead. Therefore, the correct answer is Choice *A*. Choice *B* is incorrect because, while other countries do have holidays like Memorial Day, they are called by another name, such as Remembrance Day in the UK. Choices *C* and *D* are incorrect because they get the details about these holidays wrong.

36. B: The relationship between age and time for attention span is a positive correlation because the general trend for the data is up and to the right. As the age increases, so does attention span.

37. D: An attachment is a document that is added to each email. Recipients are able to view and download the document from the email. Choice *A* is the actual email address and is where the message will be sent. Choice *B* is a feature of sending emails using BCC, which prevents recipients from knowing who else the email was sent to. Choice *C* is a feature of most email services where users can create new folders to organize their email.

38. A: The FBI and the CIA are the two major investigative agencies of the United States government. The FBI investigates crime inside the borders of the United States. The CIA is prohibited by law from collecting information about any United States citizen or resident. Therefore, the correct answer is Choice *A*. Choice *B* is incorrect because the FBI operates in both the fields of law enforcement and intelligence gathering. Choice *C* is incorrect because the CIA is under the supervision of the Director of National Intelligence. Choice *D* is incorrect because a search warrant is always required by law in order for any law enforcement authorities to enter and search a property.

39. B: Choice *B* is correct because the Gulf of Tonkin incited the US involvement in the Vietnam War. Choice *A* is incorrect because it links the attack of Fort Sumer, which served as an inciting incident in the Civil War, to the Revolutionary War. Choice *C* is incorrect because it links the assassination of Archduke Ferdinand to World War II instead of the proper conflict, World War I. Finally, Choice *D* is incorrect because it links the events of 9/11 to the start of the Gulf War; the 9/11 attacks actually lead to the War on Terror in Iraq and Afghanistan.

40. D: In common American political parlance, a public official who pushes for and advocates on behalf of military intervention is commonly referred to as a war hawk, or simply a hawk. The term is often contrasted with the dove, an individual or politician who advocates against military intervention. Therefore, the correct answer is Choice *D*.

41. D: Choice *D* is correct because all the other answer choices describe military actions that can be used to maintain a no-fly zone. A no-fly zone is a policy under which non-approved aircraft are strictly prohibited from flying in a particular zone. In order to maintain a no-fly zone, a number of military actions may be taken, ranging from surveilling the skies (Choice *C*), to targeting unauthorized aircrafts in the no-fly zone (Choice *B*), to making preemptive attacks (Choice *A*).

42. B: In common American political parlance, the term *lame duck* refers to an elected official in the final months of their term, typically after the election of their successor. The implication of the term itself is that, like a duck that can't move around very well, a public official in the last few months of their terms may find it hard to get anything done and may end up doing little more than sitting around. Therefore, the correct answer is Choice *B*.

43. A: Commas are used to separate multiple email addresses from each other. Choice *B*, *C*, and *D* are not used to separate email addresses and would not be recognized by the program.

44. C: CC, or Carbon Copy, creates a thread in the email message where recipients can see who else received the message. Choices *A*, *B*, and *D* are not what CC stands for.

45. D: The unknown quantity is the number of total questions on the test. Let x be equal to this unknown quantity. Since 75% is equal to $\frac{3}{4}$ as a fraction, $\frac{3}{4}x = 12$. To solve for x, multiply both sides by $\frac{4}{3}$. Therefore,

$$x = 12 \times \frac{4}{3} = \frac{48}{3} = 16$$

46. A: Choice *A* is correct because semper fidelis, Latin for "always faithful," is the longstanding motto of the United States Marine Corps. Choice *B*, the Coast Guard, is incorrect because that motto is *Semper Paratus*. Choice *C*, the Air Force, is incorrect because that motto is "Aim High … Fly-Fight-Win." Choice *D* is incorrect because the Navy does not have an official motto.

47. C: The answer is Choice *C*, the limited availability of a particular commodity. While too much demand, Choice *B*, might lead to scarcity, it is not the definition of scarcity. Choices *A* and *D* would be the opposite of scarcity.

48. A: Agency reports regarding all public requests for information are submitted to the US Attorney General. They are not submitted to the Speaker of the House, President, or Chief of Staff, so Choices *B*, *C*, and *D* are all incorrect.

49. D: The Occupational Safety and Health Administration (OSHA) is responsible for enforcing all worker health and safety regulations among workplaces, whether they are federal, state, or private. The Federal Health Administration does not directly enforce health and safety regulations for the workplace, so Choice *A* is incorrect. *The Workplace Safety Administration* and *Federal Internal Safety Agency* are both false terms, so Choices *B* and *C* are incorrect.

50. C: The Constitution contains provisions for how to propose and pass an amendment to the Constitution. In order to provide a balance of power between the federal level and state level of government, it was decided that an amendment to the Constitution may be proposed and passed by either a two-thirds majority vote in both the House and the Senate or by two-thirds of state legislatures calling for a constitutional convention. Therefore, the correct answer is Choice *C*.

51. A: Choice *A* is correct because it correctly identifies the three parts of the rhetorical triangle: ethos, logos, and pathos. The rhetorical triangle is a concept in rhetoric, originally postulated by Aristotle, which asserts that a speaker's ability to convince an audience of their point is based on how well they appeal to that audience in three conceptual areas. Ethos refers to the credibility of the speaker, logos refers to the logical cogency of the argument, and pathos refers to the emotional resonance of the argument. Choices *B, C,* and *D* all refer to concepts that are not part of the rhetorical triangle.

52. D: Let x be the unknown number. Difference indicates subtraction, and sum represents addition. To triple the difference, it is multiplied by 3. The problem can be expressed as the following equation:

$$3(5 - x) = x + 5$$

Distributing the 3 results in:

$$15 - 3x = x + 5$$

Subtract 5 from both sides:

$$15 - 5 - 3x = x + 5 - 5$$

$$10 - 3x = x$$

Next, add 3x to both sides:

$$10 - 3x + 3x = x + 3x$$

$$10 = 4x$$

Lastly, divide both sides by 4:

$$\frac{10}{4} = \frac{4x}{4}$$

$$\frac{10}{4} = x$$

This reduces as:

$$x = \frac{10}{4} = \frac{5}{2} = 2.5$$

53. A: The first ten amendments to the United States Constitution—which contain among them the right to free speech and assembly, the right to bear arms, and the right to be tried by a jury of one's peers—are collectively referred to as the Bill of Rights. Such amendments were made shortly after the drafting of the Constitution, as the members and factions of the Constitutional Conventions debated over what to specifically include and outlaw in the new nation. Therefore, the correct answer is Choice *A.*

54. C: Choice *C* is correct because the most recently created executive department is the Department of Homeland Security, which was founded in the aftermath of the 9/11 attacks in 2002. Choice *A* is incorrect because the Department of Energy was established in 1977. Choice *B* is incorrect because the Department of Veterans Affairs was founded in 1989. Choice *D* is incorrect because the Department of Commerce was founded in 1903.

55. C: The *.org* domain on websites is generally used by nonprofit groups or community organizations. A government website uses *.gov*, and *.edu* is used for educational institutions. Private companies and businesses use *.com*, so Choices *A*, *B*, and *D* are incorrect.

56. C: A transition will play a short animation between each slide during a presentation. Choice *A* is a hyperlink. Choice *B* is the "Font Size" option. Choice *D* is the command function CTRL + S, which is a shortcut to save progress.

57. B: Choice *B* is correct because OPEC stands for the Organization of Petroleum Exporting Countries, an intergovernmental organization consisting of thirteen countries, including Venezuela, Saudi Arabia, and Mexico. OPEC represents almost half of the global oil production and has served as means for many countries to begin to possess some national sovereignty over their resources. Choices *A*, *C*, and *D* are incorrect because these organizations do not exist.

58. C: Choice *C* is the correct answer. Commodities are raw materials or agricultural products—gold, silver, gas, oil, corn, barley, etc. Physical, tangible items are goods. Activities based on labor or skills are services. High-demand products typically have a higher price in a free-market system, depending on the supply.

59. D: A line graph represents continuous change over time. The line on the graph is continuous and not broken, as on a scatter plot. Stacked bar graphs are used when comparing multiple variables at one time. They combine some elements of both pie charts and bar graphs, using the organization of bar graphs and the proportionality aspect of pie charts. A bar graph may show change but isn't necessarily continuous over time. A pie graph is better for representing percentages of a whole. Another type of graph, histograms, are best used in grouping sets of data in bins to show the frequency of a certain variable.

60. D: The Federal Register is the official journal of the US government and is responsible for posting all new rules and regulations that result from laws or executive orders. It is available to federal agencies and the public. Both the *Federal News Bulletin* and *American Agency News* are false terms, so Choices *A* and *C* are incorrect. The Consumer Price Index has nothing to do with new US rules and regulations, so Choice *B* is incorrect.

Part Two: English Expression and Usage

1. D: Choice *A* is missing an apostrophe in *couldn't*. Choice *B* uses the clause to describe the drink, not the man in the sentence. Choice *C* does not use the adverb *unfortunately*.

2. C: Choice *A* uses *whether* instead of *weather* to describe the temperature. Choice *B* does not use the adverb *well* to describe the action. Choice *D* does not capitalize the proper noun *Around the World in 80 Days*.

3. B: Choice *A* places an extra comma after *Excuse*. Choice *C* uses *if* instead of *whether* in the phrase *whether or not*. Choice *D* uses the singular *peer* instead of *peers*.

4. A: Choice *B* inserts an extra verb *be* in the sentence. Choice *C* uses a semicolon in the contraction instead of an apostrophe. Choice *D* should use a comma instead of a semicolon since the first part of the sentence is a fragment.

5. C: Choice *A* incorrectly uses *wherever* instead of *whenever* to describe the timing of an event. Choice *B* uses the incorrect prefix to describe the opposite of suitable. The opposite of *suitable* is *unsuitable*. Choice *D* uses *do* instead of *due*.

254

6. B: Choice *A* uses the possessive *brother's* instead of the subject *brothers*. Choice *C* needs to use the adverb *slowly* to describe the verb *inched*. Choice *D* does not capitalize the proper noun, *Orlando*.

7. B: Choice *A* does not have matching tenses in the sentence. Choice *C* uses the word *effected* instead of *affected*. Choice *D* incorrectly uses *myself* instead of the subject *I*.

8. D: Choice *A* does not use the past participle *finished* to describe the past perfect tense. Choice *B* inserts an unnecessary comma after *riding*. Choice *C* uses the phrase *if or not* instead of *whether or not*.

9. A: Choice *B* does not capitalize the *Dr.* title. Choice *C* is missing an apostrophe in *couldn't*. Choice *D* uses *themselves* instead of *himself* to describe the actor.

10. C: Choice *A* uses *for* instead of *since* to describe when something specifically happened. In this case, the event is the economy crashing. *For* references a period of time, not a specific event. Choice *B* uses *for me* instead of *with me*. Choice *D* is missing a comma after *for example*.

11. B: Choice *A* is a run-on sentence and is missing punctuation on either side of *however*. Choice *C* mismatches the singular *this* with the plural word *tournaments*. Choice *D* must change the singular word *needs* to the plural *need* to match the plural subject *patients*.

12. C: Choice *A* uses the direct object *him* instead of *his* to show possession. Choice *B* is missing the verb *to be* before *shocked*. Choice *D* incorrectly uses *which* and not *who* to describe the brother.

13. C: There are two independent clauses in one sentence, so separating the two clauses with a comma is the best option. The other sentences have incorrect comma placement. Additionally, the information that Lulu was only five years old is not necessary in this particular sentence—it is out of context.

14. D: The words *accept* and *except* are often confused. Choice *B* is incorrect because *expect* is a verb with a different meaning than *except*, but it does look similar if read too quickly. Choice *C* is incorrect because the comma is not needed.

15. D: Choice *A* is incorrect because *he says* and *he have never been* are not parallel. Choice *B* is incorrect because the semicolon before *and* is used incorrectly. Choice *C* is incorrect because *Paris* should be capitalized.

16. A: Choice *B* incorrectly separates the dependent clause from the independent clause with a comma; a list with two items does not need a comma. Choice *C* uses the past tense of *talked* where it should use *talking*. Choice *D* capitalizes *City's Parks*, but there is no need to use any uppercase letters because it isn't a proper noun.

17. C: The correct answer is Choice *C* because the phrase "which took place between 1760 and 1840" should be set off with commas. Choice *B* is incorrect because it lacks a comma after "1840," and Choice *D* is incorrect because the comma after "place" interrupts the phrase "took place between 1760 and 1840."

18. B: Choice *B* does not place an apostrophe in the name *Sarah* to denote possession. The possessive form is *Sarah's*.

19. D: Choice *D* uses *there*, which refers to a place, instead of *their*, which refers to possession.

20. A: The sentence contains no errors.

21. D: Choice D breaks the parallel structure of the sentence by referring to *the perfume*. The list should read *watches, perfumes, and designer purses*.

22. B: Choice *B* uses the object *me* instead of the subject *I* to introduce the relationship between the individual and his brother. The sentence should begin with *My brother and I*.

23. B: Choice B uses *mine* instead of *my* to denote the possessive.

24. A: The sentence contains no errors.

25. D: Choice *D* is using a period to denote an abbreviation when the word has already been fully spelled out.

26. C: Choice *C* uses a semicolon instead of a colon to start a list.

27. C: Choice *C* uses *where* to refer to the time of an event instead of *when*. *Where* refers to a location.

28. D: Choice *D* uses *resisted* instead of *resist* to match the rest of the sentence.

29. A: The sentence contains no errors.

30. C: The best answer is Choice *C*. Each verb in the relative clause should show parallelism with the use of the third-person singular present tense. The clause is about words that demonstrate, words that emphasize, words that present, and so on. Therefore, *demonstrate* should be parallel with the verbs *emphasize, present*, and *introduce*. Choices *A, B,* and *D* are not parallel.

31. A: The best answer is Choice *A*. The gerund form of the verb "to connect" is *connecting*. Using this form of the verb creates a parallel structure, because the sentence also uses the gerund form of "to strengthen," which is *strengthening*.

32. D: Choice *D* is the best answer choice because it has double quotes, which are appropriate around dialogue. Additionally, the comma is inside the quotes, which is appropriate punctuation placement when it comes to dialogue.

33. A: No change is needed here, because *springtime* is one compound word. *Arctic,* when used as a noun, is capitalized.

34. B: The correct phrase is *months on end*, not *months over end*. Choice *C* is wrong because *is* does not match the plural *cries*. Choice *D* is incorrect because the word *loan* refers to something borrowed.

35. C: Choice *C* uses quotation marks to set off the quote that the football captain said to his team. Choice *B* is a passive phrase and does not correct the missing quotation marks in the sentence. Choice *D* incorrectly uses parentheses instead of quotation marks to complete the quote.

36. A: The underlined text contains no errors. Parentheses are used to add additional information in a sentence. Choice *B* creates a run-on sentence. Choices *C* and *D* do not use the correct punctuation.

37. A: The underlined text contains no errors. A comma can be used to join two independent clauses if a conjunction like *and* is used. Choices *B, C,* and *D* do not use the correct punctuation to separate two independent clauses.

38. D: Choice *D* eliminates the unnecessary comma in the sentence. Choices *B* and *C* add unnecessary punctuation that interrupts the sentence.

39. C: Choice *C* replaces the informal phrase *could of* with the correct phrase *could have*. Choices *B* and *D* do not replace *of* with the correct word to indicate a possibility or chance.

40. C: Choice *C* is a gerund, which is a form of speech that often follows the verb phrase *don't mind*. An infinitive like *to go* does not follow the phrase *don't mind*. Choices *B* and *D* are not gerunds.

41. A: The underlined text contains no errors. *Worst* is the superlative form of *bad*. Choices *B* and *D* are not the superlative form of bad. Choice *C* is the comparative form of *bad*.

42. B: Choice *B* introduces the correct subject of the initial clause, which is Jack's mother. The initial clause is not referring to Jack himself. Choices *C* and *D* do not introduce the correct subject of the initial clause.

43. D: Choice *D* is a homonym of the word *cellar*, which is used incorrectly in the sentence. As a *seller*, the man would be a vendor at the flea market. Choices *B* and *C* are synonyms of *cellar*, so they cannot describe being a seller at a flea market.

44. B: Choice *B* is the correct comparative word to describe the sentence. The comparative form of the word *good* is *better*. Choice *C* is an adverb. Choice *D* is an adjective.

45. D: Choice *D* is a comparison word used in the sentence to compare the lakes. *Then* is used to indicate a sequence of events. Choice *B* is missing the word *to*, making this an incomplete comparison phrase. Choice *C* can be used as a comparison word, but it is not used correctly in this context. For example, the sentence would need to change its word order and appear as follows: In Japan there aren't any freshwater lakes as big as Lake Biwa.

46. A: The underlined text contains no errors. The past participle, swum, is needed to complete the sentence and match the tense. Choice *B* is the base form of *swim*. Choice *C* is the past tense of *swim*. Choice *D* is a gerund.

47. A: The underlined text contains no errors. There is no need to use any uppercase letters in the name because the specific name of a contest is not being used. The words in a proper noun would be capitalized.

48. B: Choice *B* is the best answer choice here. It contains the contraction *it's* for *it is*, and also has a comma after the introductory phrase before the independent clause.

49. D: The best answer is Choice *E*, which says: "After lunch I went swimming, played with my dog, and cleaned up my room." This answer is correct because it is in parallel structure, which means the verbs "went, played, and cleaned" are all the same verb tense.

50. B: Choice *B* is the best answer because students should consider "spelling, punctuation, and content development." This is an example of a dangling modifier. The writing of the paper is not done by the spelling, punctuation, or content development. The writing is done by the students, so the clause has to use *students* as the subject.

51. A: The best answer is Choice *A*. Choice *B* is incorrect because there is a comma after "without which," and this comma interrupts the sentence. Choice *C* is incorrect because of the superfluous word *additionally*. *Additionally* is not needed here because the second sentence acts as an explanation to the first. Choice *D* is incorrect because it is a run-on sentence; there should be a semicolon or period after "writing" and before "without them."

52. D: Sentence 3 is the first sentence because it establishes the story about the concert. Sentence 1 describes the mother's reaction to the question about the concert. Sentence 2 provides more details about her reaction to Elvis. Sentence 4 explains why the mother and her friends admired Elvis.

53. B: Sentence 4 establishes the main topic, the new pizza restaurant and its owners. Sentence 3 gives more details about the owners and their recipes. Sentence 2 expands on the recipes and talks about the pizza on the menu. Sentence 1 gives details about the pizza previously mentioned.

54. C: Sentence 3 is the topic sentence and starts the discussion about factories. Sentence 2 explains why factories contributed to the growth of cities. Sentence 1 references the previous discussion about increased demand and builds upon it. Sentence 4 contrasts the previous sentence by explaining that the work was extremely difficult due to poor labor laws.

55. A: Sentence 1 establishes the parents' expectations for Meera. Sentence 2 expands on these expectations and explains what Meera did to accomplish her goal. Sentence 4 provides more detail about the effect that these extra activities had on her. Sentence 3 contrasts her effort with her pride at graduation.

56. B: Sentence 4 begins the paragraph by explaining that the printing press revolutionized society. Sentence 1 contrasts what life was like before the printing press. Sentence 2 explains what happened after the printing press was invented and mentions that books were mass-produced. Sentence 3 described what happened as a result of this mass production.

57. D: Sentence 2 introduces the main problem of the story, which is the fact that the couple has not traveled enough. Sentence 3 provides a solution to their problem. Sentence 4 builds upon their upcoming trip by explaining their worries about security once they arrived at the airport. Sentence 1 explains what happened after they got through security, and it ends the paragraph.

58. D: Sentence 2 introduces the premise for the paragraph, and the following sentences tell the story in chronological order. Sentence 4 presents the first element of the story. Sentence 1 presents an immediately following event. Sentence 3 gives the ultimate consequence of the series of events and would not be possible without the drink spilling on the computer in Sentence 1.

59. D: Choice *D* explains the consequences of the enemy breaking through their lines and presents a hypothetical situation using the word *if*. Choice *A* does not match the bleak tone of the paragraph. Choice *B* inaccurately implies that this event already happened, but it has not happened yet. Choice *C* is incorrect because the author believes the event that they describe is likely to happen.

60. C: Choice *C* describes joy and happiness, which matches the author's bright and excited tone of voice. Choice *A* describes sadness and grief. Choice *B* describes feeling hopeless about the future. Choice *D* describes feelings of anxiety or worry.

61. A: Choice *A* accurately describes the short-lived moment in time experienced by the author. This is also seen in the phrase *for only a brief second.* Something that is *fleeting* lasts for a very short time. Choice *B* is the antonym of *ephemeral.* Something that is eternal lasts forever. Choice *C* means chaotic or not in order. Choice *D* means unequaled or incomparable.

62. B: Choice *B* is correct because it serves as an introduction to the Shinkansen, which the author is evidently impressed by. Choice *A* is not supported in the paragraph. Although the cost of a train ticket is mentioned, it does not give clues as to the sustainability of the train system. Choice *C* does not match the author's generally impressed tone of voice and admiration for the train system. Choice *D* ignores the author's claim that trains are an extremely important part of Japanese travel.

63. D: Choice *D* is correct because of the details provided in the fourth sentence, which states that gelato contains lower fat and calories. This suggests that it is a healthier alternative to ice cream. Choice *A* is incorrect because no details are provided about when ice cream was invented. Choice *B* is incorrect because the paragraph discusses the main difference between gelato and ice cream, which is the amount of milk used. Choice *C* is incorrect because the paragraph does not discuss the popularity of gelato versus ice cream.

64. C: Choice *C* indicates that Alexander tried to study but didn't. The quotation marks are used ironically to show that he attempted to study but was ultimately distracted by other things. Choice *A* is incorrect because Alexander does not feel hopeful that he will complete his work. Choice *B* does not take into account Alexander's attempt to study. Choice *D* does not provide evidence about the use of quotation marks and does not explain his feelings.

65. C: Choice *C* is correct because a wide audience would be familiar with *The Time Machine* and *The War of the Worlds*, even if they aren't immediately familiar with H.G. Wells' name. Choice *A* is incorrect because the game has nothing to do with the novel. Choice *B* is incorrect because there is nothing to indicate that enjoying the game would equate with enjoying the novels. Choice *D* is incorrect because the novels do not give any indication that Wells was a military strategist, only that he wrote science fiction stories which sometimes included war.

Part Three: Situational Judgment

1. BEST: C: Focusing on current objectives provides the new FSOs with information directly relevant to their work responsibilities. The in-person presentation encourages a mentoring relationship between new and experienced staff. **WORST: A:** Because diplomatic objectives can change rapidly, training materials should be based on current goals instead of past practices.

2. BEST: A: This choice is best because it is a low-risk hands-on experience that doesn't seek to use another person's time. **WORST: B:** If a trainee FSO indicates a preferred learning process, it is reasonable for the trainer to accommodate. This hastens the trainee's integration into the team.

3. BEST: B: Each FSO swears an oath to uphold the Constitution. Emphasizing that you are a public servant required to follow elected leaders regardless of personal politics expresses integrity and a pro-democratic perspective, without inappropriately crossing professional boundaries. **WORST: D:** Until formal policy decisions or changes have been announced, it is not appropriate to confide these opinions to local officials.

4. BEST: E: The FSO's behavior reflects on the Foreign Service as a whole, especially while on an official trip. This choice is best because it avoids a situation that could compromise your integrity as a representative of the United States. **WORST: A:** This situation is not restricted to the FSO's private life, because they are being hosted for the purpose of an official trip.

5. BEST: C: Accepting the gift provides emotional support to the family seeking asylum during a difficult transition. The FSO can report the gift and privately determine the appropriate response at a later time. **WORST: A:** A hastily chosen gift is more likely to cause offense than to provide support to the family.

6. BEST: C: Choice *C* is best because it contributes an additional source of factual data to the published report. **WORST: D:** Claims made by political opponents do not increase the report's reliability because of faction-based bias.

7. BEST: D: This decision shows the best judgment because it recognizes that safety within a conflict zone cannot be assured. **WORST: A:** Although international law should protect the consulate from intentional harm, collateral damage is common in military conflict. Thus, international law is not a good reason to choose against evacuation.

8. BEST: D: The emotional component of this decision—wanting to spend time with a friend—is the most significant flaw because it is the cause of the FSO breaking from protocol. **WORST: B:** Data-based decisions are important, but this isn't a situation where specific data were present to inform the FSO's judgment.

9. BEST: C: This statement is best because multiple data points indicate that a claim is more likely to be true. **WORST: D:** The duration of the relationship has a weak correlation with reliable information. For example, the contact could be truthful, yet their information inaccurate.

10. BEST: C: As the leader, organization and task management are primary duties. It's best that the leader does not delegate these tasks to another team member. **WORST: A:** The role of primary information gathering should be delegated to another team member—probably a junior member of the team. This task requires less analysis and judgment than the other tasks. It's more effective for the team leader to spend their time and energy on different work.

11. BEST: A: In this situation, it's better to contact the head of security than your immediate superior. This is because this situation is both time-sensitive and engages issues of security and safety. This justifies contacting the most relevant authority immediately rather than following the chain of command. **WORST: D:** Although contact with the local authorities will be necessary, your first duty as an FSO is to arrange the US government's response to this crisis.

12. BEST: C: The congressperson's report has the highest priority because they are an elected official of the United States, and the Foreign Service's purpose is to work toward the foreign policy determined by elected representatives. **WORST: D:** The contracted company is not unimportant, but as an employee of the consulate they have lower priority than the FSO's superiors (Choice *A*) or colleagues in the local government (Choice *B*).

13. BEST: A: It's generally most efficient to complete a project already in progress. This requires less mental labor because a shift in focus then requires additional time for the FSO to refamiliarize themselves with the incomplete project. **WORST: C:** This task is lowest priority because it does not have a designated time for completion. Once the presentation is scheduled, the FSO can reevaluate their workflow priorities.

14. BEST: B: Assigning tasks in a single meeting is the best option because it is efficient and ensures that each team member knows their role within the context of the whole team. **WORST: A:** An oral assignment outside a structured environment risks the task being forgotten or misunderstood. A written component would help document the task, and a more structured meeting would help the employee understand their task's role in accomplishing team objectives.

260

15. BEST: A: Following the security agent's directions is the most professional decision because it emphasizes the authority of embassy security. **WORST: D:** An FSO should not seek to overrule a member of the Bureau of Diplomatic Security. Inviting the vendor in without background checks or other precautions creates a security risk.

16. BEST: D: This choice is best because it proactively suggests a solution to the problem that should require minimal expenditure of resources (e.g., staff time, paying for a new service). **WORST: A:** Advocacy is best implemented in the workplace if the advocate also has a plan of action to recommend.

17. BEST: D: It's important for the FSO to report all possible threats to security immediately. Even if a threat seems like an obvious prank, professional boundaries dictate that this is security's decision, not yours. **WORST: E:** This choice is the worst because it is the least immediate response to the threat.

18. BEST: E: The FSO should have this presentation complete and ready prior to arriving in America. Grooming yourself before the meeting provides you with a confident, professional appearance. This improves your rhetoric because outward confidence implies expertise about the topic. **WORST: D:** When a meeting is scheduled with busy people who have many responsibilities, it is imperative for the FSO to do their best to meet the official's schedule rather than cause conflicts.

19. BEST: B: Immediately responding to the official's offense reduces the possibility for further misunderstanding and demonstrates personal accountability. **WORST: A:** Following behavioral habits based on American culture does not justify a breach in local etiquette. The explanation should be accompanied by an apology.

20. BEST: A: In the case of a serious confrontation or accusation, a formal mediation process is least likely to create inappropriate drama because it creates space for the supervisor to learn about and guide the conflict resolution process. **WORST: D:** At this stage of social conflict, ignoring the teammate's complaint will escalate their frustration. This could hinder the team's accomplishment of diplomatic objectives.

21. BEST: C: This choice is best because the leader sets a good example for their employees through positive affirmation. This praise supports a healthy team environment through establishing positive opinions about teammates. **WORST: B:** One short meeting doesn't invest enough time and energy to lay the foundation for healthy teamwork.

22. BEST: B: A meeting at the new official's office gives the opportunity to develop in-person rapport while increasing their comfort level by meeting on their home ground. **WORST: D:** The document described in Choice D presumes upon the new official's time and energy while they are adjusting to the position. This could come across as rude and hinder the development of a new relationship.

23. BEST: C: Although acknowledging burnout to colleagues can be difficult, it is the best way to get support and relief until the FSO recovers. **WORST: D:** Coping skills are a useful tool for managing stress. However, due to the high-stress nature of diplomatic work, the FSO cannot safely assume that work will "return to normal" without a more proactive solution.

24. BEST: D: Some people seek privacy when grieving, whereas others seek companionship. Gentle invites encourage the grieving coworker to avoid isolation if they feel it's helpful. Often, the company of other people helps cope with grief, even if not directly addressing the loss. Choice D is better than Choices A and C because it gives the grieving coworker greater choice over how to engage with proffered support. **WORST: B:** Avoiding the topic entirely is not generally feasible in the small teams that most FSOs work with. It's better to address grief, even in a small way, than to risk coming across as callous and harming workplace rapport.

25. BEST: A: The senior representative is the best choice because seniority is increasingly important during meetings mixing attendees from several agencies. The opinion of senior officials often carries weight if the attendees do not have a strong understanding of one another's competencies. In addition, elected representatives are generally more important than appointed members of government. **WORST: B:** In general, the FSO should be backing up their superior's stance and opinion. It's better to invest time and energy communicating with other individuals.

26. BEST: A: Crossed arms often signals that the individual is closing themselves off or is feeling confrontational. Persistent observation of the woman's environment generally indicates worry or fear. Anxiety is the best answer because her physical posture is stable rather than ready to flee. **WORST: D:** The woman's body language would typically be more relaxed and open if she was feeling happy or joyful.

27. BEST: B: A formal apology accepting personal responsibility is the most professional response because it demonstrates seriousness and integrity. Choice *A* is less effective because a rush to apologize is typically undignified and will leave you in a weaker position during the negotiations. **WORST: C:** Choice *C* is the worst because it does not include an apology to the potentially offended local officials.

28. BEST: D: Choice *D* is best because it strikes the best balance between accomplishing work objectives and allowing the FSO to rest and recuperate from their illness. **WORST: B:** Attending the meetings while ill, simply because they're not on-site and the embassy's policy doesn't prohibit attendance, is reckless and disrespectful of the FSO's opposites in the local government.

FSOT Practice Tests #4, #5, and #6

The 4th, 5th, and 6th practice tests are available as digital tests along with the first three. Go to apexprep.com/bonus/fsot or scan the code below to access it.

After you go to the website, you will have to create an account and register as a "new user" and verify your email address before you begin.

If you need any help, please contact us at info@apexprep.com.

Greetings!

First, we would like to give a huge "thank you" for choosing us and this study guide for your FSOT exam. We hope that it will lead you to success on this exam and for your years to come.

Our team has tried to make your preparations as thorough as possible by covering all of the topics you should be expected to know. In addition, our writers attempted to create practice questions identical to what you will see on the day of your actual test. We have also included many test-taking strategies to help you learn the material, maintain the knowledge, and take the test with confidence.

We strive for excellence in our products, and if you have any comments or concerns over the quality of something in this study guide, please send us an email so that we may improve.

As you continue forward in life, we would like to remain alongside you with other books and study guides in our library. We are continually producing and updating study guides in several different subjects. If you are looking for something in particular, all of our products are available on Amazon. You may also send us an email!

Sincerely,
APEX Test Prep
info@apexprep.com

FREE

Free Study Tips Videos/DVD

In addition to this guide, we have created a FREE set of videos with helpful study tips. **These FREE videos provide you with top-notch tips to conquer your exam and reach your goals.**

Our simple request is that you give us feedback about the book in exchange for these strategy-packed videos. We would love to hear what you thought about the book, whether positive, negative, or neutral. It is our #1 goal to provide you with quality products and customer service.

To receive your **FREE Study Tips Videos**, scan the QR code or email freevideos@apexprep.com. Please put "FREE Videos" in the subject line and include the following in the email:

a. The title of the book

b. Your rating of the book on a scale of 1-5, with 5 being the highest score

c. Any thoughts or feedback about the book

Thank you!

Made in the USA
Columbia, SC
22 August 2024

40950074R00150